LIBRARY IN A BOOK

LEGALIZED GAMBLING

David M. Haugen

Facts On File
An imprint of Infobase Publishing

The following book is dedicated to my wife, Hayley, and my son, Jack, for giving me the precious time to complete the project. It is also dedicated to James Torr, a friend and colleague whose passion for "winning big" was a constant inspiration.

LEGALIZED GAMBLING

Facts On File, Inc.
An imprint of Infobase Publishing
132 West 31st Street
New York NY 10001

Library of Congress Cataloging-in-Publication Data
Haugen, David M., 1969-
Legalized gambling / David M. Haugen.
p. cm.—(Library in a book)
Includes bibliographical references and index.
ISBN 0-8160-6054-1
1. Gambling—United States. 2. Gambling—Law and legislation—United States. 3. Gambling—Research—United States. I. Title. II. Series.
HV6715.H385 2006
363.4'2—dc22 2005008916

Text design by Ron Monteleone
Graph by Patricia Meschino

Printed in the United States of America

MP Hermitage 10 9 8 7 6 5 4 3 2 1

This book is printed on acid-free paper.

CONTENTS

PART III
APPENDICES

PART I

OVERVIEW OF THE TOPIC

CHAPTER 1

INTRODUCTION TO LEGALIZED GAMBLING

Since the casino boom of the 1980s, gambling in America has experienced its greatest era of expansion. As of 2004, 11 states host commercial casinos, 28 states are home to American Indian casinos, and seven states possess racetrack casinos. In addition to these brick-and-mortar establishments, 39 states and the District of Columbia run lotteries. Finally, beyond these state-sanctioned gaming enterprises is the ubiquitous world of cybergambling, with wagering sites popping up on the Internet almost every day. This unprecedented growth testifies to the gambling industry's strength and popularity. According to the American Gaming Association, 53 million Americans visited casinos in 2003, and nearly half the adult population played the lottery. Furthermore, around 15 million people have partaken of the forbidden fruit of Internet gambling, which is currently illegal in the United States.

While these statistics make it clear that the majority of Americans love to gamble, they say nothing about the controversy that has accompanied the legalization of the gaming industry. Accusations of crime, corruption, and addictive gambling behavior have plagued the gaming community all along, but the state governments—which decide if, when, and how gambling will be permitted within their respective territories—have almost unanimously concluded that the benefits of legalized gambling outweigh its harms. Of the 50 states, only Hawaii and Utah prohibit all forms of gambling. The others have seen fit to sanction and regulate the industry—and to share in its profits. This, however, has not stopped a host of people, from grassroots organizers to members of Congress, from decrying gambling as a vice that America could do without. The most conservative detractors of legalized gambling, for example, view the sudden growth in the industry as just another symptom of a greater moral and social decay inherent to the late 20th century.

The controversy over legalized gambling, though, is not a modern phenomenon. Throughout the nation's history, Americans have fought for or contested the right to wager. Gambling's champions have touted it as a savior of state economies; opponents have ridiculed it as a moral demon. Gambling in America has been alternately condemned, banned, tolerated, legalized, and regulated for nearly 500 years. All this history still impacts the way in which Americans view legalized gambling today. And this legacy is so significant that any proper debates over the ethical, moral, or financial dimensions of the future of legalized gambling in America are best informed by a clear understanding of its past.

GAMBLING IN EARLY AMERICA

Gambling in North America preceded the foundation of the United States. When European settlers and explorers reached the Atlantic seaboard in the 16th and 17th centuries, they encountered Native tribes that had well-established systems of wagering. Early explorers in New York, for example, witnessed members of the Onondaga tribe placing bets on the roll of stone dice. Such gambling was a form of recreation for American Indians, but it also had a religious dimension. The Onondaga used the same dice they wagered on to predict the coming year's harvest. Indeed, for most Native tribes, casting dice or indulging in other games of chance was (and still is) a method of divining the favor of the gods. Gambling events—whether among members of a village or between two neighboring tribes—were sometimes staged as elaborate ceremonies. Drumbeats and frenzied dancing accompanied the games, and, caught up in the furor, the contestants often staked all they had on fate. Pierre-François-Xavier de Charlevoix, a Jesuit missionary writing in the 1700s, witnessed one such gambling bout during his stay with the Huron tribe of the Ohio Valley region. The Huron played a dice game in which colored stones were shaken in a dish, and according to Charlevoix: "At this game they hazard all they possess, and many do not leave till they are almost stripped quite naked and till they have lost all they have in their cabins. Some have been known to stake their liberty for a time, which fully proves their passion for this game."[1]

Like the American Indians, some of the early European colonists also had a passion for gaming. Seventeenth-century Europe was rife with gambling fever as a growing merchant economy put money—and therefore the ability to wager—in the hands of more people. While the New World colonies were founded as a haven for religious dissenters, they also attracted criminals and other desperate characters who were hoping to escape past debts or rebuild fortunes lost at Europe's gaming tables. The religious leaders may have tried to create utopias free of sinful vices, but many laymen were not content to relinquish their old habits. Card and dice games were thus as common in many of the early colonial settlements as they were in the Old World—and in some cases more so. In 1624, the Virginia colony, for example, had to post an ordinance to remind members of the clergy that card playing and dice games were forbidden to the holy order.

GAMBLING IN THE NORTH AND SOUTH

Not all New World colonies, however, were equally strict on curbing gambling. The Puritans who settled New England were perhaps the most disapproving. Their critical attitudes derived not from any belief that gambling was evil per se, but because it promoted idleness. Famed Puritan clergyman and orator Cotton Mather also condemned games of chance on scriptural grounds. He believed that since the Bible referenced the casting of lots in serious matters of divination, then any attempt to make them part of common sport would displease God. Although the Bible did not specifically prohibit gambling, New World Puritans quickly clamped down on the vice. In 1630, the same year that the Massachusetts Bay colony was established, its leaders outlawed the possession of dice, cards, and any other gaming devices. Gambling was not singled out as the only sinful vice; other entertainments such as dancing and singing were banned since they, too, were idle pursuits. The boredom engendered by banning amusements, however, only encouraged many New England colonists to flout the laws. Faced with this dilemma Puritan leaders imposed public punishments and even fines upon those who were caught gambling or engaged in other idle behaviors.

Other northern colonies cited different reasons for prohibiting or restricting gambling. New Hampshire passed an act in 1721 that barred gambling because of the impoverishment it brought upon the gambler's family. New York authorities also connected gambling with financial ruin; their colonial regulations further noted the violence that is often associated with gaming. New Jersey's laws followed the moral path set by the Puritans, but one ordinance went beyond a criticism of mere idleness. An act of 1748 charged that gambling led to widespread corruption—especially of the colony's youth.

Only in the southern colonies did gambling enjoy a degree of tolerance. The English colonists who settled Virginia, Georgia, and the Carolinas were not so unforgivingly strict in their moral outlook as the Puritans. They did not believe that gaming conflicted with Christian doctrine, and therefore they imported many traditional English pastimes that were not tolerated by their New England brethren. Both with ancient European roots, cockfighting and bearbaiting were perhaps the most barbaric wagering sports in the South. These cruel amusements were popular with the lower classes, and large crowds flocked to fighting arenas that were set up outside taverns or other community meeting places. The wealthier planters shied away from these coarse spectacles, preferring more refined diversions. Private card games fascinated some of the elite, while horse racing attracted those who had the money and inclination to breed thoroughbreds. Horse racing was in fact so popular among the gentry that racetracks were laid out in every southern colony by 1700. Virginia boasted several famous courses that drew local gamblers as well as visitors from other colonies. Before the Revolutionary War, George Washington often ran his horses at two of these courses, one in Alexandria, Virginia, and the other in Annapolis, Maryland. Because he was a well-to-do plantation owner, Washington, like other members of the upper class, not only held the privilege of entering horses in a race but also of betting on the outcome.

LOTTERIES

The English ruled all 13 of the Atlantic seaboard colonies in America after 1664, when the Dutch gave up New York (then New Amsterdam) to British invaders. Around this time, the New World witnessed the rise of another form of gaming that had already become popular in England. Lotteries had helped the British government raise revenues to fight wars and sponsor building projects in the past, but by the 1600s, English colonizing companies were using lotteries to furnish expeditions across the Atlantic. The Virginia colony was in part established by monies (£29,000 worth) received through the sale of lottery tickets. By 1620, the British Parliament even had to order the Virginia Company—the backers of the colony—to stop selling lottery tickets, as they were diverting patrons and their money away from the government's lotteries.

Although Parliament closed down the operation of colonial lotteries in England, they did not prevent lotteries from arising in the colonies themselves. Virginia continued to use lotteries held within the colonial borders to pay for roads, churches, and hospitals. Indeed, the operation of lotteries in the colonies helped to raise revenues that the mother country did not then have to pull from its own coffers. Gambling historian Henry Chafetz notes that given the success of the Virginia Company's money-making strategy in the 1600s, "the colonies gave lotteries their enthusiastic support in the eighteenth century and considered them highly respectable ventures."[2] Educational institutions were among the first civic projects to benefit from colonial lotteries. In the early 1700s, the College of Philadelphia paid for various building expenses by staging no less than nine different lotteries. In 1747, Yale College received approval from the Connecticut legislature to raise £7,500 by sale of lottery tickets. The proceeds paid for the building of a dormitory. In 1765, Harvard College also erected a dormitory with funds raised by a lottery. This lottery, however, was not very successful since it had to compete with other lotteries that were raising money to pay troops fighting in the French and Indian War.

Besides benefiting education, lotteries helped grow new industries in the colonies. Massachusetts, for example, supported its nascent paper mills through lottery ticket sales. Lotteries were also operated to fund civic works. In 1762, Massachusetts instituted a lottery to pay partially for the rebuilding of Faneuil Hall, which had been gutted by fire the previous year. Still other lotteries were held to relieve the impoverished and the bankrupt. Even some church leaders—who so often spoke out against gaming—turned a blind eye when lottery funds were used to build houses of worship. For instance, in 1794, the General Assembly of Rhode Island sold 3,000 $3 tickets to pay for the finishing of a church. All these civic lotteries enjoyed so much approbation in part because they were a voluntary means of raising money for needed improvements. Taxation had become such a controversial subject in the colonies that lotteries seemed the ideal, unforced manner of getting the public's money.

Colonial authorities tried to ensure that lotteries remained "respectable ventures," as Henry Chafetz puts it, by passing laws that approved only of lotteries that promoted civic development and forbade those that were run for private gain. Still, some strong sentiment—especially in New England—convinced local governments that lotteries were risky and immoral, and occasionally civic leaders would shut down these gaming ventures. For the most part, however, lotteries for municipal improvements enjoyed government approval and public interest throughout the 18th century.

WAR LOTTERIES

While lotteries served public works in times of peace, they were also employed in times of war to pay for raising troops and supplies. Prior to the American Revolution, colonial lotteries helped defray the English Crown's costs of fighting wars in North America. Although King George's War (1744–48) was fought mainly in Europe (as part of the War of the Austrian Succession), the American colonies took precautions to maintain their own security. Both New York and Philadelphia, for example, held lotteries to buy cannons and build defensive works to repel possible attacks from the French. Later, during the French and Indian War (1754–63), Massachusetts staged a £30,000 lottery in 1758 to outfit a military expedition against French-owned Canada. The Massachusetts volunteers who fought with General James Wolfe at the famous battle for Quebec owed their equipment, uniforms, and supplies to the proceeds of that lottery. Once the British proved the victors in the French and Indian War, they tried to recoup their tremendous expenditures by taxing the American colonies and banning lotteries (in America only). Since the war had been fought in America, the Crown believed that the colonists would be willing, even grateful, to foot the bill. The disgruntled colonists, however, turned their protest over the unfair taxation into full-scale rebellion. And, they adopted the lottery as a means of funding the fight for independence from Britain.

In 1776, a year after the first shots of the American Revolution had been fired, the Continental Congress devised its plan to pay for the men and supplies that the colonies would need to carry on a fight against the awesome might of England. The Congress estimated that it would need to raise $10 million to pursue war. Since the colonists would not stand for taxes, the Congress minted money, borrowed from foreign powers, and established a national lottery. The lottery was to offer $5 million in prizes in the hopes of taking in just over $1 million for the newly created Continental army. Like many schemes of the overzealous Continental Congress, the lottery proved a failure. Too few tickets were sold, and lottery managers kept delaying the drawing for lack of prize money. Eventually, the Congress had to admit its mistake, though it could not afford to repay the ticket buyers.

While the national lottery failed to offset the costs of the war, the individual colonies copied the idea and ran lotteries of their own. These were generally more successful than the national venture. Massachusetts, for example, operated one lottery that raised $750,000 to pay volunteers for enlisting. The colony's legislature then ran a second lottery to pay for the new army's uniforms. The Carolinas, New York, Rhode Island, and Vermont followed suit to raise and equip their own volunteer regiments. These localized lotteries seemed better managed and more trustworthy than the one operated by the central government, so similar ventures continued to flourish after the war ended in 1783.

Postwar Growth

In the years after the Revolutionary War, the nation witnessed a growth spurt. Population increased dramatically, and a number of citizens moved westward to find less crowded land. In order to continue to provide services to the expanding population, the state governments of the new United States maintained an interest in lotteries. Since taxation was still a sore subject, voluntary payment was the hoped-for savior of state and local economies. And lotteries, indeed, thrived in the postwar decades of the 1700s and into the early years of the 1800s. Much of the revenues went to improvements in transportation. Roads and bridges were constructed throughout the former colonies and into the lands to the west. These were designed to aid communication and emigration. Commerce was also given a boost by the digging of several canals that were paid for by lottery monies. The most famous of these was the Erie Canal project, which was proposed in 1808, begun in 1817, and finished in 1825.

Other capital projects also benefited from lottery income. In the states, many churches, municipal buildings, and schools were either built or repaired with lottery funds. In the new territories to the west, basic services were often obtained through lottery proceeds. Frankfort, Kentucky (which was then part of Virginia), for example, held a lottery to raise $50,000 for a town water supply. St. Louis and Detroit bought fire-fighting equipment by way of lotteries. In 1793, the new federal government embraced the lottery system to pay for a planned capital city in the District of Columbia. Inaugurating Federal Lottery No. 1, President George Washington bought the first of 50,000 tickets, which were sold at $7 apiece. A second federal lottery to expand the modest city followed on the success of the first. The states, however, opposed the national lotteries because they drew ticket buyers away from the local lotteries being operated at the same time. In his book on state lotteries, university professor Richard McGowan notes that the conflict of interest "was a precursor of competition between federal officials and state officials over various ways of raising revenue."[3]

The Decline of Early Lotteries

Besides the tinge of ill will arising between state authorities and the federal government, there were other voices of discontent over lotteries in the 18th century. The main criticism was that the lotteries fed on the meager incomes of the poorest classes and distracted them from pursuing more industrious methods of bettering their lives. These charges, however, had been around since Puritan days, and therefore did not much sway public opinion. What eventually crippled lottery mania in the United States was the growing occurrence of fraud.

As lotteries blossomed into major enterprises in the early 19th century, the methods of operating them significantly changed. In the late 18th century, two new figures had already emerged on the lottery scene. Ticket brokers and lottery contractors became lottery middlemen, acquiring the public's money and turning it over to those in charge of the lottery's worthy cause. The contractors were hired by government officials to manage a specific lottery (usually one of the citywide, statewide, or nationwide ventures), and they in turn hired or appointed brokers to sell the large number of required tickets. Both the contractors and the ticket brokers received a percentage of the lottery's earnings as their fee. Because they were paid from the total profit, many unscrupulous brokers printed and sold bogus tickets or indulged in a number of other illegitimate schemes to dupe ticket buyers. Sometimes the contractors fixed the lottery results. In 1818, newspapers blew the whistle on one such fraudulent lottery in New York. Learning of suspicious activity in the state's Medical Science Library, the newspapers informed their readers that the lottery was likely fixed. The New York legislature ran an investigation and determined that the operators of the lottery had shared the winning numbers with politicians and other prominent individuals, who would then have paid the contractors a percentage of their winnings. By 1820, public outcry forced the state legislature to ban the sale of lottery tickets in New York.

Five years after the New York scandal, a second, more highly publicized lottery fiasco rocked the nation's capital and hastened the decline of revenue lotteries nationwide. In 1823, Congress had authorized a contractor to operate a Grand National Lottery to raise money for civic improvements to Washington, D.C. Tickets were sold and winners drawn, but when authorities went to fetch the prize money, they found the contractor had skipped town. With several hundred thousands of dollars in cash awards missing, most ticket buyers felt bitter but thought they had no recourse. The winner of the $100,000 grand prize, however, believed otherwise. He sued the District of Columbia, claiming that the city was liable for the conduct of the contractor it had hired. The case eventually reached the U.S. Supreme Court, which ruled that the claimant's argument was sound and that the city had to pay him his first-prize winnings.

The Supreme Court's ruling sounded a warning to all local and state organizations that were either running lotteries or contemplating such. Legal liability might fall upon the organizers if the contractors absconded with the proceeds or in any other way defrauded ticket buyers. It was a risk that most states could not afford to take. One by one, the states began shutting down their lotteries and banning future ventures. By the beginning of the Civil War, in 1861, all states, with the exception of Kentucky and Missouri, had barred lotteries.

Two relatively new financial developments in the 19th century seemed to ease the loss of lotteries. The first of these was the establishment of regularized banking in the United States. By 1810, the new nation had 90 incorporated banks spread through the states. These institutions were fairly sound (though not federally secured) and could offer money to local building projects at reasonable rates, thus obviating some of the need for lotteries. The second development was the introduction of federal taxation in 1862. While Americans were not overjoyed with paying taxes, they did recognize that the central government needed a steady and dependable source of funds if it was to provide services to the nation. When lotteries slowly began disappearing in the years prior to the Civil War, taxes and loans would pick up the slack and become the foremost means of raising needed capital for national, state, and municipal improvements and services.

RECONSTRUCTION LOTTERIES

The loss of lotteries was a tolerable blow to state and federal finances during peacetime, but when the Civil War raged between 1861 and 1865, the national economy as a whole took a beating. Northern states—which were largely unscathed by the fighting—retained strong manufacturing economies by war's end, but the agricultural South—which had been both ravaged by Union armies and depleted of its slave labor—was in financial ruin. The North was perhaps understandably disinclined to pay for southern rebuilding efforts during the postwar period known as Reconstruction. Left to their own devices, and with no other options available, the southern states resurrected the lottery system.

The most famous of the Reconstruction lotteries was started in Louisiana in 1868. Called the Serpent, the first running of this lottery was given a touch of class and integrity when two former Confederate generals were hired to preside over the prize drawings. Ticket sales were enormous, attracting buyers in other states, North and South. Three million dollars in cash prizes were dispersed, and the proceeds went to the New Orleans Charity Hospital and various civic works in that city. The success of the initial run of the Serpent left the public wanting more, and the operators continued to hold the lottery on a weekly basis. It was a boon to Louisiana but a detriment to other southern states, which simply could not compete when they tried to stage lotteries of their own.

The downfall of the Serpent came in 1892 when the state of Louisiana declined to renew the operators' charter. Governor Francis T. Nicholls had been under pressure from the federal government, which was angered by the flagrant violation of an 1890 law banning the advertising of ticket sales through the mail. Congressmen also petitioned the governor to put an end to the Serpent because it drew millions of dollars out of their home states. The lottery operators tried to entice Nicholls to renew the charter by offering to pay a yearly sum of $500,000 (over the next 25 years) to finance a series of levees along the Mississippi. The already-harried governor declared the offer a bribe. It was widely known that the operators had bribed many public officials to keep the lottery running in previous years, but in 1892, the state legislature stood behind the governor. When the charter expired in 1895, the Serpent collapsed, and a nationwide ban on lotteries followed in the wake of even tighter federal laws against the use of the postal service for ticket sales.

THE GOLDEN AGE OF THE PROFESSIONAL GAMBLER

The ban on lotteries in the post–Civil War years was the first concerted effort to end legalized gambling in the United States. But lotteries were only one form of gambling that held Americans' fascination as the 19th century drew to a close. While the lottery was a rather anonymous game of chance that required no skill, the gamblers who enjoyed competition and preferred the chance to control their gambling fortunes played cards. Card playing was intimate; it required knowledge of the game as well as an understanding of human psychology. Professional gamblers were experts at reading their opponents, knowing when to raise the stakes and when to abandon a weak hand. The best of these card sharps made gambling a profession. They played blackjack, faro, monte, and especially poker. Sometimes they supplemented their card playing by throwing dice or betting on other games of chance.

New Orleans was the center of gambling operations in the early and mid-19th century. A crossroads for travelers moving west, the city was host to gambling halls and other dens of vice. From these "schools," well-trained gambling men graduated and moved northward along the Mississippi River to ply their trade on the riverboats that ran between New Orleans and Louisville, Kentucky. The riverboat gamblers preyed upon the wealthy southern planters and eastern rubes who often wagered recklessly with their fortunes. The gamblers' skills at gaming were their assets, and skimming from successful businessmen's profits was their trade. In this way, the riverboat gamblers, according to Henry Chafetz, symbolized young America's aspirations. Divorced from the hereditary wealth of Old Europe, Americans sought to make fortunes in the New World from nothing but their own talents. As Chafetz writes, "The riverboat gamblers, in their extreme way, reflected the contemporary temper of the country—each man for himself. Personal ambition was animated by the frenzied hope for quick gain, the everlasting urge to achieve wealth."[4]

GAMING HALLS IN THE WEST

Perhaps nowhere else in America in the 19th century was the hope for quick gain made more patently manifest than in the California gold rush of the late 1840s. While some of the New Orleans gamblers moved east to set up gaming halls in New York, Baltimore, and Washington (where such establishments were illegal but tolerated), others booked passage on the ships that made the journey from New Orleans southward around South America, and then northward up Mexico and the California coast. Their destination was San Francisco, which in 1849 was a hastily erected haven for seamen, prostitutes, and miners. The miners had crossed the continent or sailed the oceans to hunt for gold, so risk was in their blood. The gamblers who fell in with the gold hunters, therefore, had no problem finding willing partners for poker games. Furthermore, the law at the far side of the American continent was nearly nonexistent, so gamblers plied their trade openly. In his history of gambling in America, author John M. Findlay maintains that the gold rush country offered the perfect climate for the professional gamblers. To Findlay, it is not surprising that in a "society so loosely knit, and with fortune making and chance taking so highly regarded, gambling flourished."[5]

During the heyday of the gold rush, gamblers in California were so common that the territorial, and later state (1850), government decided to reap a share of their considerable incomes. From 1849 to 1855, California's legislature made gambling a legal profession, thereby allowing the government to tax the gamblers' earnings. But the golden age of the professional gambler did not last long in California. As the gold rush petered out and the state tried to mimic its eastern cousins in gentility, professional gamblers were ostracized. Laws against gaming saloons and gambling halls were enacted to curb gambling in hopes that money would be invested in business ventures that would grow and stabilize the state's economy. By the beginning of the Civil War, the gambling halls of San Francisco had closed or gone underground, and the gamblers had struck out for new territories.

Since the town's founding in 1859, Denver, Colorado (which was then in the Kansas territory), seemed to be the heir of gold-rush San Francisco. Because there was no law enforcement, the local government's tolerance of drinking, gaming, and prostitution made it a mecca for the dispossessed gamblers from other states. And despite growing antigambling sentiment across the nation, Denver retained its liberal character into the next century—even after gambling was officially outlawed in Colorado in 1900.

Other Wild West settlements in the postwar years also acquired their share of renown as gambling centers. Abilene, Kansas; Kansas City, Missouri; Cheyenne, Wyoming; and Santa Fe, New Mexico, were but a few of the frontier towns that catered to the gamblers. Increasingly, however, violence seemed to thrive where laws were lax and vice dominant. The invention of the Colt .45 revolver in 1831 made disputes over cards easily settled. As the towns grew and a respectable citizenry emerged, righteous crusaders sought an end to bar fights and gun duels. They struck at what they believed was the source of the violence—whiskey, prostitution, and gambling. Slowly the rule of law came to the West, and the crusaders forced state legislatures to close down the brothels and gambling halls. They had the support of Congress as well. In fact, as a condition of attaining statehood, Washington lawmakers required that Arizona and New Mexico ban gambling within their borders. Arizona complied in 1907, five years before it became a state. New Mexico followed in 1908, four years before its admission to the Union. Nevada remained a holdout. Although it had already achieved statehood during the Civil War, the Nevada legislature did not outlaw gambling until 1910.

HORSE RACING IN THE EAST

Congress's ultimatum to western states like Arizona and New Mexico was harsh and even hypocritical. In the congressional discussions over Arizona's coming statehood, Arizona congressman Mark Smith acknowledged that his state was willing to comply with the no-gambling restriction. But, he maintained, he and his fellow Arizonans were not bowing to pressures from eastern congressmen who, despite their puritanical stand, had let gambling continue unchecked in their own states. Smith's charge was certainly accurate. Hundreds of illegal gambling halls still operated in the major cities east of the Mississippi. Many of these remained open by paying off politicians to turn a blind eye to their activities. The East Coast also had a growing infatuation with horse racing. The members of Congress who may have feigned indignation at Smith's remark might have decried his claims about the pervasiveness of illegal gaming halls, but they could not refute the presence of several major racetracks spread throughout New England and the South.

While organized horse racing began in the South, by the end of the Civil War, it had spread northward. The South was in financial ruin during and after the war, so it was clear that if the sport of horse racing was to continue, then it would need the capital investment of the North. Racing horses required food, stables, and training, and their owners needed money to pay for this maintenance. As horse-racing historians Tom Biracree and Wendy Insinger note, "Horsemen could no longer afford to wait until a horse was five or six years old before it could race, and they needed public patronage to provide more and bigger purses to defray expenses."[6] As a result, owners had to organize themselves and create public venues that ran multiple races on a daily basis.

Saratoga Springs

One of the first and most prominent institutions devoted to wagering on horse races was erected in Saratoga Springs, New York. A mile track was laid down in 1863 by a group of investors known as the Saratoga Association. The controlling interest was held by Jim Morrissey, a champion boxer and recent don of gambling halls in New York City. The resort town of Saratoga, famed for its spa, already had a connection to gambling before Morrissey arrived. Initially attracting patients to its mineral waters, the spa catered to a more genteel vacationing set by the 1820s. By the 1850s, Saratoga's amusements grew to include discreet gaming halls and horse races. Within 10 years, 15 gambling establishments would be running wide open in the small town. And in 1861, Morrissey opened his first gambling hall in Saratoga, a few years prior to his racing venture.

By 1867, Morrissey was already the boss of horse racing and gambling operations in Saratoga. Reform elements in the community had tried to run Morrissey out of town but with no success. Part of Morrissey's appeal was that he kept his establishment orderly and always donated money to local philanthropic causes (and to local politicians). In that year, Morrissey built the Saratoga Club House. It was the realization of a lifelong dream to own the greatest gambling house in America, one that would rival the luxurious pleasure palaces of Europe. In time, the Saratoga Club attained that reputation. A salon, drawing rooms, and large gaming rooms occupied the lower level, while private rooms for high-stakes games were housed on the second floor. As per Morrissey's house rules, no women were allowed in the gaming areas, no Saratoga citizens could gamble at all, and no credit was extended to any visitors. Even with these restrictions, gamblers flocked to the club and the racetrack by the tens of thousands each year. Within the first two years of operation, the Club House and track racked in half a million dollars.

The professional gamblers who came to Saratoga were a different breed than their western counterparts. Unlike the Trans-Mississippi gamblers, who acquired their incomes at the card table or roulette wheel, the racetrack and clubhouse clientele was initially composed of wealthy farmers, industrialists, and men born to money. They were the social elite who had the spending cash and free time to vacation at resort towns like Saratoga. They did not gamble as a trade, but many were "professional" in their skill at betting and gaming. Because he had aspirations to be part of the social aristocracy, Jim Morrissey made sure that his patrons were of the best character, and he brooked no boorish conduct that would upset the decorum of his establishment. He even dressed himself up as an eastern dandy, and his wife was covered in jewels befitting one of Old World wealth. Unfortunately, despite Morrissey's pretensions, the clientele of the Club House never looked upon him as anything more than a fine host and businessman. Morrissey's spendthrift ways and his ill-advised investments in Wall Street (another of his pretensions to high social status) eventually depleted his fortune. Having already served twice as a congressman from New York (1866–70), Morrissey returned to politics in 1875. He won a seat in the New York Senate. He made a successful bid for reelection in 1877, but before he could complete his term, he died of pneumonia on May 1, 1978. He was still the operator of Saratoga Club House and racetrack, but his estate by then had dwindled to $75,000. Ownership of the successful gambling hall and track passed to other hands.

The Saratoga Springs venture was the model for all other big racetracks in the nation. When East Coast investors realized the potential of racetracks, they began setting up courses up and down the Atlantic seaboard. One of the first of the imitators was Leonard W. Jerome. A financier and partner of Jim Morrissey, Leonard had watched the growth of the Saratoga enterprise and decided to duplicate its success in New York City. He joined with his friend, August Belmont, to purchase an estate in Fordham, Long Island. There, in 1866, the new partners established Jerome Park, a fancy racecourse coupled with an extravagant clubhouse. As Tom Biracree and Wendy Insinger relate, "Included in the facilities were spacious dining rooms, a huge ballroom, a skating rink, a trap-shooting range and overnight accommodations."[7] Jerome and Belmont were after the same moneyed clientele that had been patronizing Saratoga. To this end, the financiers organized a jockey club that boasted 1,300 members selected from the social register. But it was the out-of-town guests of Saratoga and Jerome Park that helped the spread of horse racing in the country. Impressed with the gambling, entertainment, lodgings, and quality of patronage, wealthy visitors would return to their home states and set up jockey clubs of their own.

Emergence of Bookmakers

"While the wealthy members of the newly formed jockey clubs provided the impetus for the new growth of racing," Biracree and Insinger assert, "it was the gambling that provided the fuel."[8] To facilitate the wagering, a new figure emerged on the racing scene in 1866. Bookmakers were so named because they originally placed so many bets with opponents that they had to keep a book with records of their transactions. They operated then, as they do now, by giving odds on each horse in a race. The odds are determined by the bookmaker, increasing the payouts for horses that have little chance to win while dropping the odds on horses that are favorites. Bookmakers skew the odds slightly to take in more money than they pay out. The difference is their profit.

Small time bookmakers, also known as handbook operators, frequented saloons and other public hangouts to find customers. These men preyed on the poorer classes, and therefore they did not need a lot of capital to back up their bets. Handbook operators took wagers as low as a nickel but never more than a few dollars. They did not make much money in their racket, but it was enough to survive. And keeping the stakes low meant they were never a threat to the poolrooms.

Poolrooms were betting establishments run by bigger bookmakers. With fixed locations, they catered to a slightly wealthier clientele who stopped in to get racing odds and make wagers. The odds at poolrooms changed as the odds at the track changed. The updates for each race were sent by telegraph from the track. Patrons could wait in the poolroom to see if more favorable odds would appear or until an employee called "time." Then the results of the race would be read from a ticker tape, and all bets would be settled. The process would begin again for the next race that day.

Poolroom operators gave worse odds than those bookmakers who worked the racetrack. Sometimes the odds were cut by half. The poolroom managers rationalized the lower odds as part of their fee for convenience and for being able to cover large bets. The bookmakers who conducted business at the track, on the other hand, paid fees to the track owners. The owners usually encouraged the presence of bookmakers at their tracks because it brought in customers. And bookmakers did not mind paying the fees because the wealthier patrons at the track meant substantially larger profits. At the more prestigious tracks, this system worked well, and bookmakers typically ran an honest business in order to maintain their lucrative positions. At some of the smaller racecourses, however, abuses were more common.

Nearing the End of the Race

Unscrupulous bookmakers possessed all sorts of means to fix races in their favor. Some would bribe jockeys to throw races; others might drug or cripple the odds-on favorites. Even poolroom operators could prove dishonest by continuing to take bets on losing horses between the time the race results were relayed to the poolroom and the time the operator announced the results to the waiting gamblers. Checking the misdeeds of dishonest bookmakers was one of the many jobs of the Jockey Club. Formed in 1894, the Jockey Club was an organization of track operators and horse owners that wrote the rulebook for the running of races in the United States. In an attempt to monopolize and standardize the racing scene, the Jockey Club licensed the competitors, hired the officials, and investigated any corruption on all major courses. Anyone tied to racing could be fined, suspended, or barred from member tracks if the Jockey Club revealed a trace of fraud or dishonesty.

Unfortunately, the Jockey Club could not address the amount of reported and unreported abuse in the bookmaking racket. In 1894, there were 314 tracks in America, and the number of bookmakers was many times that. Although a good portion of these bookmakers remained honest in their dealings, the criminal element among them brought an increasingly bad reputation to the business. Furthermore, the antigambling crusaders who were at this time shutting down gambling halls across the nation also set their sights upon horse racing and the perceived evils of bookmaking. In league with the powerful temperance movement that swept turn-of-the-century America, the antigambling forces painted all forms of wagering as a great social ill. Pressured by the temperance lobby, politicians who once sanctioned gaming halls and racetracks (usually for a cut of the profits) tried to remain in office by turning against the gambling operators. Other candidates won their political campaigns by running on a temperance ticket. The result was a clamping down on the bookmakers.

With the shift in public opinion, the bookmakers no longer enjoyed the protection of the big-city political machines. Many poolrooms were raided and run out of business by politicians who were hoping to show their commitment to cleaning up vice in their cities. Other bookmakers were forced underground. The repercussions for horse racing were severe. Without bookmakers at the track, fewer people went to see the races. Dwindling attendance coupled with the loss of revenue generated by bookmaker fees forced the tracks to close one by one. In 1908, only 25 of the original 314 tracks in America remained open. That same year, New York banned bookmaking. Within three more years, Belmont Park, the pride of New York City, closed its doors to ride out the wave of antigambling sentiment.

Horse Racing's Salvation

The tracks that remained in operation in the early years of the 20th century were under the patronage of the Jockey Club, which had considerable political and economic clout. But it was not the protective arms of the Jockey Club that ensured the future of horse racing in America after the turn of the century. With bookmakers banned, the tracks had to find a new way to generate money through wagering. The answer was provided by Colonel Matt Winn. As manager of Churchill Downs in Louisville, Kentucky, Winn was desperate to save his track when the city enforced its bookmaking ban in 1908. He recalled that several pari-mutuel wagering machines had been left in track storage since the 1870s. He had the machines installed in time for the running of the Kentucky Derby. To Winn's surprise, the machines pulled in more than $67,000, far more than was earned through bookmaking in the previous year's derby.

The pari-mutuel machines issued tickets to bettors that only identified (by number) the horse they backed in the race. The odds for that horse, indeed all horses in the race, were determined after betting had ceased—not before, as bookmakers had done. The method of tabulation was based simply on how the number of bettors divided their wagers in the race. Thus the odds were true odds, not the skewed odds offered by bookmakers. The only difference was that the track levied a 5 percent fee that was skimmed from the machine's total intake. Pari-mutuel machines had arrived in the United States in the 1870s, but bookmakers strongly opposed them, and the tracks acquiesced. With bookmaking outlawed, pari-mutuel betting became the salvation of American horse racing. During the reform years, the system kept racing alive in Kentucky, but in the 1930s, pari-mutuel betting would spread. Track operators appreciated the system for its mechanical ease. Gamblers approved of pari-mutuel betting because it eliminated the suspicious oddsmaking of the bookmakers. The states also gave their support to the system because the pari-mutuel earnings were taxable income for the tracks. As Biracree and Insinger write, "The latter became increasingly attractive during the Depression, when ten states authorized pari-mutuel wagering and the number of tracks increased by 70 percent."[9] Until that time, American horse racing by and large relocated to Canada, where it thrived.

A New Cultural Climate for Gambling

Between the turn of the century and end of the First World War, the reform movement held sway in America. Frugality, temperance, and modesty were the bywords of the times, and leagues of reform-minded individuals (such as the Woman's Christian Temperance Union and the Anti-Saloon League) successfully lobbied local, state, and federal politicians to make the war against vice part of their campaign agendas. The most notable manifestation of the power of the dominant Puritan outlook was the enactment of the Eighteenth Amendment, which prohibited making, transporting, or selling alcoholic beverages. Adopted in August 1917 and becoming law in 1920, the amendment ushered in the era of Prohibition. Although liquor was the ostensible demon named in the Eighteenth Amendment, the reform movement grew to such power and influence that all vices—including gambling—felt the sting of the nation's moral crusade. Like the tavern trade, gaming operations and bookmakers moved underground during Prohibition. There the gambling business remained until the dawning of the next decade.

According to Vicki Abt, a professor and board member of the National Council of Problem Gambling, legalized gambling was destined to make a comeback in the 1930s because of changing economic and cultural conditions that significantly impacted America during the decades between the two world wars. "Culturally, the central event of the period was the start of the breakdown of the Protestant morality," Abt argues.[10] This change in the nation's moral structure was a product of the Roaring Twenties, a time in which the urban middle class rebelled against the ideals of Prohibition by reveling in all of the taboos of America's Puritan past. Dancing to frenetic jazz beats, smoking in public, and drinking in speakeasies (illegal, underground bars) became the fashion among those who could afford those pleasures. For women, the times were especially liberating. The new Jazz Age "flappers" drank, smoked, and donned revealing clothing as they toyed with more openly sexual personas. Although critics labeled this behavior "licentious," advocates of the new hedonism viewed it as a celebration of the pleasures that had always been part of America yet were repressed by Protestant ethics.

In addition to the weakening of culture values, Abt asserts that the Great Depression of the 1930s "expanded the climate for acceptance and legislation of gambling."[11] In Abt's view, the depression belied the Protestant work ethic by destroying the notion that an individual's hard work always earned the just reward of economic security. Secondly, the depression taxed the states' loosely organized systems of social security (mainly local church charities and politically financed relief organizations) to such an extent that the central government under President Franklin Roosevelt felt compelled to remedy the situation with the federal relief programs of the New Deal. Trying to regain their legitimacy—as well as to raise needed capital—the states looked for ways to generate quick income. One of the obvious means was to legalize gambling and tax the profits. Following the example of Kentucky (and other states such as Illinois and Louisiana that had converted in the recession years of the late 1920s), several more state legislatures (such as Michigan, New Hampshire, and Ohio) authorized pari-mutuel betting at racetracks in the early 1930s. One state, Nevada, went even further and unsuspectingly ushered in the modern age of American gambling.

BIRTH OF CASINO GAMBLING

Between 1910 and 1931, Nevada maintained only a shaky allegiance to the edicts of the national reform movement. The liberal attitudes of the populace made enforcing the bans on gambling an unpopular move for any zealous politician. Most Nevadans simply ignored the law; others called for repeal. In 1915, public opposition was strong enough that the stringent antigambling laws were amended to legalize slot machines and card games. The business of gambling, however, remained underground until 1931. In that year, the state government, faced with economic ruin from the Great Depression, convinced itself and the citizenry that reaping a share of the lucrative but illicit economy could save the state's finances. The state legislature lifted its restrictions on gambling, and the underground gaming houses moved into the light to become legitimate businesses that could be taxed accordingly.

New "above ground" gambling enterprises opened immediately. These were not the small, one or two-story gambling halls that dotted the West in the previous century but larger clubs that were modeled on the swank resorts of the East. Their clientele included not only the local denizens who had frequented the underground betting parlors but also visitors from California who had been crossing into Nevada since the 1920s to take advantage of the state's market in quickie marriages and divorces. Thus, with the gambling clubs came the first stirrings of Nevada's soon-to-blossom tourist trade.

LAS VEGAS: FROM CLUBS TO CASINOS

The Nevada town most notably associated with modern gambling was also one of the first to host a gambling club. The Meadows Club opened in Las Vegas in 1931. The owner, Tony Cornero, was a former owner of gaming clubs in California. He relocated to Las Vegas when California authorities chose to crack down on gambling operations in the 1920s and 1930s. Cornero's new venture offered customers an assortment of table games such as blackjack, poker, craps, and roulette. Unbeknownst to Cornero at the time, these games would become standard fare in most clubs and casinos from then on.

When Cornero arrived, Las Vegas was just another provincial outpost in the desert. Most of the money that came into town was in some way connected to the nearby Hoover Dam. Workmen spent their dollars in town during the dam's construction (1930 to 1936), and then the tourist trade picked up once the dam was completed. In fact, when the people of Las Vegas learned that gambling enterprises were opening in their town, they were tolerant of the trade, but they had no conception that gambling would come to define the community as well as become its economic focus. As

John M. Findlay writes, "Bettors generally risked only little sums, and observers mostly agreed that the business was small, even harmless."[12] Other operators followed Cornero's lead, and more clubs popped up in downtown Las Vegas in the 1930s, but throughout the decade, gambling remained only one of many attractions for visitors.

It was only in the 1940s that gambling took off in Nevada. The more modest clubs gave way to larger enterprises that could, by modern standards, be called casinos. Two large casinos, the El Rancho Vegas and the Last Frontier, moved into downtown Las Vegas in 1941 and 1942, respectively. And in 1946, William F. Harrah built the first elaborate resort casino in Reno. Harrah was not interested in attracting the local patron or the casual visitor; he aimed at marketing his casino to bring in a steady stream of tourist dollars. To this end, he employed buses to pull in thousands of middle-income tourists who otherwise might have not made the trip to Reno. His fleet fanned out to 31 neighboring cities, most of which were in California. The scheme worked, and soon gambling resorts themselves became tourist destinations.

The first huge casino—one on par with Harrah's—came to Las Vegas in the same year that Harrah's opened. Benjamin "Bugsy" Siegel, a New York mobster, built the Flamingo Hotel and Casino with $6 million of underworld proceeds. Set seven miles away from the downtown area, the Flamingo was a huge complex with 75 lavish accommodations, a golf course, a shooting range, a gym, an array of expensive gift shops, and, of course, a casino. It was the first step in realizing Siegel's dream of transforming Las Vegas into a gambling and resort community. Siegel's mobster backers were not so taken by his vision; they were more unnerved that Siegel's Flamingo enterprise lost money as soon as it opened. Within months of its inauguration, the Flamingo closed. It reopened after another couple of months, but the business continued to waver next to insolvency. Siegel's mob connections—including Lucky Luciano, one (of the founders of the National Crime Syndicate) suspected Siegel of siphoning off part of the casino's earnings. Wanting to make sure their investment was appropriately managed, the mob had Siegel murdered. Under new management, the Flamingo eventually became successful, and it set the stage for other resort-casino complexes (such as the Desert Inn, the Dunes, and the Tropicana) to fill in the soon-to-be-famous Las Vegas "Strip" within the next 10 years.

The Criminal Connection

Although not every casino operator was tied to the mob (as Cornero and Siegel were), "modern Las Vegas," in the words of reporter and author Timothy L. O'Brien, "could never have been erected without the vast sums of money organized crime eventually poured into it."[13] The criminal bosses who settled in Las Vegas were either former bootleggers who became obsolete when Prohibition was repealed in 1933, or they were illegal gaming-hall operators from Southern California who had to relocate when California clamped down on gambling. Despite their nefarious dealings, these underworld characters at least brought with them a level of experience in operating gaming enterprises that helped Las Vegas's earliest casinos become big business. Furthermore, as John M. Findlay concedes, "The legal nature of betting in the Silver State enabled gamblers to practice their livelihood respectably, bringing them above ground from the underworld, so they in turn helped to ensure the success of the urban gambling resort which gave legitimacy to their way of life."[14]

The operators from Southern California also contributed to Las Vegas's rise by enticing their former clients to make the pilgrimage to the new gambling haven. Knowing how to treat their Los Angeles friends ensured that these big gamblers would continue to visit Las Vegas. Some of these big gamblers were also members of the other select clientele that the casino operators hoped to attract. The Los Angeles underworld had always had a connection to Hollywood, and movie stars, directors, and writers were both friends and patrons of the Southern California operators. Once these celebrities began showing up in Las Vegas (at the invitation of the casino owners), the chamber of commerce recognized the advantage of marketing the town as a unique place where common people could rub elbows with their film idols while standing at the roulette table or sitting in on a hand of poker. The mobsters even concerned themselves with the management, upkeep, and promotion of their casinos to draw bigger crowds. Las Vegas was big business, and it was a legal business. So those who once had been skilled at evading the law now concentrated on maximizing their profits by working within it.

The time and money spent by casino owners made Las Vegas thrive in the years between the end of World War II and the 1960s. Not only did visitors flock to Las Vegas to gamble, but the number of permanent residents rose to more than 100,000 by 1960. With the rapid expansion, however, came many of the urban-development problems that are common to any community transforming from town to metropolis in such a short time. Amid lavish casinos and tidy bankrolls were housing shortages and poverty. And the local citizens were still not reconciled to the idea that vice and the criminal element had completely hijacked the future of Las Vegas.

The degenerate aspects of the city came under fire in November 1950 when the Senate Special Committee on Organized Crime in Interstate Commerce decided to hold hearings in Las Vegas. Headed by Senator Carey Estes Kefauver of Tennessee, the committee openly deplored the fact that the civic authorities had let known racketeers manage the gambling operations in Las Vegas. By the time the senators had drawn up their report, however, the Kefauver Committee's criticism went beyond a condemnation of the criminal element. Citing the city's lack of economic security, its absence of a cultural life outside of casinos, and its corruptive influence on visitors who indulged a vice that was illegal in their home states, the committee concluded that gambling was "not healthful"[15] to the residents of southern Nevada.

THE FIRST STEPS TOWARD REGULATION

The Kefauver Committee had little immediate impact on disrupting organized crime in the United States. The committee was purely an investigative body, not a regulatory commission with teeth to weed out corruption. But by broadcasting the hearings in which gangsters testified to the extent of mob influence in many facets of American life (including gambling), the Kefauver Committee did make the public aware of the scope of criminal activity in the country. Even the head of the Federal Bureau of Investigations (FBI), J. Edgar Hoover, was compelled to admit that the underworld existed—a fact that the FBI had publicly denied for so long. Ultimately, with increased publicity came a heightened nationwide fear that the mob would continue to grow and infect other communities in the way it had taken over Las Vegas. A backlash against the unseen menace resulted in the formation of more than 70 local crime commissions in cities all over America in the early 1950s. Furthermore, since legalized gambling appeared to be clearly in the hands of the mob, the legislatures of Arizona, California, Massachusetts, and Montana voted down proposals to allow legalized gambling to spread to their states.

Incredibly, it would not be until 1955, four years after Kefauver's hearings ended, that Las Vegas would establish its own Gaming Control Board. This move came not as a show of voluntary concern for crime; instead it was prompted by public outcry over underworld kingpin Meyer Lansky's use of mob funds to finance the Thunderbird casino. The state shut down the Thunderbird and gave the control board the power to investigate future applicants for casino licenses as well as to enforce current gambling regulations. Four years later, after growing public suspicions that the Gaming Control Board may have been less than scrupulous in its duties, the Nevada legislature passed the Gaming Control Act, which created a five-member Gaming Commission to oversee the three-member control board.

The Gaming Commission was the brainchild of Governor Grant Sawyer, who had won election in 1958 on a platform that promised, if not to rid Las Vegas of the criminal element, to at least make sure that no more undesirables took a hand in operating the casinos. Sawyer's commission created a "Black Book" of those who were to be excluded from even entering a casino. Sawyer's men routinely patrolled the casinos, looking for any characters named in the Black Book. His agents were mostly former law-enforcement personnel, and Sawyer encouraged his men to "hang tough" in the face of resistance from the casino owners.

Despite the governor's interest in cleaning up the racketeers, Sawyer's commission was largely ineffectual. In 1961, President John F. Kennedy and U.S. Attorney General Robert Kennedy decided to take matters into federal hands. Their long-range goal was to outlaw gambling altogether. The first step was to show how gambling and crime were inextricably entwined. To achieve this, Robert Kennedy asked the Nevada attorney general to deputize federal agents to conduct raids on the casinos. Fearing the move would not only reveal the criminal element but also ruin the state's economy, Governor Sawyer convinced Washington that he was stepping up his own efforts to regulate the casino business. The Kennedys backed off, but when Sawyer's words were put to the test, his administration proved too weak to handle the crooks.

In 1965, the co-owner of the Desert Inn—a mobster by the name of Ruby Kolod—was entered in Sawyer's Black Book. His name was removed two weeks later after mob boss Moe Dalitz put pressure on the Gaming Commission. To show his overall displeasure, Dalitz then funded Sawyer's opponent in the next gubernatorial race. Sawyer lost to his lieutenant governor, Paul Laxalt. Timothy L. O'Brien finishes the story by stating that "during [Laxalt's] occupancy of the governor's mansion no new names were added to the Black Book's ranks. For good measure, Laxalt named Dalitz a 'special assistant to the governor.'"[16] Sawyer succeeded in blocking the federal government's attempt to grab the reins of gambling from the states, but he had failed to divorce Nevada's casinos from their criminal origins.

LAS VEGAS MAKEOVER

Despite Paul Laxalt's tolerant opinion of men like Dalitz, it was under his term as governor (1966–70) that the face of gambling in Las Vegas changed most dramatically. In 1966, the first new casino to open on the Strip in eight years heralded the new style and image of Las Vegas. Caesar's Palace was a huge resort complex that drew upon every imaginable classical Roman motif—a columned portico entrance, fountains shooting water high into the air, replicas of famous classical statuary, and employees dressed as centurions. There was a standard gaming room (though oval-shaped), but it was surrounded by the unreal Roman-esque spectacle that offered the hotel and casino visitors a unique experience unavailable in the other casinos in Las Vegas (or anywhere in the world, for that matter). Caesar's Palace was the creation of Jay Sarno, a mob front man who was also part showman. Like many of his fellow operators, Sarno was unconcerned with daily receipts or casino management, but unlike his brethren, Sarno was a marketer. Caesar's opened its halls to conventions, and in the 1970s, it began hosting high-profile boxing matches that were televised. Soon, when people thought of Las Vegas, they thought of Caesar's Palace.

The advent of the "themed" casinos was only one of the key occurrences that would transform Las Vegas in the late 1960s. A second major change was as important but less visible. In 1969, the Nevada legislature passed the Corporate Gaming Act. This legislation allowed public corporations to invest in casinos. Suddenly gambling was in league with capitalism, the lifeblood of America, and gambling became just another industry. Corporatizing also tempered the image of Nevada casinos as mob fronts since these enterprises were now answerable to a board of stockholders and the Securities and Exchange Commission.

By merging spectacle with corporate sanitization, the chamber of commerce hoped to reshape utterly public attitude toward Las Vegas in the 1970s and 1980s. The mobsters still ran several of the older casinos into the 1980s, but the last of the big-time bosses, Tony Spilotro, was arrested and extradited back to Chicago in 1983. From then on, the mob was out and big business was in. Bigger corporate hotel-casinos were constructed around various themes (from an ancient Egyptian pyramid to a one-stop tour of Hollywood), and more sections of these complexes were devoted to stage shows, shopping, and family amusements. The MGM Grand Casino and Hotel even added a theme park with seven amusement rides. It was a conscious attempt to rid Las Vegas of the "Sin City" image and create a family-friendly vacation spot. Of course, gambling was not forsaken in this makeover. As former *Time* and *New Yorker* editor Kurt Andersen explained in a 1994 article: "People who won't take vacations without their children now have places to stick the kids while Mom and Dad pursue the essentially unwholesome act of squandering the family savings on cards and dice."[17]

Anderson maintains that the success of Las Vegas as a family-friendly destination was not due to some cleansing of the vice-laden elements of the city, but rather it came as a result of the nation's increasing "collective tolerance for vulgarity."[18] According to Anderson, the rise of vulgarity is part of a general relaxing of rigid Protestant ethics that has been transforming America since the 1960s. This liberal and libertine attitude is reflected in such cultural mainstays as the media, consumer spending, architecture, and entertainment. And as each these cultural arenas become more accepting of the vulgar or garish, they reinforce the notion that permissiveness is the norm. Las Vegas embraces the vulgar extreme in nearly all these categories. Thus, Las Vegas reflects America as America reflects Las Vegas. "If it is now acceptable for the whole family to come along to Las Vegas," Anderson writes, "that's because the values of America have changed, not those of Las Vegas. Deviancy really has been defined down."[19] While this trend toward permissiveness has had a glaringly noticeable effect on Las Vegas (i.e., the

Strip of the 1960s looked like an alluring adult playground, while the Strip of the 1980s and beyond appears to have more in common with Disneyland), it has also redefined public attitudes toward gambling nationwide.

THE MODERN WAVE OF LEGALIZED GAMBLING

The fiscal crises of the 1930s (and again in the 1970s) and the growing permissive culture that derived from the 1960s were the two forces that changed the way the public and federal and state legislatures viewed gambling in the late 20th century. Because of unpredictable economic downturns coupled with expanding populations, the states struggled to find money to maintain public services. Furthermore, since they cannot operate on a deficit for long (the way the federal government can), the state legislatures were constantly seeking steady sources of income. Legalized gambling has always been an obvious option, but many states were reluctant to embrace it because of the moral taint that seemed to adhere to it. One reason they were able to avoid serious consideration of legalized gambling was because of the post–World War II industrial boom that funded many state economies. But by the 1960s and 1970s, the boom had ended, and state incomes would soon fail to meet the needs of the still-growing population.

Charting the progress of legalized gambling in America in the 20th century is a study in both economic need and a growing tolerance of this vice. In the 1930s, the Great Depression prompted Las Vegas to inaugurate casino gambling and encouraged 21 states to reauthorize horse racing. Between the 1930s and the 1960s, postwar development held sway. In the 1950s, some states tolerated charity bingo games, while Florida permitted betting on the old Basque sport of jai alai. But the next great wave of legalized gambling did not occur until 1963. In that year, New Hampshire resurrected a relic of the previous century—the state lottery.

LOTTERIES RETURN

As the 1960s dawned, residents of New Hampshire were faced with rising costs of increased public services. The state's constitution prohibits progressive taxes to keep up with inflation, so in the past the state legislature often relied on raising "sin taxes" on such items as alcohol and tobacco products. In 1963, the people of New Hampshire were vehemently against bearing any more tax burdens. Acknowledging the resentment, the legislature asked the voters consider an initiative to raise money through a lottery system, the proceeds of which would support education (half the sales earnings were kept by the state and the other half were returned to the winners as prizes). The chosen form was a sweepstakes that was tied to two horse races run in the course of each year. The government would hold a monopoly on the sweepstakes so that the fear of tampering or fraud was eliminated. The other enticing aspect of the lottery was that it was designed to attract bettors from neighboring states. In effect, New Hampshire was banking on the hope that the needed revenue would primarily come from out-of-state ticket sales. For residents of New Hampshire, the lottery appeared to offer a solution to the state's financial needs without dipping further into the people's pocketbooks. The voters overwhelmingly approved the initiative, and the first state lottery run in roughly 70 years began legal operation in 1964.

During its first year of operation, the New Hampshire sweepstakes sold tickets at $3 apiece. As predicted, many of the tickets were purchased by residents of nearby Massachusetts and New York. But overall sales fell short of expectation. Of the $10 million predicted earnings, only $5.7 million in tickets were sold. Each year thereafter, sales continued to decline. By 1967, only $2.5 million was generated through the sweepstakes. In that year, New York, recognizing that a good portion of its residents' income was crossing the border, decided to start a lottery of its own. The New York Lottery was a monthly drawing, which, by law, was limited to not more than 12 drawings per year. The tickets, priced at $1 and $2, were sold only at such reputable establishments as banks, hotels, and municipal offices. Still, like the New Hampshire sweepstakes, the New York Lottery failed to live up to expectations. Sales declined to the level of New Hampshire's disappointing results by 1970.

In their 1985 book, *The Business of Risk: Commercial Gambling in Mainstream America*, Vicki Abt, James F. Smith, and Eugene Martin Christiansen attribute the failure of the New Hampshire and New York lotteries to their structure and operation. Both lotteries, the authors claim, were designed—albeit unknowingly—to limit the public's participation. Abt, Smith, and Christiansen attest, "The long intervals between opportunities to play dictated very slow rates of gambling, with the likelihood that many persons would lose interest in the games altogether once their novelty had worn off." Very low odds of winning a prize and so few winners per prize period also contributed to waning interest in the games. Most important, however, was that the random drawings left little room for players to try to manipulate their own fates. "Neither lottery offered opportunities for player participation or the exercise of skill," Abt, Smith, and Christiansen conclude, "and while the games were very easy to learn they had little or no intrinsic play value."[20]

New Jersey's and Massachusetts's Innovations

Learning from its neighbors' mistakes, the state of New Jersey launched its own lottery in 1970. The New Jersey State Lottery was based on correctly picking a six-digit number. Instead of monthly drawings, this lottery was held weekly to encourage frequent playing and to hold players' continual interest. More significantly, the price of tickets was only 50 cents, to make the game more affordable. Cheap tickets and more chances to gamble and win per month proved a winning combination for New Jersey. Within six months, ticket sales reached $78 million, and just over a decade later sales topped $417 million. It was an astounding success that was instantly copied. New York dropped its lottery ticket prices to 50 cents and even began selling tickets through common retail stores to increase visibility and convenience. Weekly drawings also became the standard for all state lotteries that would eventually follow in the wake of New Jersey's success.

New Jersey, however, remained at the forefront of lottery experimentation for several years. At first, payouts increased, and in 1971, a New Jersey resident became the first person in lottery history to win $1 million in prize money. Then in 1972, New Jersey inaugurated the first daily-drawing game, which greatly increased gamblers' frequency of play. Massachusetts took the idea one step further in 1974 by marketing the first "instant game" lottery tickets. Commonly known as "scratchers," instant-game lottery tickets rely on purchasers scratching off a thin coating that covers hidden numbers or symbols. A correct pattern or grouping of these characters yields a winning ticket. Most winning tickets pay out small sums, which for most players is enough since the gratification is instant and player participation is high. In the year following the Massachusetts innovation, New Jersey trumped its own daily-drawing lottery by allowing for even greater player participation. The new "Pick-it" lottery was a "daily numbers" game that permitted players to choose the three-digit number they wanted to play. The new "Pick-it" game was so successful, it replaced the old daily game in 1976. The following year, half the lottery tickets sold in New Jersey were for the "Pick-it" game. In less than a decade, 15 states adopted the "Pick-it" formula.

Lotto and Powerball

Although the feeling of controlling one's fate enticed players to flock to the daily games, the increasing prize amounts of all lotteries also reeled in a sizable portion of the population. In 1976, New York combined the New Jersey "Pick-it" principle with an old Italian game called Lotto. Every week the lotto prize was offered to anyone who could correctly choose six numbers (each ranging from 1 to 36). Since the odds of choosing the correct set of numbers are astronomical (about 1.9 million to 1), few people ever won, and the prize money would then accumulate from week to week. In a matter of weeks, the jackpot would swell to tens of millions of dollars. This time the low odds of winning did not deter gamblers; instead the huge rewards waiting for the lucky guesser kept up public interest. New York grossed $197 million in 1977. Five years later, the lottery took in $425 million. In 1984, a year after the state began running the Lotto drawings twice a week, ticket sales reached nearly $900 million.

Lotto drawings caught on in other states, but not every state could boast the kind of jackpots New York offered. The prize amounts were (and are) still subject to the number of tickets sold. Therefore, the states with fewer residents could only afford to award cash prizes in relation to their population size (not including out-of-state sales). That meant by the time California began hosting lotteries in 1985, the smaller states had an increasingly difficult time competing with the huge cash prizes available in the states—like New York and California—that have bigger populations. To remedy the inequality, Iowa, Kansas, Oregon, Rhode Island, West Virginia, and the District of Columbia banded together in September 1987 to form the Multi-State Lottery Association (MUSL). Missouri joined the confederation one month later. Operating out of Des Moines, Iowa, the MUSL ran a game in which players were asked to pick seven correct numbers (each ranging from 1 to 40) to win the coveted multimillion-dollar jackpot. The new Lotto America was not a grand success on its first outing. After six months, ticket sales brought in only $32 million (an insignificant sum that had to be split seven ways).

The MUSL was quick to revamp its lottery when proceeds did not meet expectations. In 1988, Lotto America changed from a challenge of picking seven numbers to one of picking six numbers. The range of numbers also changed from a field of 40 choices to a field of 56. The new game was statistically more difficult to win, but that only increased the size of the prizes. By 1991, Delaware, Idaho, Indiana, Kentucky, Maine, Minnesota, Montana, South Dakota, and Wisconsin joined the MUSL, and the total yearly intake was around $400 million. After dividing the proceeds 16 ways and allowing that half was returned as prizes, each state fared only a little better than the inaugural run five years previously.

The Multi-State Lottery Association tried to bolster its intake by starting another high-jackpot game. In 1992, they unveiled Powerball. The new game was still based on picking numbers, but this time players were to choose five numbers (from a field of 45) and then select a sixth "Powerball" number (also out of 45). The combination of the six numbers could yield nine different ways to win a prize (the lowest were in single-dollar amounts, while the grand prize was worth millions). The odds of winning the Powerball jackpot were worse than winning the Lotto jackpot, but this only sent the prize totals even higher. That, in turn, brought player interest. After two years of steadily rising ticket sales, the annual sales between 1994 and 1996 reached well over a billion dollars. Then, unexpectedly, in 1997, ticket purchases dropped below the billion mark. Part of the blame was attributed to competitive lotteries in other states and to the rise of other legalized forms of gambling. Perhaps more significant, though, was the defection of the state of Georgia from the MUSL. Georgia had joined the MUSL in 1995 but quickly abandoned ship to join another multistate lottery organization. When the state changed games, anti-lottery forces—spurred greatly by religious fundamentalists—staged a statewide campaign to end Georgia's participation in any lottery scheme. The grassroots campaign had great momentum and membership, but it lacked the money to win its crusade. Still, the strength of the anti-lottery movement made Georgia and other states aware of the growing opposition.

Lottery Criticisms

For the MUSL, there was a fearful moment that Georgia's decision was the herald of a coming backlash against lotteries. Yet no great push toward prohibition followed. That is not to say, however, that modern lotteries have enjoyed universal applause. Besides the religious right condemning gambling as a corrupting influence, there have been many other criticisms of government-sponsored lotteries. One argument against lotteries is that an inordinate amount of lottery play comes from the less privileged, less educated, and least wealthy strata of American society. Citing statistics from economists Charles Clotfelter and Philip Cook, political science professor Michael Nelson states that "eighty-two percent of lottery bets are made by just 20 percent of players—and this group is disproportionately poor, black, and uneducated."[21] If lotteries are designed to generate revenue in the manner of a voluntary tax, then the government is targeting those people who can least afford the expense. In this respect, lotteries are equivalent to regressive taxes because they fall hardest on those citizens from the lowest income levels. Even if participation in the lottery is voluntary, Nelson and others ask whether it is ethical to run a lottery knowing that the income is derived from the poor and could otherwise be raised by "an increase in sales tax of less than 1 percent."[22]

Clotfelter and Cook's statistics, however, are not the only ones to weigh in on this question. For example, the North American Association of State and Provincial Lotteries (NASPL) disputes the notion that the poor are paying the burden of this voluntary tax. According to the NASPL, critics should refrain from even thinking of lotteries as a tax, since taxes are compulsory. But even if the poor were somehow coerced into participating in lotteries, the NASPL argues that they do not—as a whole—make up the largest percentage of ticket purchasers. In a public information pamphlet released in 2000, the NASPL cites surveys from various lottery states that reveal a completely different trend. In Colorado, less than 7 percent of the population had an annual income below the poverty line ($15,000) in the late 1990s, but only 5 percent of all the state's lottery players had incomes in that range. Similarly, a 1998 survey in Minnesota showed that while 9 percent of that state's lottery players had incomes below $20,000, a disproportionate number of players had incomes over $50,000. The NASPL maintains that of all lottery players in the nation, those with incomes of at least $75,000 spend three times as much on lottery tickets as do those with incomes under $25,000. The conflicting findings suggest that the question of lotteries' impact on the poor will likely remain a subject of debate for some time.

Perhaps a more serious question raised by legalized lotteries, though, regards the new complicity between government and gambling. One reason that lotteries were banned in the 19th century was that they were privately run (even if state-sponsored) affairs in which fraud was not uncommon. In order to remove the fear of wrongdoing from the minds of modern players, the states not only had to regulate the lotteries but own and operate them as well. While calming public fears may be a benefit of government ownership, the fact that state governments operate the games means that they are actively promoting gambling in society. This statement has an obvious ethical dimension, but it also has an economic one. In order to make money, the governments have to advertise—in effect, to persuade—citizens to continually support a grand-scale get-rich-quick scheme. In this light, the lottery operates as a business on which the state governments have a monopoly. The question then is, "Should it be a function of government to promote any business venture?" To answer positively or even tolerantly would blur the distinction between traditional notions of government and the private sector (where business has always remained).

An Unclear Future for Lotteries

Reasoned critiques of the lottery system have won over some state legislatures in recent years. Prior to 1999, of the 34 initiatives to legalize lotteries in various states, only two failed to win approval (both were defeated in North Dakota). Those that did pass did so by wide margins of votes. But since 1999, the margins have begun to shrink. In South Carolina, for example, residents approved a state lottery in 2000 but not without a hard fight against religious leaders and Republican opposition. In 1999, just over half of Alabama's voters struck down a constitutional amendment to initiate a lottery. In 2004, the lottery bill will likely be put back on the table, but this time at least 61 percent of those polled are expected to vote for the measure. As of the first half of 2004, 10 states have held out against mounting pressure to institute lotteries. Most of these states are in the South, which may seem unusual given that the Reconstruction lotteries once ran in every southern state. The reluctance, however, may be explained in part by the anti-gambling stance of the strong religious lobbies and, as professor Richard McGowan suggests, because the South "is also the section of the country that spends the least amount of tax dollars on social and welfare projects."[23]

One of the reasons lotteries enjoy public sanction in most of the country is because they are tied to specific social programs in the host states' budgets. Like the original New Hampshire sweepstakes, California, Florida, and Illinois are just a few of the states that use lottery proceeds to fund education. Massachusetts channels its lottery income to police and fire departments. Pennsylvania alleviates Medicare costs with lottery earnings. Connecting lotteries with social welfare programs gives players an impression that their gambling habits are supporting good causes. The link, however, may not hold in the future. As McGowan (among others) points out, the rising costs of these social programs will outpace the revenues generated by lotteries.

Examining the life cycles of the major types of state lottery games (Lotto, numbers games, and instant games) illustrates why experts like McGowan believe the forecast is not so rosy. Lotto sales are typically erratic, soaring when jackpots are so high that they become newsworthy and then plunging when interest wanes. Daily-numbers games tend to provide a steady income but without growth. Only instant games have shown successful increases in sales over time (which is why a vast majority of lottery states have relied on them for the greatest part of lottery revenue). Still, as McGowan comments, instant-game ticket sales "do not appear to be able to match the necessary increases in funding" that social programs require. He also warns: "Hence state governments need to reconsider seriously earmarking lottery revenues for a specific cause. If they do not, either the good cause will be underfunded or that state will have to permit other forms of gambling to cover the shortfall in revenue."[24]

THE CASINO BOOM

States that run lotteries have kept a close eye on the life cycle and revenues of those games. Recognizing that, in the long run, lotteries alone would not bring the revenues needed to fund social services, many of these states began considering the legalization of other forms of gambling. They wanted to back a form of gambling that could be run by private operators so that the state was not tainted—as with lotteries—by promoting a vice. Casinos were an obvious choice. But before 1978, the only model for casino gaming was Las Vegas, and its connection to crime and licentiousness would make casinos a hard sell to state constituencies. Then, in 1978, casino operations received a boost in credibility. That year, casino gambling came to New Jersey.

Atlantic City

Between 1900 and 1945, Atlantic City and other New Jersey shore communities were tourist havens. Atlantic City, especially, was a well-known resort town that catered to summer visitors from New York City and other nearby metropolises. The town's famous boardwalk (popularized in the game Monopoly), its luxury resorts, and its entertainment pavilions drew tourists by the thousands, as did the Miss America Pageant, held in Atlantic City every year. After World War II, however, several events contributed to the decline of New Jersey's seaside resort communities. Television stole away the audiences who had once come to see acts that were mainstays of Atlantic City venues. Furthermore, improved roads and the burgeoning of major airline travel changed the conception of the family vacation. People no longer felt confined to frequent the same nearby haunt year after year; tourism for many in the postwar decades meant the freedom to visit destinations across the United States. Without a steady stream of summer guests, Atlantic City and the whole New Jersey shore began to suffer. Lacking capital, the hotels and resorts couldn't keep up with the times. Some fell into disrepair. Sensing future decline, civic and business leaders in Atlantic City came together in the early 1970s to solve the crisis and bring tourism back to the community.

The proposal laid before the state in a 1974 referendum called for a reinstating of casinos to Atlantic City. The resort had once been home to the Millionaires Club, the Bath and Turf Club, and other popular betting venues in the early part of the century. The Atlantic City committee expected that golden age prosperity could easily return to the Jersey shore. What they did not count on was how resistant other New Jersey provinces were toward bailing out the tourist resorts. Many of the northern sections of the state felt only disdain for seaside communities that had never bothered to build any indigenous industries (outside of tourism) to help strengthen their local economies. With this strong opposition, the referendum was easily defeated.

Atlantic City's leaders did not give up, however. They pushed for a second referendum in 1976. This time, the town waged an advertising campaign to inform voters of the advantages gambling would bring to the state. Chief among the benefits was the assertion that gambling revenues would actually make the resort communities less dependent—and therefore less financially draining—on the rest of the state. James F. Wortman, the director of the Office of Gaming Education and Research at the University of Houston, maintains, "Most experts were skeptical that it would have a great impact, but at this point, it was something." Even with this grudging acceptance, according to Wortman, rumors suggested that the second referendum was still headed for defeat. "Some last-minute compromising enabled the caveat '. . . in Atlantic City only' to be added. This quieted the homeowners in the northern counties, who were afraid that having casinos nearby would lower property values."[25] The initiative passed by a narrow margin in November.

Even though casinos were given the green light in Atlantic City, the first one did not open until 1978. In the meantime, the town assembled a panel to consider how best to implement and regulate this foreign industry. The main concern was to keep organized crime from setting up shop and making Atlantic City into an East Coast Las Vegas. To ensure this, the panel established a cautious and thorough licensing department. Part of the license requirements stipulated that casino employees had to be drawn from the local community. This was to safeguard against racketeers simply filling casinos with experienced hands from Las Vegas or underground dealers from other cities like Chicago. The new casinos also had to provide for the possibility of advancement for entry-level employees so that there would be guaranteed turnover in the higher echelons. The strict regulations worked to the town's benefit. The first casino to open was in the recently refurbished Chalfonte-Haddon Hall Hotel, a property on the historic boardwalk. The owner and operator was Resorts International, a relatively new gaming corporation that ran casinos in the Bahamas (and had once been the Mary Carter Paint Company). On the first day of operation, the newly created New Jersey Casino Control Commission expected less than a thousand visitors to satisfy their collective curiosity by peeking into the new hotel game room. But, as Wortman attests, "When the doors opened, they found a line three abreast, three city blocks long. These lines continued for weeks."[26]

Lessons Learned from Atlantic City

Resorts International's success encouraged other corporate interests to invest in Atlantic City. Soon Bally's, Harrah's, and Playboy opened casinos there. In fact, the corporatization of casinos in Atlantic City was one of the positive legacies of this New Jersey experiment. While Las Vegas had to go through a transformation to become corporate in the 1970s and 1980s, Atlantic City began as a big-business venture. New Jersey casino operators did not have to muscle mobsters out of gaming halls, and that did a lot to bolster public confidence in the integrity of the New Jersey gambling enterprise. The other Atlantic City legacy that had not been part of Las Vegas's initial conception was immediate state regulation of the industry. As the renovation of the Chalfonte-Haddon Hall Hotel was underway, Governor Brendan T. Byrne selected the members of the New Jersey Casino Control Commission. The commission set down rules on casino operation as well as regulations for any subsidiary support and training facilities. To monitor casino compliance, the government inaugurated the New Jersey Division of Gaming Enforcement (an extension of the state police). These regulatory agencies worked to keep racketeers out of Atlantic City and inspire confidence in the aboveboard operation of its casinos. Coupled with corporate management of the casinos, immediate regulation helped calm public fears that this state revenue machine was really lining the pockets of organized crime. In addition, since the casinos were privatized industries, Atlantic City was funding the government without being managed by it. Concerns over the questionable government ethics in running state lotteries did not apply to the mere regulation of this money-making venture.

Atlantic City's embrace of casino gambling was, indeed, a moneymaking venture. According to Wortman, within 10 months of operation, Resorts International was able to pay off the principle loan amount of $77 million used to renovate the Chalfonte-Haddon. The community has also been benefiting from the new investment. Yearly per capita incomes that averaged $8,000 in the 1970s have roughly quadrupled in the new century. The new money has brought changes in civic infrastructure and public lifestyle. As Wortman details:

> *New housing starts are increasing in both counties [Atlantic and Cape May], and new malls, restaurants, and businesses are changing the face of their landscape. Poverty has not been eliminated, but a diverse compendium of noncasino jobs is available for those who are willing to work. Attendance at schools and colleges is on the rise, since families are better able to afford personal enrichment programs, job skill upgrades, and their children's education.*[27]

The story of New Jersey casinos, however, is not entirely rosy. "A succession of inept, and sometimes corrupt, politicians kept Atlantic City from realizing its growth potential," Wortman argues. As an example, he cites the suspect workings of the Casino Redevelopment Authority, a government organization founded along with the advent of the casinos. The Casino Redevelopment Authority was given the task of managing a fund built up through compulsory casino contributions. For the first six years, the fund was earmarked for civic improvement projects in Atlantic City. After that, other New Jersey communities could benefit from the proceeds. During the initial six-year period, the fund grew into the millions but, oddly, only one project was supported with fund money. "Infighting in the city council and lack of leadership from the mayor's office were largely responsible for this wasted opportunity," Wortman contends.[28] This was only one of the problems spawned in the new alliance between state authorities and casino interests. Others include overly strict casino regulations and a state law that bars anyone connected to the casinos from running for government office or even taking a hand in civic matters. This latter piece of legislation effectively keeps casino personnel from ever offering help in solving community problems and promotes an antagonistic relationship between two forces that could be working in greater partnership.

With the examples of the mismanaged funds and other problems since the 1970s, Atlantic City's legalization of casino gambling remains an experiment—one that still is being reviewed and amended even as the resort town continues to be the second-largest gambling center and the top resort destination in the United States. As a major tourist attraction, the revenues brought by casino gambling have been considerable. In 2003, the casinos grossed nearly $4.5 billion. The incredible income is a fact that has never been lost on other states contemplating the expansion of legalized gambling. Yet until 1989—13 years after Atlantic City passed its referendum—Nevada and New Jersey were the only states to have sanctioned casinos.

Several reasons may account for the long period of delay. First, the 1980s were dominated politically by the Republican Party, and many conservative politicians—especially those backed by the religious right—spoke out against the moral ills of gambling. Second, no reliable studies had been conducted to discern the impact of gambling on specific communities. Since casino gambling had mainly been the province of Las Vegas, few states had bothered to conduct research on the predicted social and economic costs of legalizing casinos in their own domains. Finally, as William R. Eadington, director of the Institute for the Study of Gambling at the University of Nevada-Reno, has suggested, the fortunes of the gambling industry rise and fall with the economy. When the economy is fairly strong, as it was in the early 1980s, gambling initiatives face stiffer opposition. In these times of relative prosperity, politicians can afford to take the moral high ground because the states and the federal government don't need the extra revenues. In times of economic adversity, however, legislatures look to the expansion of gambling as a way to boost budgets and increase employment. According to Eadington, the casino boom that coincided with the 1989–91 recession followed that principle. During that slow period, Eadington maintains, "There was a very strong impetus at the state level to introduce casinos for economic-development or job-creation purposes."[29]

Riverboat Casinos

In 1989 the legislatures of both Iowa and South Dakota passed initiatives that allowed casino gambling to take root in their states. Iowa took the lead in April but restricted this new enterprise to casinos operated aboard riverboats only. In 1991, the first five floating commercial casinos plied the waters of the Mississippi River. Later that year, Illinois launched its first riverboat. Over the next four years, four other states approved riverboat gambling: Mississippi in 1992, Louisiana in 1993, Missouri in 1994, and Indiana in 1995. In these states, the restriction of casinos to riverboats was a planned move. Professor Cathy H. C. Hsu, a researcher on gambling impacts, explains that state legislatures pushed for this type of casino because the riverboat's nostalgic image made them an "easier sale" to voters. "People also have the perception that riverboat casinos are easier to control because of the limited space and restricted locations," Hsu contends, "therefore, it is possible to have a low-crime gaming environment that attracts respectable patrons." These factors convinced voters to approve the initiatives with the comforting assumption that, in Hsu's words, "their communities would not turn into Las Vegas or Atlantic City."[30]

Iowa took to riverboat gambling because its agricultural economy had suffered in the late 1980s. Its embrace of the new venture was tempered by cautious regulation. Initially, riverboat casinos could only be licensed to nonprofit organizations or to corporations that were willing to pay a fee (or a percentage of their profits) to the state. The 1989 Iowa Excursion Boat Gambling Law further restricted gaming by mandating hours of operation and limiting the maximum bet per hand to $5. Both these laws were dispensed with in 1994 when the legislature revised the law in an attempt to please customers, increase revenues, and keep the state competitive with other gambling markets.

Illinois, Mississippi, Louisiana, Missouri, and Indiana had reasons similar to Iowa for instituting riverboat gambling. Each state had suffered economic setbacks in the 1980s, and all viewed riverboat casinos as a means of boosting revenues and increasing tourism at the same time. Like the casinos in Las Vegas and Atlantic City, the riverboats are privately owned commercial enterprises. All are subject to some kind of state gaming commission that oversees their lawful operation. One of the first rules in each state was to insist that the riverboats cruise while their game rooms are active. That mandate was slightly altered when Mississippi chose to tolerate dockside casinos—river barges that float on the water but are permanently moored at a dock. The other four states then began toying with dockside gambling but usually by allowing the riverboats to remain active only while tied to the dock during bad weather. The increased patron traffic (and therefore greater profits) at dockside, however, was too great a temptation, and one by one the riverboat laws changed. In 1999, Illinois dispensed with cruising requirements. Trying to keep competitive, Indiana then allowed some of its riverboats to become dockside facilities in 2002. Missouri had already allowed continuous boarding in 2000, but unlike Mississippi, the casinos are not open 24 hours. Louisiana's riverboats are now required to remain dockside and be open all day. In Iowa the mandate for cruising, which forced boats to take to the water from June through October, has been lifted in 2004.

In 2003, Illinois raised its casino tax to 70 percent, the highest in the nation. Tax revenue from the nine riverboats in Illinois reached $719.9 million in that year, making it the state with the second-highest revenue from gambling enterprises (only Nevada earns more). With 10 riverboats in operation, Indiana pulled in $702.7 million in tax revenues. Missouri derived $369 million from its 11 floating casinos. Louisiana's 14 riverboats provided $335 million in state taxes. Twenty-nine dockside casinos in Mississippi generated $325 million in tax revenue. Finally, Iowa reaped $209.7 million in revenues shared between its 10 riverboats and three racetrack casinos.

Legalized Gambling

Limited-Stakes Casinos

While Iowa waited two years between passing legislation and launching its first riverboat casinos, South Dakota opened its first land-based commercial casinos in 1989, the same year state lawmakers and the public approved the initiative. The Black Hills town of Deadwood was selected as the host community, and in April of that year, three-quarters of Deadwood's voters agreed to permit casino gambling within the limits of the town. It was a bold move for a small community of fewer than 2,000 people, but the town's economy was in decline after its mining and lumber industries dried up. Wanting to reinvigorate tourism to the historic frontier town (the resting place of famed frontiersman and gambler "Wild Bill" Hickok), the legislature adopted limited-stakes casinos. By definition, limited-stakes initially meant that all games—from slots to poker—had a maximum single bet of $5. Regardless of the limited states, the casino business thrived in Deadwood. In the new century, the maximum single bet was raised to $100 per bet. Around 80 gambling halls are in operation as of 2004, bringing in more than $65 million and generating more than $5 million in tax revenues. To add an atmosphere of respectability, the casinos, by law, must offer a second form of business on the premises—whether gift store, restaurant, or bar. With the money invested in these establishments and the community, Deadwood has rebuilt itself, refurbishing its frontier architecture and resurrecting its cultural heritage.

The success of Deadwood prompted Colorado to consider limited-stakes casinos in 1990. That year, just over half the state's voters approved a constitutional amendment that legalized casino gaming. Three towns—Central City, Black Hawk, and Cripple Creek—were slated for the renewal possibilities offered by hosting casinos. Like Deadwood, all three communities had been mining centers in the 19th century, and all were now suffering the last stages of economic decay. Their populations had dropped to well under a thousand residents by the time gaming arrived in 1991. In October, 11 casinos popped up in the three towns. Each offered standard casino games, but wagering limits were set at $5. Within a year, the number of casino jumped sevenfold, but the boon did not last. Competition has since forced more than 30 establishments to close.

Given the slim margin that passed the initial amendment, Colorado has proved to be a state resistant to gambling expansion. Since 1992, several initiatives have been brought before the voters to allow casinos to spread to other parts of the state. Each of these has been defeated. It is also unlikely that Colorado will increase its betting limits (as South Dakota has done), for to do so would require the state's voters to further amend the state's constitution. Still, with three gambling centers, the state has reaped the benefits. Tax revenues are more than $100 million, and these are channeled to historic preservation and community improvements. Some of these funds are used to offset the impact of gambling—such as increased traffic and the need for more law enforcement—on other towns in the host counties.

LOUISIANA'S UNIQUE STRUGGLE

Louisiana's experience with casino gambling has been markedly different from that of its predecessors. In 1992, having passed the riverboat initiatives during the previous year, the state legislature decided to take the reins of gambling expansion. The purpose was to stimulate economic development and create jobs. Without proposing the matter to the voters, the government put into action the Louisiana Economic Development and Gaming Corporation Act. This law permitted the construction of a single gaming center in a Louisiana parish with a population of more than 490,000 (leaving Orleans Parish as the only candidate). The facility could only offer gambling; it could not host restaurants, a hotel, or other businesses. It would be managed by a single corporation that was under exclusive license to the government.

The chosen site for this grand casino was the 100,000-square-foot Rivergate Convention Center in downtown New Orleans. The government brokered a deal with Harrah's Jazz Company to run the operation, and the opening date was set for the first quarter of 1994. Delays kept the project on hold, but in 1995, a temporary casino was opened in a nearby municipal building while construction of the main complex was still underway. Within six months, however, Harrah's Jazz Company filed for bankruptcy, and the temporary facility closed. The building remained unfinished, and the project languished for four years. Then, in 1999, Harrah's reopened the project, and the building was completed.

All was not well, however. In 2000, the company was again close to bankruptcy. Fewer visitors than expected came to the casino, preferring instead to head to the established riverboat casinos in Shreveport, Bossier City, and Lake Charles. The legislature stepped in to bail out the company by cutting its tax bill and allowing for construction of a hotel and restaurants. Harrah's New Orleans is still limping in the new century. Revenues have yet to meet projections, and only 2,500 of the promised 50,000 jobs have materialized in relation to the casino project. As University of New Orleans economist Tim Ryan concludes, "What we've probably learned is that if you want to legalize gambling because you want it to be economic development, you're probably making a mistake."[31]

Michigan and Beyond

Michigan passed its Gaming Control and Revenue Act in 1996. Like Louisiana's law, Michigan's act stipulates that gaming is allowed only in a city with a population of at least 800,000. Furthermore, that city must be located within 100 miles of another state or county that permits gambling.

These requirements effectively narrowed the choice of host cities to Detroit. Voters in Detroit had to approve the measure, however, before tolerating casinos. By the slimmest of margins, the initiative passed with 51 percent of the voters in support of gaming. In 1999, three casinos began 24-hour operation, and within three years, these establishments were taking in more than $1 billion per year. The tax money derived from the casinos is spent on city improvements, public safety, and aid for primary and secondary schools.

Michigan is the most recent state to permit commercial, land-based casinos. Other states have forms of casino gambling, but no permanent casinos on lands that are not under the sovereign control of Native American tribes. Florida, for example, has many day cruises that operate casino-type games (e.g., blackjack, poker, roulette) once the ships have sailed beyond the three-mile territorial limit. Similarly, South Carolina has two cruises. Georgia, Massachusetts, and Texas each have one such cruise in operation.

INDIAN GAMING

The boom in commercial casinos was not a herald of change but actually the following of a trend. In the 1970s and 1980s, one of the nation's more disenfranchised ethnic groups—Native Americans—struggled to improve reservation life. To achieve this, in part, the tribes looked for ways to become self-reliant in order to fund the social improvements they envisioned. Noting how states had reinstated lotteries for renewal projects and welfare programs, some tribes turned to gambling enterprises as a solution to their financial needs. The move was controversial, sparking a fight with state authorities. After court battles, the tribes proved their sovereign rights, and in 1988, Native Americans entered into the high-stakes gaming market. This lucrative move then prompted states like Iowa and South Dakota to push into the casino business in 1989 to try and cash in on the millions (and later billions) of dollars that Americans were now spending on tribal lands.

The Seminole Raise the Stakes

Although the 1980s would prove to be the watershed for Indian gaming, the first stirrings of this enterprise occurred in the previous decade. The 1970s were a time of consolidating what gains had been won for Native Americans in the turbulent 1960s. In that decade, the administrations of three presidents encouraged Indian tribes to develop industries and work to improve social infrastructure such as schools and medical facilities. In many ways, however, the rhetoric from Washington was full of promise but not much action. Native Americans were among the most impoverished of the nation's citizens. Without capital, the tribes relied on government handouts that were never large enough to support large-scale economic changes. In the early

1970s, this situation changed slightly when the Nixon administration passed the Indian Education Act and the Indian Financing Act—both of which offered government monetary assistance for schools and businesses. Further acts in the decade strengthened tribal autonomy and self-reliance.

As part of the trend toward self-reliance, some tribes began hosting charity games in the 1970s. These operations were fairly small and usually in accordance with state laws that permitted charity gaming and low-stakes bingo. In 1978, however, the atmosphere changed. The Seminole Nation in Florida started running bingo games with jackpot prizes worth $10,000. As an explanation, they argued that other charity games in the state were keeping patrons from visiting the reservations and spending money. To keep competitive, the Seminole claimed they had to raise the stakes 100fold. The result had both positive and negative consequences. As William N. Thompson, the chair of public administration at the University of Nevada, Las Vegas, explains, "Players flocked to the Miami suburb of Hollywood where the Seminole bingo hall was located. Rival bingo games run by charitable groups took a major hit. Their sponsors were not amused."[32]

Backed by the charities, the county officials took action. Robert Butterworth, the Broward County sheriff, insisted that the Seminole game was in violation of Florida law. He filed criminal charges against the tribe to have the bingo game shut down. The sheriff's complaint stemmed from congressional law that allowed the states to enforce criminal laws on reservations. The Seminole protested, and a series of court cases followed. Eventually, in *Seminole Tribe of Florida v. Butterworth* (1981), a federal court of appeals declared that the state had no authority to prohibit games played on Indian land. In addition, the court maintained that because bingo was legal in Florida, the Seminole's game may be a civil violation but not a criminal offense. Because states are severely restricted in how they enforce civil law on reservations, it was therefore unlikely that Florida could regulate tribal gaming. The sheriff and his champions sought to have the U.S. Supreme Court reverse the decision, but the high court declined even to review the case. The dismissal, rendered in 1982, was based on the grounds that the Seminole were not operating an illegal game; they were only changing the way in which the game was played. This was, as the appellate court stipulated, a civil matter and not, in the Court's view, a case for federal interdiction.

The Supreme Court Rules on Indian Gaming

With a favorable court decision to encourage them, other Native American tribes immediately began running high-stakes bingo games. At the time, only five states had barred any form of gambling, so most tribes had the freedom to set up and run legal bingo parlors. By 1988, more than 100 Indian tribes were engaged in this type of gaming. Most state governments were apprehensive at this new phenomenon, not only because prizes were in the thousands of dollars, but also because the revenues were estimated to be in the hundreds of millions and no state board or official tribal council as yet regulated Indian gaming.

A bigger scare to the states came in 1987 when the Supreme Court decided to hear a case similar to the one involving Florida's Seminole tribe. In this instance, the state of California tried to regulate or close down high-stakes bingo games operated by the Cabazon and Morongo Indians. The pretext of the state's argument was that organized crime may have infiltrated the games. In *California v. Cabazon Band of Mission Indians*, the Court stuck to the opinion it rendered when dismissing the Florida case. Because California had legalized bingo, the Cabazon and Morongo Indians were not violating any criminal law. As for the concern that criminal influence should prompt state involvement, the Court maintained, "The State's interest in preventing the infiltration of the tribal bingo enterprises by organized crime does not justify state regulation. . . . State regulation would impermissibly infringe on tribal government."[33] While this rhetoric echoed the Seminole verdict, the justices went further in stipulating that no non-tribal authority could regulate gaming on Indian land unless it was empowered to do so through an act of Congress.

This assessment was extremely disturbing to state governments. It was easy to interpret the Supreme Court ruling as an open door to vastly increased and unregulated gaming whether state voters wanted it or not. For example, the governments of Nevada and New Jersey feared that the Court's decision gave the tribes in their states the power to build and run casinos without any input or interference from the state. The Native American tribes remained closemouthed on the issue, seemingly tolerant of the current trend. To the states, however, the proposition of increased gaming had momentous consequences. They began petitioning the federal government to address the situation—through an act of Congress—before things, from the states' point of view, got out of hand.

Indian Gaming Regulatory Act

After much pressure from the states, the federal government and American Indian tribes reached an agreement concerning the expansion and regulation of Indian gaming. The result was the Indian Gaming Regulatory Act (IGRA), which was signed into law in October 1988 by President Ronald Reagan. Fundamental to this law was the creation of a National Indian Gaming Commission. The commission has three members, two of whom are Native American. The commission's duty is to oversee and regulate the types of games run on reservation land and to draw up guidelines on which the tribes could contract with outside corporations to assist in these ventures. The IGRA also stipulates that Native American tribes had to negotiate with the states to expand any gaming enterprises beyond bingo or similar games. In making their case, the tribes had to prove that revenues were to be earmarked for tribal benefit. The states were then required to consider and act on these negotiations in good faith. If the state governments proved obstinate, the tribes could file suit and federal courts would step in to compel the states to act. In short, the IGRA was a damage control measure. The law expected the states to accede to tribal demands or show just cause why they should not.

Despite its rather progressive rhetoric, the IGRA was not supported by all Native American tribes. The Red Lake band of Chippewa in Minnesota and the Mescalero band of Apache in New Mexico immediately challenged the constitutionality of the act. They argued that the law insisted that tribes negotiate over matters that should be within the bounds of tribal sovereignty. Federal courts dismissed this objection, and in 1990 the U.S. Supreme Court refused to hear an appeal.

For the most part, though, it has been the states that have objected to the IGRA. Perhaps the most mercenary complaint is that Native Americans are exempt from state sales taxes, taxes on income earned while on reservation land, and property taxes. Therefore, the states would receive nothing from the huge business generated through tribal gaming. In fact, because Indian gaming may draw dollars away from lotteries or other legalized forms of gambling (which are heavily taxed), the states are forced to compete with the tribes for revenue. While this may not seem significant in relation to $10,000 jackpot bingo games, it became a serious concern when some tribes decided to angle for expanded operations. In states that permit charity "Las Vegas nights," for example, tribal authorities argued that since the state tolerates casino-type games on those occasions, the tribes have a right under the law to run similar games. Furthermore, because the IGRA does not specify jackpot amounts or the frequency of gaming activity (both of which would be matters of civil regulation), American Indians have a insisted that they have the power to run unlimited-stakes casino games 24 hours a day.

Negotiating Gambling Compacts

According to the IGRA, Indian tribes must enter into a compact, or legal agreement, with the states in order to run any casino-type enterprise. The compact outlines the types of games the tribes intend to operate and the kind and degree of involvement the state will have in the gaming. The state, for example, may ask for wagering limits, jurisdiction over civil or criminal violations regarding the casino, fees for such regulatory measures, and the power to administer and approve gaming licenses on Indian land. It is up to the tribe and the state to negotiate these matters, but the state must show that it is willing to compromise and negotiate "in good faith," as the IGRA insists. If the compact goes through, the secretary of the Interior records the deal in the federal registry. If the state tries to stonewall the compact, then the tribes can turn to the federal courts.

Since the adoption of the IGRA, a few states have tried to block or delay the expansion of Indian gaming. Some of these have paid the price of negotiating "in bad faith." Connecticut was the first to lose its case in federal court when it tried to block casino gaming on Indian land by maintaining that casino gambling was illegal in the state. In 1990, the Mashantucket Pequot, noting that Las Vegas nights were tolerated, convinced a federal court that the state was acting in bad faith. The court ordered the Connecticut government to reconsider its position and conclude a compact within 60 days. The state complied, but by failing to negotiate on friendly terms, Connecticut forfeited any advantages it could have gained in the compact.

Other states learned from Connecticut's folly and entered into compacts with the hope of gaining as many concessions as possible. Minnesota, for example, signed compacts with 11 tribes, each of which agreed to limit casino-type gaming to blackjack. In Kansas, four tribes negotiated compacts in 1995. Thanks to friendly dealings, the state obtained the privilege of performing background checks on all casino operators and merchants working with the casinos. The Kansas tribes are also required each to have a regulatory commission, but the state has the power to oversee any licensing done by these commissions. Even Connecticut learned from its previous experience. When the Pequot came back in 1992 to negotiate for slot machines in their casinos, the state was more amenable. In the new compact, the state agreed to allow slots on the condition that the tribe pay an annual fee of 25 percent of its machine-game revenues (at least $100 million).

The trend toward conciliatory agreements came to an abrupt halt, however, in 1996. In that year, the U.S. Supreme Court was again brought to bear on Indian gaming. Five years beforehand, the Seminole tribe of Florida petitioned the state to allow Las Vegas–type casinos on Indian land. Florida's electorate was against the move, and Governor Lawton Chiles refused to enter into compact negotiations. The Seminole sued the state for bad faith. When the case reached the Supreme Court, Florida's attorney general argued that the lawsuit was unconstitutional because of the provisions of the Eleventh Amendment. That amendment prohibits states from being sued in federal court except by other states, the federal government itself, or foreign nations. In effect, the Florida attorney general contended that the clause in the IGRA that provided Native American tribes with this recourse was unlawful and invalid. In deciding *Seminole Tribe of Florida v. Florida*, the Supreme Court justices voted 5 to 4 in support of Florida's claim. Florida's Seminole were denied their casino. More significantly, all states were now granted immunity from suits brought against them by Indian tribes.

With the leverage of federal lawsuits unavailable to Native Americans, the future of expanded gaming operations on Indian land became uncertain. Some states voluntarily entered into compacts with tribes, believing that more concessions might be gained now that the recourse to federal courts was no longer an option for the tribes. In 2004, Texas governor Richard Perry offered to allow two tribes in his state to operate video slot machines in casinos if they sign a compact that no dice or card games will be offered. But Native Americans are not powerless in the compact-making process. In 1999, the Seminole of Florida decided to open a casino regardless of the state's wishes. The state sued the tribe, but the Seminole appealed. In a stunning decision, the 11th Circuit Court of Appeals maintained that if Native American tribes could not sue the states, then the states could not sue the tribes. In effect, by not entering into a compact, the state could do nothing to stop the tribes from expanding their gaming.

The Department of the Interior also tried to weigh in by adopting a revised Indian Gaming Regulatory Act in 1998. This document amended the compact-making process by putting forth guidelines that would allow the secretary of the Interior to force a compact between a state and a tribe if voluntary discussion had ceased, a mediation process failed, and the state had asserted its immunity from legal suit. Seven tribes—including Florida's Seminole—sought to exploit this new channel, but the secretary's hands were immediately tied. The Senate barred the secretary of the Interior from forcing compacts until federal courts decide any lawsuits questioning the legality of this method. So far, Florida and Alabama have sued the secretary of the Interior over this matter. In the wake of all this legislation, some tribes have entered willingly into compact negotiations, while others have chosen to run casinos without a compact. The Spokan tribe of Washington, for one, has opened four casinos (offering table games and slots) while still battling the state over the right to operate.

Pari-Mutuel Wagering Fights for Survival

While Indian gaming rose in the late 1980s and early 1990s, another form of legalized gambling tapered off. Pari-mutuel betting on horse racing, dog racing, and jai-alai matches was in a state of decline in the 1980s because other types of wagering were simply more convenient. Since jai alai has a small share of pari-mutuel income (since it is a legal wagering sport in only four states), racing took the noticeable hit in revenues. While a select clientele of racing fans still frequented the track, the average gambler was more likely to pick up a daily-numbers lottery ticket at a convenience store rather than spend the day at the races. When casinos multiplied in the early 1990s, pari-mutuel revenues fell to a distant third, claiming only about $4 billion, or one-tenth of what tribal and commercial casinos were amassing, by decade's end.

Off-Track Betting

Greyhound racing reached its peak in 1992. In that year more than 3 million people visited the nation's 50 dog tracks and wagered $3.5 billion on the races. Since then a few tracks have shut down as attendance declined. Animal rights organizations have also taken issue with the sport. Idaho, Nevada, and Washington are just three of seven states that banned dog racing due to political pressure in the 1990s (though none of those states ever had dog tracks). In the new millennium, 46 tracks in 15 states remain in operation, but revenues have been cut in half. The introduction of slot machines at dog tracks in Iowa, Rhode Island, and West Virginia is the only thing keeping those businesses afloat.

Horse racing fared much better in the 1990s, mainly because of the prestige and media coverage associated with major events like the Triple Crown. State governments also threw their weight behind horse racing because they had come to depend on the tax revenues. One way the states have supported racing was to permit the widespread implementation of off-track pari-mutuel betting (OTB). New York City offered the first OTB sites in 1970. The altruistic purpose was to cut down illegal bookmaking. The practical reason was to increase wagering by allowing bets to be made at select off-track locations that would be more convenient to gamblers. The move was successful. As Vicki Abt, James F. Smith, and Eugene Martin Christiansen assert, "OTB effectively eliminated the geographic and demographic barriers to horse-race betting."[34] In the 1980s and 1990s, many states, hoping to retain their gambling revenues, followed New York's lead. Of the 33 states running horse races and 11 operating dog tracks in the new millennium, 22 have off-track betting facilities.

Not every state population has been charmed by the idea, however. In 1991, Minnesota's government added a constitutional amendment to permit OTB, but it was declared unconstitutional the following year. In 1994, the legislature held another referendum to allow the public to decide if off-track betting should be tolerated. The initiative was soundly defeated by a campaign condemning OTB as another example of legalized gambling poison spreading unobtrusively into more and more communities.

The states have always had a special partnership with racing that has no parallel in relation to other forms of gambling. When many racetracks began to close down due to waning attendance in the 1970s, some states took a hand in bailing the industry out. In New Jersey, for example, the state funded the construction of the Meadowlands in 1976. The Meadowlands is operated by the state (the governor is listed as one of the many managers of the arena), and its pari-mutuel revenues went first to paying off the debt incurred for erecting the massive racing complex. New York operates its three major racetracks (Aqueduct, Belmont, and Saratoga) through a state-franchised nonprofit organization. In the early 1970s, when the state found it necessary to legalize off-track betting to keep revenues flowing, the legislature created a public benefit corporation to manage these affairs.

Electronic Novelty and the Racino

While the states' support of racing has kept the sport and the revenues alive, the expansion of the pari-mutuel industry is due to technological innovation. Gamblers can now place bets by phone in some states, and currently 41 states allow Internet users to wager legally on races over the World Wide Web. Gaming is increasingly turning toward electronic media, and horse racing is keeping abreast of the trend. For instance, in the late 1990s, the AmTote Corporation created one of the more interesting innovations. The company partnered with Oaklawn Park racetrack in Arkansas to experiment with an electronic pari-mutuel system that runs like a video game and allows gamblers to bet on previously run races. The system, called Instant Racing, was unveiled in 2000 at Oaklawn and the Southland Greyhound Park in West Memphis, Arkansas. The games have been a success, bringing Arkansas $5.8 million in 2004. In 2003, Oregon became the second state to offer Instant Racing (but the state dropped the machines after only a brief trial); Wyoming has since adopted the game at certain off-track betting locations.

The embrace of Instant Racing reflects a growing trend in the industry toward a reinvention or perhaps an evolution of the idea of the racetrack. While once patrons were content to pass the hours watching and wagering on the races, today's visitors want more instant gratification. Richard McGowan argues that the horse-racing business has had to conform to this shift in public preference. As McGowan contends, horse racing was the most tolerated form of legalized gambling in America during the early to mid-20th century because of the "society's preference for games that involved a certain amount of skill" (in picking winning horses, for example).[35] But over time, as slot machines and lottery tickets became more ubiquitous, horse racing—and the gaming industry in general—had to transform in the 1990s. McGowan concludes, "The primary reason for this transformation has been the public's new-found tolerance, and indeed preference, for games of chance rather than games of skill."[36]

To cater to this demand—and therefore to keep gamblers coming to the track—some tracks have evolved into racetrack/casino hybrids called "racinos." Typically, racinos are veteran tracks with new rooms set aside for slot machines and other video-wagering games. In 1990, West Virginia was the first state to operate video poker terminals. The initial machines were installed at Mountaineer Park racetrack, and the combination of racetrack and casino proved so popular that slots were implemented in 1997. Since then, six other states have opened racinos: Rhode Island in 1992, Delaware and Iowa in 1995, New Mexico in 1999, and Louisiana in 2002. New York opened its first racino at Saratoga Springs in April 2004 and raked in $6 million in its first month of operation. Maine has legalized racinos, but none has yet opened there. At least 10 other states are considering racino proposals.

Racinos have helped revive declining track attendance. This is due to both the variety of games (some racinos now offer full-fledged casino gaming) and the increased winners' purses resulting from casino revenues. *Global Gaming Business* reports that for racinos in Delaware and West Virginia, for example, "the average purse is nearly 80 percent more than racetracks without slots." The gaming periodical goes on to mention how these increases are affecting the industry: "This advantage of supplemented purse amounts gives less prestigious tracks the ability to attract top horses, trainers and jockeys—and, in turn, draw them away from more established tracks without slots."[37] Besides paying out large prizes, racinos are able to pocket quite a bit of money to expand their operations. In New Mexico, slot machines earned $87.6 million in 2001. Of that, $17.5 million was dispensed as prize money, while $48 million was kept by the track. The rest went to a Compulsive Gambling Fund ($219,000) and to the state ($21.9 million). Powerhouse racinos could, therefore, come to dominate the field and possibly consume or drive other non-casino tracks out of business. In 2001, Richard McGowan predicted such a future for racing when he speculated, "There will likely be a major consolidation of horse-racing tracks throughout the US, with 10 to 15 'supertracks' emerging as the only racing outlets."[38]

THE FUTURE OF LEGALIZED GAMBLING

While the racing industry may be consolidating, other forms of gambling are expanding. Specifically, the future of gambling may reside less with brick-and-mortar structures like casinos and racetracks, and more with innovations in technology. Electronic gambling through video terminals or Internet connections is already heralded as the newest gambling revolution. As such, it inspires wild optimism in some and worry in others. Access to cyberspace, for example, could put casino gambling within reach of every household in America. This possibility strikes fear in those who oppose legalized gambling just as much as it troubles the owners of brick-and-mortar casinos who may be financially harmed by the competition. Thus, it is the impact of the new technology that will determine whether the gaming industry and the public take to electronic gambling.

VIDEO LOTTERY TERMINALS

The slots and video games placed in America's racinos are not the same as those found in Las Vegas or Atlantic City casinos. These new machines are called video lottery machines (VLTs), and they are an outgrowth of the state's lottery system. Although the machines look and play the same as their casino counterparts, they are, in the skeptical view of professors Thomas Barker and Marjie Britz, "different according to the states that allow them." As Barker and Britz explain:

> *States allowing VLTs argue that the classic casino gambling machines (video and slot) are house-banked and coin-in, coin-out machines. Video lottery terminals, on the other hand, are state-banked (banked by the state's lottery commission) and dispense redeemable tickets to winners, not coins. Some states also point out that the VLTs have buttons, not the pull levers of one-armed bandits found in casinos.*[39]

The main distinction, then, is that losses are paid into the state's lottery pool and winnings are drawn from it. Because of this, the state can insist that playing the machine is comparable to buying an instant-game lottery ticket.

While video lottery terminals are commonly found at racinos, they are not confined to them. South Dakota was the first state to employ VLTs in 1989, and these machines were installed in restaurants, taverns, and convenience stores. More than 10,000 VLTs—offering video bingo, blackjack, keno, and poker—flourished in these establishments until a state supreme court decision in 1994 declared them unconstitutional. A subsequent statewide referendum later that year made the machines legal again. Current laws allow up to 10 machines in each business location. Fifty percent of the income from VLTs goes to the state, and the other half is divided between the owner of the machine and the owner of the establishment. The revenues have proved to be quite high—especially since the machines are convenient and require little maintenance. Only two years after their initial installation, VLTs were bringing in four times the income as traditional lottery ticket sales.

Some states such as Oregon and West Virginia imitated South Dakota's permissive laws and allowed VLTs to spring up in various locations, but other states such as Rhode Island and Delaware have restricted VLTs to racinos. Delaware's VLTs are unusual because they are traditional coin-in, coin-out machines (both slots and video games). Barker and Britz claim that this makes Delaware's racetracks "in effect state-run casinos without table games."[40] New York, which legalized VLTs at racetracks in 2004, has the newest innovation. Although they are the more traditional paper-receipt machines, the state's VLTs are connected so that patrons are competing in a separate "true" lottery in which the odds are determined by the number of players.

The current inability to expand VLT operations in states such as New York and Delaware is, in part, a result of popular backlash against gambling in recent decades. While some state officials favor expansion to increase lottery revenues, sections of the public are concerned over the social costs of more VLTs. Unlike the building and running of casinos, video lottery terminals do not provide jobs, and therefore they benefit only the states and the owner of the machines. Also troubling is the problem of compulsive gambling in relation to VLTs. Opponents of video lottery terminals (and all forms of video gambling) refer to these devices as the "crack cocaine" of legalized gambling because they are allegedly extremely addictive. In 2002, after co-conducting a study of problem gambling and VLTs in Rhode Island, Robert Breen of the Brown University School of Medicine concluded that "the men and women who 'got hooked' on video gambling became compulsive gamblers in about one year. Those who got hooked on other kinds of gambling (such as horses, sports betting, blackjack, etc.) became compulsive gamblers after about three and a half years."[41]

One final concern is that legalization of VLTs gives Native American tribes in those states the precedent necessary to push for tolerance of gaming machines in tribal casinos. This has been a major focus of debate in Texas in 2004. State officials are proposing that Texas invigorate its sagging racetrack revenues by tolerating VLTs and granting permission to three of the state's tribes to operate such terminals as well. Some opponents of the legislation fear that more of the Texas tribes will argue that tolerating VLTs is tantamount to tolerating any slot or video game—regardless of whether it is connected to the state lottery. The potential consequence is profound, for states that legalize VLTs may, through the loopholes of the IGRA, be authorizing Vegas-type slots on their American Indian reservations.

INTERNET GAMBLING

Video lottery terminals illustrate how the gaming industry has continued to embrace new technologies to make gambling more convenient to players as well as to operators. Yet as convenient as these machines may be, VLTs still rely on patrons leaving the comfort of their own homes. In this respect, they are—like casinos and lotteries—subject to the wax and wane of players' interest. In the most recent marriage of technology and gambling, new operators have tried to overcome the industry's reliance upon a player's motivation to visit a casino or even a local grocery store by moving gambling from the digital age into the information or virtual age.

In 1991, Minnesota experimented with online betting when it partnered with the Nintendo Corporation to make lottery wagering available through select Nintendo game machines hooked up to homeowners' television sets. The project received so much public protest that it was quickly canceled. The failure caused Minnesota and other states to reconsider any plans to move ahead with interactive television gambling. But while the states dallied, online technology took off. By the end of the decade, the Internet—a system of communication that linked computers across the country—had become accessible by the hundreds of millions of Americans who had personal computers in their homes. All these people were now residents of cyberspace, the name given to the virtual world that exists within the confines of the Internet, and they could chat, shop, conduct business, or even gamble in this new world that seemed beyond the reach of most state or even federal controls.

In this unregulated community, independent operators set up virtual casinos or other gaming sites on privately owned web sites. The Internet gaming halls offer video versions of common casino games—from poker to blackjack to slots. The non-casino sites take wagers on horse racing and sporting events. Regardless of the type of site, customers typically register with the sites by using a credit card to establish an account. This account acts as the patrons' bankroll from which they can wager on the individual games or events. As a lure, some casino sites even offer a complimentary starting sum, knowing full well that gamblers are likely to lose more than they will win and eventually will have to turn to their credit cards to keep playing. But because online gambling is illegal in the United States, the site's bank and the players' accounts are established through offshore or foreign corporations. Therefore, even though the operator and the players may reside in the United States, the game's server (the host of the web site) and the money accounts are held outside the country—in South America or various Caribbean island nations, for example. There they are free of federal regulation and taxes.

Currently, "cybergambling" makes up only about 1 percent of the total gaming revenues in the United States. Still, that is an impressive $5.7 billion—an amount that leads investors and operators to predict that Internet gambling may be the way of the future. At the dawn of the 21st century, around 200 companies run 2,000 Internet gambling sites. That is about 100 times the number of gambling sites that existed in 1996. And the number is growing, since setting up and running a site is fairly simple. Some companies in the United States even manufacture software necessary to begin operation.

The Questionable Legality of Cybergambling

The illegality of Internet gambling sites is still the subject of debate in America. According to federal laws, it is legal for horse-racing states to take wagers from other parts of the country, so Internet betting does not, in this case, conflict with any known statutes. The opposite is true for sports wagering. Since this form of gambling is only legal in Nevada, only bets from within the state are legal. This, however, does not stop most sports betting sites from taking bets from across the country. As yet, the federal government has been reluctant to chase down the many citizens who place these illegal wagers, but some state authorities have threatened a crackdown in their own jurisdictions. Online casinos and lottery sites have also escaped most persecution, although the government attests that online casinos are illegal. According to Robin Gareiss and John Soat, two reporters for the tech journal *Information Week*, the lack of strong legal action is because these sites both fall into a "gray area" in terms of federal legislation:

> *The statute most cited as governing lotteries and electronic casinos is the 1961 Federal Interstate Wireline Act. In essence, this law says that any bookie who uses wire communication between states or between a state and a foreign country to take bets on any sporting event or contest is guilty of a felony. The confusion relates to the words "sporting event or contest." The Justice Department says "sporting" modifies "event," and the word "contest" covers everything else. Online gambling advocates say the word "sporting" modifies "event" and "contest," and therefore applies only to sports betting. . . . What's more, some question whether the Internet is covered under "wire communication" because the law referred to phone wires when it was written.*[42]

Despite the controversial interpretations of federal laws, many groups—from the American Gaming Association to the Christian Coalition—are calling upon the government to ban all forms of Internet gambling in the United States. Some fear that such easy access to gaming is a danger to both problem gamblers and the country's computer-savvy youth. Others, like the gaming associations, see Internet gambling as unwelcome competition. Of course, even if Internet gambling is banned in the United States, some legal scholars still debate how the laws could be applied to U.S. citizens who are patronizing the sites of offshore hosts.

Even though laws have not yet caught up with Internet gamblers, the Department of Justice stands by its position that online casino operation is illegal. But few prosecutions have been made against online casinos, mainly because their operators have relied on offshore hosts. Instead, federal authorities have been focusing their efforts on crippling the industry by targeting its lifeblood. In 2002, government prosecutors were successful in convincing Citibank, one of the largest credit-issuing corporations, to bar its customers from using their credit cards to place bets on online casinos. Other credit companies such as Bank of America, Chase Manhattan, and Fleet had already banned transactions with online gambling sites. Federal lawyers orchestrated the coup by suggesting that since the Justice Department considers online gambling illegal, any U.S. corporation dealing with gambling sites could be prosecuted for "aiding and abetting." Ron Carter, the chairman of the Internet Gaming Commission (an advocacy group), claims that since most online gamblers place wagers with credit card funds, the ban has cut deep into online casino profits. Paraphrasing Carter's estimates, Gareiss and Soat write,

"Since banks began rejecting the transactions, the online-gambling industry has lost $500 million to $1 billion in revenue."[43]

The government has also pressured Internet providers to ban online casino advertisements from their web browsers. In 2004, Google and Yahoo!, two of the Internet's largest search engines and web hosts, agreed to pull these advertisements after a grand jury investigation began to subpoena select online media companies. Yahoo! executives stated that they would ban casino advertisements from their U.S. market but not those foreign markets where gambling is legal. Google chose to drop these ads from all its markets. Critics of the move argue that the Internet service providers (ISPs) shouldn't have caved in so easily. Some legal scholars suggest that Yahoo!, Google, and other ISPs are within their First Amendment rights to run any ads they choose. David Carruthers, an online casino and sports betting operator, implores the ISPs to bring their collective muscle to court. "I urge these search engines and other service providers to stand up for themselves and challenge these pressure tactics by federal prosecutors," Carruthers has stated.[44] The implication is that the rather unclear legislation being used to ban online gambling would not stand up to legal scrutiny. As yet, no service provider has contested the ban. In fact, more and more search engines and ISPs have decided to yank all online gambling ads as a result of looming grand jury investigations.

CURRENT ISSUES IN LEGALIZED GAMBLING

The future of Internet gambling—like all forms of gambling in America—is still uncertain. While brick-and-mortar casinos, riverboats, racetracks, and lotteries appear entrenched in society because of state governments' desire for revenue and because of people's general acceptance of these institutions, many of the current controversies relate to further expansion of gaming. Few Americans are calling for a prohibition of gambling, but many are contending that society has reached the saturation point. "Before 1988, the trip to Atlantic City or Las Vegas required a plane trip and time, not to mention money," Thomas Barker and Marjie Britz point out. "Today a visit to a casino—land-based, riverboat, dockside, Indian, or day cruise—is within driving distance for all Americans."[45] In addition, lottery tickets are available at most neighborhood convenience stores, and now the Internet has brought gaming within the reach of those who do not want to leave their homes to gamble. Is it possible, critics ask, that the ease of gambling in America has turned a potentially dangerous vice into a socially acceptable form of entertainment?

The gaming industry (both legal and illegal) has done everything in its power to make it easy for people to wager their money in the slim hope of striking it rich. Keeping that dream alive has paid off for the industry and the states' treasuries. For the gamblers, the dream of instant wealth has occasionally come true, but for most players, the thrill and excitement of the games has been the only reward. And since gaming venues have become so ubiquitous, concerned Americans are asking whether these types of benefits have outweighed or even blurred the costs of gambling's expansion in America.

DOES GAMBLING BENEFIT OR HARM LOCAL ECONOMIES?

Ignoring the indeterminate contributions of Internet gaming sites, gambling's main impact upon a host community—the community where a specific structure such as a casino, riverboat, racino, or other gaming hall is located—is undeniably economic. At the beginning of the 21st century, gamblers lose around $48 billion a year to the gaming industry. A hefty percentage of that money is handed to the states in the form of taxes and fees, and these revenues are then ideally channeled back into state or civic projects. According to gambling proponents, the primary beneficiary is the host community.

Tunica, Mississippi, has often been used as the poster child for positive civic revitalization through gambling. Tunica, which was one of the poorest locales in the nation, opened its first riverboat casino in 1992. Ten more quickly followed. A town that once had 16 hotel rooms suddenly had more than 6,000. The casino business in Tunica created 14,000 jobs, and the tourism industry is on the rise. Before 1992, the county drew about $4 million a year in revenues, but after only five years of casino operation, Tunica was bringing in $35 million annually. The money was spent on roads, a river park, and an airport. And in 1999, the casino tax revenues were so high that the community no longer needed to levy a property tax. The transformation in Tunica was impressive.

These benefits were not limited to Tunica; they occurred in many host communities across the country. From East St. Louis, Illinois, to Deadwood, South Dakota, the infusion of gambling revenues brought drastic change. The gaming industry and its advocates maintain that, in most cases, jobs were created, welfare payments dropped, and new civic improvements received needed funding. The National Gambling Impact Study Commission (NGISC), an independent research body appointed by Congress, supported these findings. In 1999, after conducting the most extensive review of legalized gambling to date, the NGISC reported that "research conducted on behalf of the Commission confirms the testimony of . . . casino workers and government officials that casino gambling creates jobs and reduces levels of unemployment and government assistance in communities that have legalized it."[46] Frank J. Fahrenkopf, Jr., the CEO of the American Gaming Association (an industry advocacy group), takes these findings one step further by suggesting that gaming is an ideal investment for struggling communities. "It is a clean industry from the standpoint that you don't have smokestacks polluting the environment," Fahrenkopf states. "Secondly, it promotes capital investment and economic development. Third, it produces jobs. And finally, you can tax the hell out of it."[47]

Opponents of legalized gambling, however, argue that casinos and other gaming halls are not the solution to a host community's economic woes. Blake Hurst, a concerned citizen in Missouri—where riverboat casinos are tolerated—argues that "casinos serve as a gigantic sump, sucking sales from surrounding businesses."[48] According to Hurst and others, since casinos offer shopping, food services, and entertainments, patrons who flock to them rarely feel the need to step outside them to visit non-casino businesses in the area. In some communities where casinos are permitted, local restaurants and retail outlets have experienced no rise in sales; some have even reported a loss. For these business people, the economic benefits of increased tourism promised by casino gambling were never delivered.

In addition to noting the negative impact on community businesses, those who oppose casinos as a community's means to economic salvation insist that the casinos themselves do not provide a worthwhile boost to the local job market. While casinos do require large staffs to operate, the majority of jobs offered are menial, low-paying, and without an opportunity for advancement. Table dealers, for example, may be paid well, but they are only a small percentage of the casino staff. The majority of employees serve as money counters and cleaners, waitstaff, and hotel maids. These unskilled positions likely pay just a bit more than minimum wage. Furthermore, the boon in new jobs offered by the casino may mask the loss of jobs suffered in the community as local restaurants and retail shops are driven out of business from their inability to compete.

While local politicians who favor casinos in their communities might hype the economic promise of these ventures, anti-casino spokespersons are quick to point out that legalized gambling has many costs as well as benefits. Some of these may be tangible civic problems, such as traffic congestion and the need for more police services. Other costs may be less visible, such as an increase in problem gambling (and the resulting family crises and lost workplace productivity). Professor Patricia A. Stokowski goes further by arguing that the undeniable civic revitalization that occurs when casinos move into a host community also has a down side. According to Stokowski, the improvements are often made at the expense of the poorest residents of the community. Low-income housing may be swallowed up and turned into upscale rental space that caters to those drawn in by the revitalization. The poor are then pushed farther away from the casino redevelopment site and are sometimes left with no means to reach that area and take advantage of the new economic opportunities. Citing outside research, Stokowski maintains that this dilemma confronted the impoverished residents of Tunica, Mississippi. "Without a car," Stokowski writes, "low-income residents could not get jobs in a casino because no buses ran between the poorer neighborhoods and the riverboat areas."[49]

Does Legalized Gambling Benefit American Indian Tribes?

While citizens and state legislatures question the costs and benefits of casinos on communities such as Tunica or even Las Vegas, the debate over the impact of legalized gambling is perhaps most poignantly being waged in relation to Indian gaming. Tribal territories are historically among the poorest regions of America, so when gaming was legalized on Indian land—with the IGRA stipulating that the proceeds had to fund economic development—any changes were expected to be momentous. After almost two decades since the IGRA was enacted, Indian gaming has certainly blossomed, yet the fruits have not been evenly spread. While more than 300 gaming ventures are run by about 200 tribal governments, two-thirds of the total profits are reaped by the 39 largest casinos. According to Virginia representative Frank Wolf, "About 80 percent of the revenues are going to 3 percent to 5 percent of the tribes."[50]

For small groups, the economic benefit of a casino operation is life changing. The Mystic Lake Casino in Minnesota, for example, pays about half a million dollars annually to each of the 100-odd members of the Mdewkanton Dakota band. Of course, most Native American groups are not so small, and not every tribe holds a class III gaming license that allows them to run a casino. Some tribes are permitted slot machines that often are situated in gas stations or convenience marts. These gaming devices offer little in the way of jobs or incredible yearly payouts. Even those larger tribes benefiting from high-income casinos often channel their funds into housing, business infrastructure, health care, and "donations" to the states for upkeep of roads and other necessities. Some have also built tribal colleges to offer higher education to tribe members. With these expenses, few Native American tribes are left with luxury funds. Michael Parrish, president of Bay Mills Community College, an institution built and run by the Chippewa of upper Michigan, says that after taking care of necessities and investments for the future, "There's very little disposable income left."[51]

Critics of Indian gaming continue to argue that the boon of economic prosperity is being enjoyed by only a few of the country's 550 tribes. Some Native American governments that have gaming licenses are too isolated to realize any benefits. This was apparently true for the Hualapai tribe in Arizona. After opening a casino in the 1990s, the Hualapai had to close shop within a year because tourists seemed to favor sightseeing at the Grand Canyon over the gambling opportunities on the nearby reservation. Instead of gaining instant wealth, the Hualapai were left $1 million in debt. According to many reports, the tribes that have gaming enterprises near major population centers receive the most benefits; those in isolated locations see very little change. In 2000, an Associated Press review maintained that "in counties that include reservations with casinos, the average poverty rate declined only slightly between 1989 and 1995, from 17.7 percent to 15.5 percent."[52] To explain this, some critics point to the fact that 75 percent of the jobs in Indian casinos are filled by non-tribal personnel, leaving most tribe members without the opportunities offered by much-needed gainful employment.

Such statistics, however, are made to serve more than one master. The National Indian Gaming Association (NIGA) is credited with the above statistic, yet this pro-gaming institution touts the non-tribal employment rate as an unanticipated benefit of Indian gaming. As the NIGA and others attest, Indian gaming impact positively not only the reservation but also the surrounding communities. In addition to providing 300,000 jobs, tribes give millions of dollars to the states as fees and assessments every year from gaming revenues. These monies are used to support state projects that benefit every resident. Furthermore, a research group in Cambridge, Massachusetts, examined data from the 1999 National Gambling Impact Study Commission (NGISc) and found that per capita incomes rose for non-tribal residents who simply lived near a Native American casino. In these same communities, welfare payments dropped. As Jim Adams writes in a 2000 issue of *Native Americas*, "From Arizona to Minnesota, regional studies show that the benefits for non-Indians have far outweighed the costs."[53] Other findings that Adams cites suggest that the benefits are also manifest for the tribes themselves. According to one unpublished survey, tribes that operate casinos have cut jobless rates on Native American land by as much as 25 percent. But even with such impressive findings, it is still far from certain that Indian gaming has proved to be the panacea for the poverty and other social ills that still plague the majority of the nation's reservations.

Do Individual Rights Come Before Society's Good?

Many of the debates over the impact of legalized gambling on Native American reservations, other host communities, or even the states in general tend to focus on gambling's economic benefits or shortcomings. In these arguments it is almost tacitly assumed that gaming is an acceptable pastime to Americans and that its tolerance in a community is based primarily on whether the money and jobs it generates outweigh any social problems—such as crime or problem gambling—that may ensue. Not all Americans, however, believe that the legalization of gambling is an economic issue. Previous bans on gambling in the United States have typically been enacted on moral and ethical grounds. Christian temperance committees, for example, have traditionally viewed gambling as a vice that, though perhaps not intrinsically evil, can lead to sinful behavior when indulged in excessively. In addition, the corruption and crime that have plagued legalized gambling's past convinces many that if wagering is not wicked, the atmosphere that springs up around it may warrant the abolishment of gaming for society's good.

The main argument that arises from the ethical debate concerning legalized gambling is whether the individual's right to wager should take precedence over the possible harm gambling does to society as a whole. Those who wish to protect the right to gamble (as it is afforded by the states) point out that the majority of Americans approve of legalized gambling. According to a survey released by the American Gaming Association (AGA) in 2004, 86 percent of Americans believe they have the right to gamble with their own money if they so chose. The same survey indicated that about one in four gambling-age citizens visited a casino in the past year (2003), and similar polls reveal that about half the population plays the lottery regularly. AGA spokesman, Frank Fahrenkopf, Jr., maintains that there is no secret to the preference for gambling. People flock to casino resorts to gamble, Fahrenkopf states, "because it's fun." Fahrenkopf, like a great percentage of Americans polled about gambling preferences, claims that gambling is a form of harmless entertainment. For those who visit Las Vegas or any other gambling resort, gambling is just part of the attraction. "They come to our resorts," Fahrenkopf asserts, "to see a concert or a show, shop, dine at one of our fine restaurants, and, yes, to gamble."[54] In this respect, gambling is portrayed as a diversion that is just one of many ways in which responsible people spend their money for personal enjoyment.

Those who oppose gambling (or at least its spread) in the United States, however, interpret the "responsible gaming" argument as a smokescreen to hide serious problems that result from a culture based on risk. Some critics have noted that gambling is not akin to other forms of entertainment. Unlike dining or moviegoing, gambling offers the chance of winning money. According to the critics, if the possibility of financial reward was removed from the formula, gambling would not be an attractive pastime. Therefore, gambling caters to the "get rich quick" philosophy that flies in the face of one of the mythic ideals of the nation—namely, that prosperity is earned through hard work.

According to James F. Smith, a professor and gambling researcher, the undermining of the work ethic is a result of living in a modern age in which there are "diminishing real opportunities to match the dreams fuelled by advertising and . . . television exposés of the lifestyles and runaways of the rich and famous."[55] As Smith and others have noted, declining economies and poor job prospects dampen the spirits of working-class Americans who are, at the same time, awash in pop culture images of wealth and consumerism. The contrast between reality and the imagined good life tempts many people to risk their hard-earned money on the possibility of striking it rich to reach the level of comfort and satisfaction that advertisers suggest everyone deserves. And, unfortunately for the majority of gamblers, the odds are stacked heavily against winning big.

While many gamblers may be able to control the impulse to wager everything on the hopes of hitting the jackpot, some gamblers cannot. But even if the most compulsive gamblers are ignored in the debate over the ethics of gambling, those who wager more than infrequently may be taking time away from work, family, or other responsibilities. Gamblers of all stripes are also diverting money from household budgets to pay gambling expenses. While this may not be financially ruinous to those who make six-figure salaries, it can be draining to lower-income families. Speaking of the lure of Iowa's riverboat casinos, columnist Marc Cooper writes:

> *Statistics show that the poor are likely to spend two-and-a-half times the percentage of their income on gambling as the middle class. And with the stock market and limited-partnership opportunities not much of a draw among K Mart workers, gambling is the only "investment" many of the working poor think they can afford. A full 27 percent of lower-income gamblers polled in one study said they were in the casino "to get rich." Yet the average result of each gambling visit is a loss of between $25 and $100.*[56]

Both the willingness to wager more than one can afford and the accruing of debilitating personal losses are signs of what many experts term problem gambling, and it is the destructive effects of problem gambling that has critics of the industry championing an end to legalized gambling or at least a rethinking of its regulation. Like most other aspects of the gambling debate, however, problem gambling is a controversial issue. Though no one argues that problem gambling is an illusory phenomenon, spokespersons on both sides rarely agree on its pervasiveness, its costs to society, or even how to define and contend with it.

Is Problem Gambling a Serious Problem?

The 1999 National Gambling Impact Study Commission (NGISC) determined that of the 125 million Americans who gamble, about 7.5 million are problem gamblers. Of that number, 2.2 million were deemed pathological gamblers, a subpopulation that suffers from a mental dependence on gambling despite losses. Therefore, not all problem gamblers are compulsive gamblers even though the two terms are often used interchangeably in unscientific literature. Furthermore, the NGISC made note that the American Psychiatric Association refers to pathological gambling as an abuse or dependence, not an addiction. Unlike drug addiction, for example, there is no physical craving for repeated wagering. Some analysts still dub pathological gambling an addiction, however, because of the repetitive and overriding impulse to gamble, but this terminology is generally confined to the lay community, especially to critics who wish to show that the ruinous effects of pathological gambling are similar to those experienced by substance addicts.

Problem gamblers are certainly preoccupied with gambling in the same way drug users might be preoccupied with cocaine, heroin, or alcohol. When problem gamblers are winning, they ride a psychological high; but when they are losing, they do not cut their losses and call it quits. Instead, problem gamblers believe they can make up their deficit by gambling more. Often this means they will return to their favorite gambling hall (e.g., racetrack, casino, bingo parlor, lottery terminal) day after day to chase their losses. Inevitably, more money is gambled away, and debts begin to mount. Typically, problem gamblers will keep their debts a secret from family and friends, believing that the next big wager will erase their source of shame. To cover their losses in the meantime, problem gamblers will often use any available credit sources and, when those are exhausted, turn to selling off possessions or even stealing. According to Ronald M. Pavalko, a spokesperson for the National Council on Problem Gambling, a study of 394 members of Gamblers Anonymous in Illinois, Wisconsin, and Connecticut revealed that 57 percent admitted to stealing to pay gambling expenses. "The most common crimes committed by problem gamblers," Pavalko states, "are embezzlement, forgery, misappropriation of funds, and tax and insurance fraud. 'White collar' crimes predominate, but robbery, burglary, shoplifting, and drug dealing also occur, although less frequently."[57]

The criminal costs to society, gambling's critics say, only tell part of the story. Referring to statistics compiled in 1995 by Henry Lesieur and Christopher Anderson (who had polled members of Gamblers Anonymous in Illinois), Senator Paul Simon of Illinois reiterated before Congress in that year: "A survey of compulsive gamblers found 22 percent divorced because of gambling, 40 percent had lost or quit a job due to gambling, 49 percent stole from work to pay gambling debts, 23 percent alcoholic, 26 percent compulsive overeaters, 63 percent had contemplated suicide and 79 percent said they wanted to die."[58] Antigambling forces contend that these problems associated with compulsive gambling are sometimes "hidden" costs to society because they impact the gambler and—with the exception of workplace theft—do not stray into criminal violations. The dollar amounts of some of these hidden costs, however, are significant, critics argue.

Problem gamblers are believed to declare bankruptcy more often than nonproblem gamblers. According to statistics cited by the NGISC, problem gamblers can leave behind bankruptcy debts between $75,000 and $150,000. Such debts drive up interest rates that are passed from banking and credit institutions to consumers. In addition, the NGISC cites statistics provided by the National Opinion Research Center (NORC) at the University of Chicago that estimate "the annual average costs of job loss, unemployment benefits, welfare benefits, poor physical and mental health, and problem or pathological gambling treatment is approximately $1,200 per pathological gambler per year and approximately $715 per problem gambler per year."[59] Lifetime costs for bankruptcy, arrest, imprisonment, and legal fees for divorce were $10,550 per pathological gambler and $5,130 per problem gambler. Using these figures for an overall assessment, NORC concluded that pathological gambling costs roughly $5 billion per year plus $40 billion in lifetime expenditures.

Prohibitionists maintain that with such high costs, gambling is an obvious detriment to society. More lenient critics argue that the costs are evidence the industry needs more regulation—especially self-regulation. One of the common complaints leveled against the gaming industry is that casinos and other gambling operations prey upon problem gamblers. According to these charges, the industry acknowledges that a good percentage (estimates run as high as 30 percent) of its income comes from habitual gamblers and therefore willfully lags on addressing problem gambling or taking effective measures to counter it. One sign that the industry is supposedly abetting problem gamblers is the routine installation of ATMs on the gaming floor of most casinos (although some states have banned this practice). Industry advocates, on the other hand, contend that most gaming operators are concerned about problem gambling. About half the largest casinos (including those on Native American land) hire professionally trained staff to spot and intercede with problem gamblers in order to refer them to treatment programs. According to casino managers, problem gamblers are undesirable customers because they run up debts they cannot pay and end up costing the casino money. To help curb this, casinos also voluntarily post signs that both warn patrons about problem gambling and provide phone numbers of local and national help lines.

In addition to the "in-house" measures, many gaming institutions contribute part of their earnings to state organizations that raise public awareness about problem gambling and offer treatment for those affected. These contributions are made on top of the percentage of gaming revenues that the states automatically set aside for such programs. The NGISC reported that in 1998 the states allocated a combined total of $20 million to 45 different institutions devoted to problem gamblers. The commission admits that this is only .01 percent of the total revenues paid to the states by the gaming industry. Critics charge that this incredibly small percentage reveals that the state governments are aiding the industry by merely paying lip service to a serious social problem affecting millions of Americans.

Pro-gambling activists believe government involvement in the issue of problem gambling is already sufficient without being disruptive. For one thing, the American Gambling Association consistently points out that despite its funding of research on the topic, no hard facts have proved that problem gambling is linked to the myriad social ills that are commonly but unscrupulously pinned on the gaming industry. In essence, the defenders of gambling fear that wild exaggerations without statistical proof help promote an atmosphere that makes prohibition or unwarranted regulation seem necessary. To ward off this feeling, the gaming industry advertises how committed it is to curbing problem gambling while keeping the democratically sanctioned entertainment of gambling free from government control.

WHAT ROLE SHOULD THE STATE GOVERNMENTS PLAY?

Two of the most troublesome aspects of problem gambling are the pervasiveness of Internet gambling and the high rates of underage problem gamblers. Various sources, including NORC, estimate that the number of underage pathological gamblers in the United States runs upward of 1 million. Some studies indicate that much of the problem gambling in the country can be traced to early experiences with gambling in a person's teenage years. That is, young gamblers are likely to become compulsive gamblers as they grow into adulthood. This problem may be exacerbated by the Internet gaming parlors, which, though requiring a credit source to access, have no way of knowing the age of their clients. Critics of the industry claim that besides facilitating underage gamblers, the easy access and clandestine nature of Internet gambling is also a danger to adult problem gamblers. These issues are but two of the many reasons that some antigambling activists advocate more government regulation of the gaming industry.

In its opening letter to the federal lawmakers, state governors, and tribal leaders, the NGISC assessed the gambling explosion in America in the latter half of the 20th century and recommended a halt to any further spread. The NGISC was careful to point out that they were not advocating a ban on gambling but rather a temporary cessation so that state governments, local authorities, and tribal leaders could assess the costs of gaming on host communities and each state as a whole. Antigambling forces were quick to pick up on the recommendations of the NGISC. Some organizations such as the National Coalition Against Legalized Gambling (NCALG—founded in 1994) used the NGISC's findings to bolster its own claims that the consequences of gambling's expansion had never been properly assessed. Even before the NGISC published its report, the NCALG had helped defeat several gaming bills and measures in various states by arguing that gambling ruined the economies of host communities and corrupted society. But with the NGISC's call for a moratorium, the NCALG hoped that a general sentiment against gambling would sweep the nation.

Indeed, in the late 1990s, the spread of gambling—at least in the form of brick-and-mortar structures such as casinos, pari-mutuel facilities, and racetracks—did seem to slow. Shannon Bybee, director of the International Gaming Institute at the University of Nevada, Las Vegas, noted that the casino industry's stalled growth at the end of the decade had much to do with the public's mindset. "Anytime something gains visibility, it becomes much more of a target," he says. "Many people don't like casino gambling, but they didn't get upset about it as long as it was confined to Nevada and New Jersey. But when it began spreading to other states, they did get upset. It was a natural reaction to the gambling industry's success and expansion."[60] Reaction to gambling's spread manifest chiefly on the local level in the form of NIMBY ("not in my backyard") organizations that were often tolerant of gambling as long as it did not take place near the members' community. There was still a general fear that erecting gambling halls in a respectable community would invite crime, prostitution, and other social problems that were popularly associated with Las Vegas.

NIMBY backlash and debates in the state legislatures helped keep casino expansion at bay at the turn of the millennium, but so, too, did corporate mergers, faulty financing, and internal wrangling within the industry itself. As for state regulation of casino gambling, the common cry was for tighter background checks on operators, restricted hours of casino operation, and detailed files of casino conduct and income. There is still a concern that in Las Vegas, for example, the relatively few number of government regulators concentrate their time and efforts on the major casinos while leaving the thousands of other gambling license holders less thoroughly examined. Yet after years of complaint, most states had efficient regulatory agencies in place in the 1990s, and even today, policing strategies are not likely to change radically. Casino gambling, however, was only one part of a larger picture. Lotteries were still in full force at the end of the 1990s and continue strong in the 21st century. Unlike casinos, lotteries are tied to the state governments. Therefore, gambling's opponents believe that if the industry is ever to be defeated, lotteries will have to be severed from government control. For, as the argument runs, if the government has a stake in protecting one aspect of gambling, how can it be objective in regulating other sectors of the industry?

To some of gambling's detractors, lotteries are an obvious example of corrupted ideals because, to these critics, the states have gone beyond complicity to become promoters of gambling. In 1999, the NGISC acknowledged this argument by stating:

> *For some, state governments have exceeded their stated objective of using the lottery to modestly enhance public services, and instead have irresponsibly intruded*

> *gambling into society on a massive scale through such measures as incessant advertising and the ubiquitous placement of lottery machines in neighborhood stores. In this view, states have become active agents for the expansion of gambling, setting the stage for the introduction of commercial gambling in all its forms. The question arises: Is this a proper function of government?*[61]

To Thomas A. Kelly, a public-policy researcher who served as the NGISC's executive director, the answer is no. In Kelly's words, "Lottery states cannot avoid a conflict of interest between the public good and the public treasury."[62] For that reason, he advocates that if lotteries are to continue, then they should be run by private organizations. As the NGISC notes, other critics argue that the state governments need to be held accountable for how they promote lotteries. In recent years, critics have charged the states with excessive advertising (billboards, convenience-store signage, radio and television spots) and with false advertising by neglecting to emphasize the slim odds players have of winning a jackpot. There is also an ethical component to this argument that suggests by heavy promotion, the state governments are advocating the "get rich quick" mentality and downplaying the value of hard work.

Countering all these arguments is a daunting task, but gambling advocates believe that the professed outrage is confined to a narrow segment of the population. Gambling's defenders acknowledge that lotteries, casinos, bingo parlors, and all other wagering outlets are in business to make money. They do not need to prey on the public because the public willingly plays these games as a form of entertainment and to satisfy the very human love of risk taking. The clamoring for more state regulation or even the banning of gambling is comparable to the outcry against tobacco use and alcohol consumption—two other forms of personal enjoyment that seem to have the sanction of the majority of the public. But unlike these two vices, gambling is not apt to cause lung cancer or cirrhosis. To proponents of gambling, casinos, racetracks, and lotteries are simply entertainment venues for people to spend their money, and they help the state governments fill their coffers without resorting to new or higher taxes.

Of the many reasons cited by gambling's opponents to bring about more state regulation or prohibition, gambling's defenders insist that none seems to stand up to scrutiny. While detractors claim that gambling breeds crime (such as money laundering, muggings, theft, and fraud) in host communities, the Public Sector Gaming Study Commission (PSGSC), a nonpartisan collective of state legislators, dismisses this notion in their 2000 report by remarking, "This conception appears to be based on fictional portrayals of the industry and unsubstantiated anecdotal evidence."[63] Ironically, the commission suggests that some areas benefit from reduced crime because police forces are enlarged thanks to gambling tax dollars. The PSGSC also refutes the sense of alarm that the NGISC raised about problem gambling. According to the PSGSC, the research on problem gambling trends is inconclusive and the incidence of pathological gambling is extremely low. The executive committee of the PSGSC affirms that because gambling incurs no serious social costs, no extra regulation is needed. Gambling advocates support this conclusion. To them, more regulation would just increase the costs to casinos and other gambling ventures, and these costs could force gaming halls to cut jobs or possibly close up shop—both of which would negatively impact a host community's economic strength.

Finally, moving beyond its dismissal of more state regulation, the PSGSC maintains that because the responsibility of tolerating gambling is already well managed by the states, no federal involvement is warranted. In its executive summary, the committee avers, "The states are fully competent to continue handling this responsibility. The federal government should exert authority over gaming and gambling only when interests beyond the state level are directly involved."[64] To gaming interests, this sentiment has always been something of a mantra. For one thing, by keeping gambling decisions at the state and local level, the people impacted by new gambling ventures have a say in how gaming will be implemented into their community or whether gaming is right for their community at all. Gambling's defenders argue that to invite federal regulation is to open the door to the possibility of national prohibition, thus robbing America's communities of the right to decide for themselves.

SHOULD THE FEDERAL GOVERNMENT REGULATE GAMBLING?

The majority of state representatives have traditionally been silent on the issue of gambling regulation or even on the industry itself. Since all but two states currently tolerate some form of gambling within their borders, few members of Congress are willing to call for changes in the status quo. And siding with the industry might alienate powerful sections of the electorate, which could jeopardize reelection. Some members of Congress, though, have refused to shy from the issue. Republican Senator Jon Kyl of Arizona is a vocal opponent of gambling, arguing that it is corruptive to individuals, families, and society. Before he retired, Illinois senator Paul Simon, a democrat, was another critic of the industry. Simon was adamant in claiming that gambling was not living up to its economic promises while, in the meantime, further impoverishing the poor and burdening society with a host of ills. He was instrumental in winning Senate approval for the creation of the NGISC to assess legalized gambling's impact on the nation.

With only a few strident voices punctuating the silence in Washington, the federal government's main role in the gambling debate has been to create commissions like the NGISC to "look into" the problem and make recommendations. These recommendations typically call for changes at the state level, since the regulation of gambling has traditionally resided with the states, and the federal government seems unwilling to take the reins unless compelled. Critics argue that this is an example of the federal government "passing the buck" so that any ill effects of gambling might be blamed on lack of state regulation or enforcement. But others, including the NGISC, maintain that the states are already doing an effective job of managing gambling, and thus there is no cause to strip them of that authority. In addition, the NGISC points out that the states have also excelled at policing the gambling industry, ridding its upper echelons of mobsters and others directly connected to organized crime. Effective regulation coupled with enforcement has convinced the federal government that the states are still in control of gambling despite its vast and unprecedented spread in recent decades. For their part, the states have been content to maintain the status quo. Seeing that Washington is committed to its hands-off policy, no state has felt compelled to adopt any of the major recommendations made by the NGISC (such as a moratorium on gambling expansion, the reduction of convenience gambling outlets, or the limiting of gambling advertisement).

Gambling's opponents, however, interpret the relinquishing of gaming authority to the states as potentially dangerous. Richard A. McGowan suggests that since the business is competitive, especially for casinos and lotteries that thrive because of interstate patronage, the fact that states vie over customers could lead to unscrupulous practices. "As states compete more and more for gambling revenue," McGowan predicts, "many states will be tempted to cut corners in order to protect or increase this source of revenue."[65] Given this scenario, McGowan concludes that only federal regulation could curb such behavior. Until that time, however, the federal government willfully lacks any power to intrude in state-sanctioned gambling ventures.

The hands-off policy of the federal government does not mean that it has no stake in the expansion of gambling in the United States. Because of the unique status of Native American tribes, the federal government does have authority over Indian gaming. Tribal lands are held in trust by the federal government, which has a duty to protect the welfare of the tribes. The tribes have sovereignty over their lands (a fact that has been confirmed in many U.S. Supreme Court cases), but it is within the federal government's power to limit Indian sovereignty. To do so, however, requires judicial review of the constitutionality of any proposed limitations. One of the government's main objectives in fulfilling its trust duties is to ensure the economic well-being of the tribes. Therefore, Washington's attitude toward tribal gaming has always been one of encouragement, as long as the gaming revenues have been shown to support the welfare of the various tribes. While there is an altruistic motive for self-sufficiency, the underlying financial truth is that the more those tribes become self-sufficient, the less they will rely on government handouts.

Given this desire to allow Native Americans self-sufficiency, the Indian Gaming Regulatory Act was not the government's attempt to manage gaming on Indian lands. Instead, it was a measure to bring Indian gaming in line with state-sponsored gaming. By requiring that tribes enter into compacts with states, the IGRA structured Indian gaming along the lines of a contract, so that states could install controlling measures up front while granting Indian gaming enterprises an air of legitimacy (which undoubtedly would benefit them in advertising, transacting with non-Indian merchandisers and service providers, and maintaining cordial relationships with the state governments). The IGRA is not above criticism for all its promises of creating "good faith" between tribes and their home states. One of the most telling objections has been leveled by states such as Washington and California, in which tribes have opened casinos without entering into compacts with the state governments. In these cases, the states have no authority to stop the Indian operations. And while state authorities have appealed to federal agencies to step in and end the "uncompacted" gaming ventures, the government has done nothing for fear of setting a precedent that might jeopardize the whole system established by the IGRA.

The federal government has also been somewhat slow in taking action against Internet gambling. Although the states and the Justice Department contend that Internet gambling is illegal, the government has not found a means of directly closing down cyberspace casinos, most of which operate through overseas service providers. Instead, Congress is trying to pass a law that would make it illegal for credit institutions to allow their patrons to use credit cards to conduct online gambling transactions. The Unlawful Internet Gambling Funding Prohibition Act passed the House of Representatives in 2003. The Senate's bill of the same name (pushed by Senator Jon Kyl) was reviewed by a senate committee but never came up for vote before the end of the congressional session. Both bills show the government's willingness to take on Internet gambling merchants, but they also reveal the limitations of any regulation measure. Since the majority of online casinos reside outside U.S. jurisdiction, the government can only block the means of accessing them. Internet casino operators, however, are finding ways to skirt the barriers. Some, for example, are taking wire transfers for payment instead of credit card debits.

Because of the flaws in the "build a better mousetrap" mentality, many of those who oppose government bans on Internet gambling do so not because they are in favor of the vice but because they believe that Internet gambling only can be controlled if it is legalized. If Internet gambling remains an illegal activity, critics say, then it will likely thrive underground where there will be no recourse for those fleeced by shady dealings. If Internet gambling were legalized, however, then it would probably remain in the United States, which, as economics professor Koleman Strumpf claims, "would allow policies to be put in place that could limit the potential excesses of gambling and minimize the role of the criminal element."[66] Other proponents of legalization maintain that making Internet gambling lawful would be healthy for the gaming industry and consumers because it would promote competition.

The American Gaming Association disagrees. Spokesperson Frank Fahrenkopf, Jr., states, "We are opposed to [Internet gambling]. We don't believe the technology exists to properly regulate it."[67] Yet while methods of regulation may be part of the industry's opposition to Internet gambling, there is also a more obvious consequence of legalization—namely, that increased competition would dig in to the current industry's profits. And since state-run lotteries share in those profits, some critics assert that there is a natural bias in government against Internet gaming.

The revenues of Internet gaming coupled with its popularity in America, however, may prove to be the prohibitionists undoing. In his testimony before the NGISC in 1998, law professor Tom W. Bell argued that both the state and federal government will eventually rethink their policies when they realize that substantial amounts of money are being lost to overseas gaming operations. "State governors and legislatures will soon demand a share of that bounty," Bell asserted. Thus, in Bell's view, besides their inability to banish Internet gambling successfully, the government will be motivated to adopt legalization once the states recognize that they will be losing out on "a huge new cash cow" if prohibition persists.[68]

Currently, though, the federal and state governments maintain that Internet gambling is too dangerous to regulate. The potential for operators to manipulate the odds in their favor or otherwise take advantage of patrons would always exist in cyberspace, some analysts suggest. But the most often cited reason for continuing the ban on Internet gaming is that easy and unmonitored wagering will exacerbate problem gambling. Critics fear that once removed from the social milieu of the casino floor, for example, many gamblers will feel no sense of restraint as they sit alone in front of a computer for hours. Furthermore, for those already suffering from problem gambling, Internet gambling would prove a cruel means of feeding their addiction.

Such problems, though, are not beyond the purview of the states. The danger that seems to necessitate federal involvement is the interstate nature of Internet gambling. Because Internet gambling can reach customers in all 50 states, it has no way to adhere to the various laws and restrictions inherent to each individual state. In this respect, Internet gambling is heedless to the manner in which each state has tailored its gambling laws to balance financial interests with public welfare concerns. Critics, therefore, contend that Internet gambling is likely to remain outlawed until such a time—if ever—the federal government can work out an effective means of regulating it.

No Certain Outcome for the Business of Risk

Any attempt for the federal government to become more actively involved in gambling in the United States, however, will likely be met with stiff opposition. According to the American Gaming Association's survey of casino gambling, 87 percent of Americans polled believe that gambling is a personal choice or freedom that should not be abridged or violated by the government. In addition, part of this percentage is made up of people who do not care to gamble themselves but believe that the right should exist for those who do enjoy it. Thus, the government's struggle would be to convince not only the gamblers but also those who fear any increase in the prohibitionary or regulatory powers of federal or state authorities.

Perhaps, then, the market, and not the government, will curb the current expansion of gambling in America. With the increased number of brick-and-mortar casinos, lottery terminals in every convenience store, and Internet gaming available to the majority of the nation's households, competition for customers and revenue is fierce. Some analysts insist that, under such conditions, the expansion of the industry cannot last. Or perhaps the moral backlash, which has stalled the industry to some extent since the 1990s, will contain the spread of gambling if not reverse it.

On the other hand, gambling is one of the more popular entertainment activities in America. According to the AGA survey, almost three times as many people visit a casino each year than attend baseball parks, where America's national game is played. In its final report, the Public Sector Gaming Study Commission made the more ominous assertion that "Whether it is legal or not, gambling is going to occur in America on a large scale, and it is going to be widely endorsed or at least tacitly condoned."[69] Therefore, although the future of its legality or even its regulation is far from certain, gambling is likely to remain active in America. As many gambling historians have pointed out, risk taking and individualism are part of the national character. From the nation's pioneers to Wall Street speculators, Americans have gambled everything on making a better life for themselves. The promise of winning big in the lottery or hitting a casino jackpot is just another manifestation of that fundamental American desire.

---

[1] Pierre-François-Xavier de Charlevoix, quoted in Henry Chafetz. *Play the Devil: A History of Gambling in the United States from 1492 to 1955.* New York: Clarkson N. Potter, 1960, p. 11.

[2] Chafetz, *Play the Devil,* p. 20.

[3] Richard McGowan. *State Lotteries and Legalized Gambling: Painless Revenue or Painful Mirage.* Westport, Conn.: Quorum, 1994, p. 12.

[4] Chafetz, *Play the Devil,* p. 73.

[5] John M. Findlay. *People of Chance: Gambling in American Society from Jamestown to Las Vegas.* New York: Oxford University Press, 1986, p. 88.
[6] Tom Biracree and Wendy Insinger. *The Complete Book of Thoroughbred Horse Racing.* Garden City, N.Y.: Dolphin Books, 1982, p. 142.
[7] Biracree and Insinger, *The Complete* . . . , p. 142.
[8] Biracree and Insinger, *The Complete* . . . , p. 143.
[9] Biracree and Insinger, *The Complete* . . . , p. 144.
[10] Vicki Abt. "The Role of the State in the Expansion and Growth of Commercial Gambling in the USA," in Jan McMillen, ed. *Gambling Cultures: Studies in History and Interpretation.* New York: Routledge, 1996, p. 191.
[11] Abt, in McMillen, *Gambling* . . . , p. 191.
[12] Findlay, *People of Chance*, p. 121.
[13] Timothy L. O'Brien. *Bad Bet: The Inside Story of the Glamour, Glitz, and Danger of America's Gambling Industry.* New York: Times Books, 1998, p. 26.
[14] Findlay, *People of Chance*, p. 123.
[15] Kefauver Committee, quoted in Findlay, *People of Chance*, p. 173.
[16] O'Brien, *Bad Bet*, p. 32.
[17] Kurt Andersen and Priscilla Painton. "Las Vegas, USA." *Time*, January 10, 1994, p. 44.
[18] Andersen and Painton, *Time*, p. 44.
[19] Andersen and Painton, *Time*, p. 51.
[20] Vicki Abt, James F. Smith, and Eugene Martin Christiansen. *The Business of Risk: Commercial Gambling in Mainstream America.* Lawrence: University Press of Kansas, 1985, p. 56.
[21] Michael Nelson. "The Lottery Gamble." *The American Prospect*, June 4, 2001, p. 20.
[22] Nelson, *The American Prospect*, p. 21.
[23] McGowan, *State Lotteries and Legalized Gambling*, p. 18.
[24] Richard A. McGowan. *Government and the Transformation of the Gaming Industry.* Northampton, Mass.: Edward Elgar, pp. 59–60.
[25] James F. Wortman. "Personal Recollections of the New Jersey Gambling 'Experiment' in Atlantic City." in Cathy H. C. Hsu, ed. *Legalized Casino Gaming in the United States: The Economic and Social Impact.* New York: Haworth Hospitality Press, 1999, p. 27.
[26] Wortman, in Hsu, *Legalized* . . . , p. 30.
[27] Wortman, in Hsu, *Legalized* . . . , p. 38.
[28] Wortman, in Hsu, *Legalized* . . . , p. 36.
[29] William R. Eadington, quoted in Richard L. Worsnop. "Gambling Under Attack." *CQ Researcher*, September 6, 1996. Available online. URL: http://library.cqpress.com/cqresearcher/cqresrre1996090600. Downloaded on June 17, 2004.
[30] Cathy H. C. Hsu. "History, Development, and Legislation of Riverboat and Land-Based Non-Native American Casino Gaming," in Cathy H. C. Hsu, ed. *Legalized Casino Gaming in the United States*, p. 64.
[31] Tim Ryan, quoted in Alan Sayre. "After Promises of Prosperity, N.O. Casino Struggling." *Las Vegas Sun*, June 24, 2002. Available online. URL: http://www.lasvegassun.com/sunbin/stories/sun/2002/jun/24/513623519.html. Downloaded on June 17, 2004.

[32] William N. Thompson. "History, Development, and Legislation of Native American Casino Gambling," in Cathy H. C. Hsu, ed. *Legalized Casino Gaming in the United States*, p. 46.

[33] *California v. Cabazon Band of Mission Indians*, 480 U.S. 202 (1987).

[34] Abt, Smith, and Christiansen, *The Business of Risk*, p. 94.

[35] McGowan, *Government and the Transformation of the Gaming Industry*, p. 61.

[36] McGowan, *Government. . .*, p. 72.

[37] "Back in the Saddle." *Global Gaming Business*, February 1, 2004. American Gaming Association web site. Available online. URL: http://www.americangaming.org/Press/op_eds/op_eds_detail.cfv?ID=252.

[38] McGowan, *Government and the Transformation of the Gaming Industry*, p. 71.

[39] Thomas Barker and Marjie Britz. *Jokers Wild: Legalized Gambling in the Twenty-first Century*. Westport, Conn.: Praeger, 2000, p. 88.

[40] Ibid., p. 90.

[41] Robert Breen, quoted in "Video Slots: The Most Addictive Form of Gambling in History." Lifespan web site. Available online. URL: http://www.lifespan.org/Services/MentalHealth/RIH/Gambling/Research/. Posted (n.d.) 2002.

[42] Robin Gareiss and John Soat. "Let It Ride: Sure Gambling Seems Like a Perfect Business Model for the Web, but Is It Legal?" *Information Week*, July 8, 2002, p. 59.

[43] Gareiss and Soot, *Information Week*, p. 59.

[44] David Carruthers, quoted in Matt Richtel. "Google, Yahoo Dropping Internet Gambling Ads." *Las Vegas Sun*. April 5, 2004. Available online. URL: http://www.lasvegassun.com/sunbin/stories/gaming/2004/apr/05/516641983.html. Downloaded June 17, 2004.

[45] Barker and Britz, *Jokers Wild*, p. 185.

[46] Report of the National Gambling Impact Study Commission, June 18, 1999, chapter 7, p. 7.

[47] Frank J. Fahrenkopf, Jr., quoted in Patrick Marshall. "Gambling in America." *CQ Researcher*. Available online. URL: http://library.cqpress.com/cqresearcher/cqresrre2003030700. Posted March 7, 2003.

[48] Blake Hurst. "The Government as Gambling Partner." *The American Enterprise*, March/April 1996, p. 63.

[49] Patricia A. Stokowski. "Economic Impacts of Riverboat and Land-Based Non-Native American Casino Gaming," in Cathy H. C. Hsu, ed. *Legalized Casino Gaming in the United States*, p. 168.

[50] Frank R. Wolf, quoted in Marshall. "Gambling in America," *CQ Researcher*, March 7, 2003, p. 203+.

[51] Michael Parrish, quoted in Ron Selden. "Gaming No Panacea for Meeting Tribes' Needs." *Journal of American Indian Higher Education*, June 30, 2003, p. 24.

[52] David Pace. "Indian Casinos." *Investigative Reporters and Editors, Inc. The IRE Journal*, March/April 2001. Available online. URL: http://www.findarticles.com/p/articles/mi_qa3720/is_200103/ai_n8950335. Downloaded June 17, 2004.

[53] Jim Adams. "Gaming's Flush: High Stakes in Indian Country." *Native Americas*, December 31, 2001, p. 18.

[54] Frank J. Fahrenkopf, Jr. "Gambling Opponents Forget One Thing: It's Fun." American Gaming Association web site. Available online. URL: http://www.americangaming.org/Press/op_eds/op_eds_detail.cfv?id=20. Posted August 1, 2000.

[55] James F. Smith. "When It's Bad It's Better: Conflicting Images of Gambling in American Culture," in Jan McMillen, ed. *Gambling Cultures*, p. 111.
[56] Marc Cooper. "America's House of Cards: How the Casino Economy Robs the Working Poor." *The Nation*, February 19, 1996, p. 11.
[57] Ronald M. Pavalko. "Problem Gambling: The Hidden Addiction." *National Forum*, Fall 1999, p. 28.
[58] Paul Simon. "The Explosive Growth of Gambling in the United States." Congressional Record of the 104th Congress, July 31, 1995, p. S10912.
[59] Report of the National Gambling Impact Study Commission, June 18, 1999, chapter 4, p. 14.
[60] Shannon Bybee, quoted in Richard L. Worsnop. "Gambling Under Attack,"
[61] Report of the National Gambling Impact Study Commission, June 18, 1999, chapter 3, p. 4.
[62] Timothy A. Kelly. "Gambling Backlash: Time for a Moratorium on Casino and Lottery Expansion." Family Research Council web site. Available online. URL: http://www.frc.org/get.cfm?i=IS00C1. Archived March 13, 2003.
[63] Report of the Public Sector Gaming Study Commission, March 2000, final report, p. 37.
[64] Ibid., executive summary, p. 2.
[65] McGowan, *Government and the Transformation of the Gaming Industry*, p. 121.
[66] Koleman Strumpf. "Why Prohibitions on Internet Gambling Won't Work." Cato Institute web site. Available online. URL: http://www.cato.org/dailys/02-19-04.html. Posted February 19, 2004.
[67] Frank J. Fahrenkopf, Jr., quoted in Marshall. "Gambling in America,"
[68] Tom W. Bell. Testimony before the National Gambling Impact Study Commission. May 21, 1998.
[69] Report of the Public Sector Gaming Study Commission, final report, p. 4.

CHAPTER 2

THE LAW AND LEGALIZED GAMBLING

The following chapter discusses legislation and court cases that have significantly affected legalized gambling in America. Because the decision to make gambling legal and subsequently regulate it falls mainly to the individual states, the bulk of gambling legislation has no relation to the federal government. However, with the expansion of tribal gaming since the 1980s and the relative novelty of Internet gambling, federal legislators have assumed the power to decide issues of regulation when the states' authority has been exceeded. Furthermore, despite the federal government's overall willingness to let the states manage their own affairs when it comes to gaming, the U.S. Supreme Court has been called upon to adjudicate some gambling-related matters. Because it maintains that gambling is a state concern, the Court remains reluctant to hear many related cases, but it has often felt compelled to render verdicts when the issue appears to have national repercussions.

This chapter will begin by examining the federal laws that relate to gambling, then move on to discuss important state laws. The chapter concludes by identifying relevant federal and state court cases that have shaped the definition and progress of legalized gambling in the United States.

FEDERAL LEGISLATION

Federal gambling laws are codified in several different sections (called "titles") of the U.S. Legal Code. Definitions of illegal gambling and Indian gaming codes, for example, are part of Title 18. The laws and statutes outlined hereafter have all become part of this large and ever-changing body of federal regulations.

ANTI-LOTTERY ACT OF 1890

Background

In the atmosphere of reform that characterized government in the 1800s, state legislatures tried to end the corruption associated with many state lotteries by terminating the lotteries altogether. The state leaders recognized that the way to cripple lottery operators was to strike at their source of funds. They surmised that enacting local laws would be ineffective since the most successful lotteries sold most of their tickets to residents of other states; so the state governments appealed to the federal government for help.

In 1872 Congress made it illegal for anyone to use the U.S. mail to transmit circulars, advertisements, or any materials that related to "illegal" lotteries. Four years later, the term *illegal* was stricken from that law, and it was therefore amended to include any lottery—even those that were still tolerated by state governments. Skeptics argued that the 1876 law was still inadequate in curbing lotteries because it did not apply to newspapers, which enjoyed First Amendment protection and carried many lottery advertisements across state lines. As time went on, however, this argument seemed inconsequential in a broad sense since lotteries were on the decline in the 1880s.

The collapse came not from restrictive laws but because the lotteries could not compete with Louisiana's Serpent lottery, the largest, longest running, and most popular game in the nation. The Serpent drew money from every state in the Union and therefore earned the focused wrath of the state governments in the last two decades of the century. But to bring down the mighty Serpent, the states again had to appeal to the federal government.

Key Aspects of Legislation

Knowing that the Serpent received 90 percent of its revenue from out of state, Congress enacted the Anti-Lottery Act of 1890 to prohibit the mailing of "any newspaper, circular, pamphlet, or publication of any kind containing any advertisement of any lottery or gift enterprise of any kind offering prizes dependent upon lot or chance, or containing any list of prizes awarded at the drawings of any such lottery or gift enterprise, whether said list is of any part or all of the drawing." The new statute effectively extended the 1876 law to include newspapers, the main means by which the Serpent (and other lotteries) had notified the public of drawing dates and prizes.

Impact

It is unknown how much impact this law would have had on the Serpent because the lottery's demise came not because of failing ticket sales but because Louisiana's governor declined to renew the operator's charter. In

1893, the Serpent relocated to Honduras and tried to continue its operation by pulling in American money through a postal address in Florida. This prompted Congress to pass an 1895 law that made it illegal to transport lottery tickets through the mail. This was the final nail in the Serpent's coffin and a significant act of Congress in its own right.

Once radio was developed, the federal government extended the prohibition of lottery advertising to all broadcast media in the Federal Communications Act of 1934. In 1975, however, that law was amended to allow newspapers and broadcast media to advertise lotteries if the lotteries are state-sanctioned and the newspaper is published in or the broadcast station is licensed to the state in question. The Charity Games Advertising Act of 1988 later permitted charities to use the mail to advertise gaming events. Otherwise, the Anti-Lottery Act of 1890 survives to this day with only slight amendment.

FEDERAL COMMUNICATIONS ACT OF 1934

Background

In 1927, Congress passed the Radio Act to regulate the new medium in "the public interest, convenience, or necessity." At the time, however, radio was under the aegis of both the Department of Commerce and the Interstate Commerce Commission, leading to some confusion and disputed areas of control. In 1934, President Franklin Roosevelt asked Congress to streamline the old act and make it applicable to all broadcasting methods. In response, Congress enacted new legislation, known as the Federal Communication Act of 1934, part of which dealt with the unlawful advertising of games of chance.

Key Aspects of Legislation

The Communications Act is an extensive bill that covers the regulation of commercial broadcasting. In bringing together the various forms of broadcast media, the act gave birth to the Federal Communications Commission (FCC) as the sole legislative body to police the airwaves and telecommunications networks. In relation to gambling, the act empowers the FCC to prohibit the transmission of any gambling advertisements by radio, television, or telephone wire. This is an extension of the powers granted to the U.S. postal service in barring the transmission of gambling advertisements in print media.

Impact

The Communications Act has been altered over the years to make it relevant for more modern forms of communication (such as cable television). It has also been amended in 1975 to lift the ban on broadcasts for state-sponsored lotteries, and then in 1988, it was further amended to allow Native American casinos to advertise on the airwaves. Until 1999, however, non-Indian casinos were still barred from broadcast advertising. In that year, the U.S. Supreme Court struck down that prohibition because it made the law seem inconsistent and gave lotteries and Indian casinos an unfair advantage in the gambling marketplace.

There have been several attempts to rewrite the act to bring it in line with the digital age, but none have passed Congress. Most recently, the Communications Act is being employed in the fight against Internet casino advertising. However, in this respect, many critics call the act outdated and of debatable use.

Transportation of Gambling Devices Act of 1951 (Johnson Act)

Background

In 1950 and 1951, when the Kefauver Committee revealed the vast extent to which organized crime had infiltrated the casino industry in Nevada, an angered nation was motivated to take action to stop the spread of what it perceived as a troublesome vice. For Washington lawmakers, part of the backlash manifested in the passage of the Transportation of Gambling Devices Act (commonly known as the Johnson Act).

Key Aspects of Legislation

The Johnson Act makes it illegal to transport slot machines, roulette wheels, or any other gaming device (or even part of such a device) across state lines unless both states permit such devices to be operated within their jurisdictions. In 1951, Nevada was the only state in which gambling was legalized, so the act was primarily an attempt to keep gambling confined to that state. The law, however, does include a clause by which states can exempt themselves from the restrictions if they so choose. In addition to banning the transportation of gaming devices, the Johnson Act requires manufacturers and distributors of these devices to register each year with the U.S. Department of Justice.

Impact

The law effectively eliminated various gambling devices that cropped up at county fairs and other public venues outside Nevada (and some parts of Idaho and Maryland). A few manufacturers tried to beat the law by fashioning slot machines that did not match the "drum or reel" type named in the law, but none of the resulting devices were popular or successful. The law has been amended over time to include more modern gaming platforms. For example, any software or physical components used in Internet casino gaming is illegal to transport across states lines.

Interstate Wire Act of 1961

Background

In the early 1960s, the administration of President John F. Kennedy sought to clamp down on organized crime, which seemed to have set up a national network that infiltrated business and politics. The zealous attorney general, Robert Kennedy (the brother of the president), focused on curtailing gambling because he believed it was the lifeblood of the grand criminal syndicate. With a sympathetic Congress, the administration was able to institute several federal statutes to restrict gambling. The Wire Act was one such piece of legislation.

Key Aspects of Legislation

The Wire Act of 1961 sought to prohibit bookmakers from taking bets over the telephone. Exactly what activities the bookmakers are not allowed to take bets on is the subject of much debate. The law in part reads:

> *Whoever being engaged in the business of betting or wagering knowingly uses a wire communication facility for the transmission in interstate or foreign commerce of bets or wagers or information assisting in the placing of bets or wagers on any sporting event or contest, or for the transmission of a wire communication which entitles the recipient to receive money or credit as a result of bets or wagers, or for information assisting in the placing of bets or wagers, shall be fined under this title or imprisoned not more than two years, or both.*

The disputed wording of this law resides in the phrase "sporting event or contest." Some lawmakers and scholars interpret the adjective *sporting* as modifying both *event* and *contest.* This narrow definition restricts the Wire Act to prohibiting only bets taken on sports-related games. In 2002 a U.S. district court in Louisiana, in fact, dismissed a case because the indicated type of wagering had nothing to do with sporting events. That case was appealed and the appellate court upheld the original verdict. Other legal factions argue that *sporting* only modifies *event,* therefore leaving *contest* open to broader application against any form of betting conducted over a wire service.

Another controversial aspect of the Wire Act is that it only holds the bookmakers, and not the bettors, accountable for the crime of transacting wagers via phone lines. The courts, however, have upheld this strict definition, and only those who run gambling operations have been targeted by the law.

Impact

The Wire Act has been the subject of much recent controversy. In the Internet age, gambling's opponents insist the broader definition of the act can be used to shut down online casinos as well as target credit card institutions that, by extension, abet illegal wire transactions. Online casino operators, however, argue that the wording of the act—specifically in reference to its use of terminology such as "common carrier"—limits the government's jurisdiction to regulating telephone companies. The U.S. Justice Department, though, maintains that the Wire Act covers all forms of wire and wireless communications, including Internet service providers.

INTERSTATE TRANSPORTATION OF WAGERING PARAPHERNALIA ACT OF 1961

Background

Enacted at the same time as the Wire Act, the Wagering Paraphernalia Act is another piece of legislation aimed at illegal gambling and organized crime. Unlike its companion pieces, the Wagering Paraphernalia Act is narrow in its scope and seeks only to outlaw the interstate transportation of materials related to sports betting.

Key Aspects of Legislation

The Wagering Paraphernalia Act is designed to throttle sports wagering bookmakers by making it illegal to transport or send the tools of their trade across state lines. The text of the act reads:

> *Whoever, except a common carrier in the usual course of its business, knowingly carries or sends in interstate or foreign commerce any record, paraphernalia, ticket, certificate, bills, slip, token, paper, writing, or other device used, or to be used, or adapted, devised, or designed for use in (a) bookmaking; or (b) wagering pools with respect to a sporting event; or (c) in a numbers, policy, bolita, or similar game shall be fined under this title or imprisoned for not more than five years or both.*

The wording of the act is specific enough to target bookmaking tools and practices but loose enough to include all types of sport-wagering games.

Impact

Since the Wagering Paraphernalia Act was created to thwart one form of illegal gambling, its concise nature has meant that this law has never been the subject of much debate. Some of its precise wording, such as the use of the term *knowingly,* has made the law particularly useful even in cases in which defendants claim they sent wagering materials without the intent of breaking the law. In addition, the inclusion of some broad language, such as *paraphernalia* and *device,* has given federal prosecutors the ability to keep the law abreast of changing times and technology.

THE TRAVEL ACT OF 1961

Background

Along with the Wire Act and Wagering Paraphernalia Act, the Travel Act is the third piece of federal legislation enacted in 1961 when Attorney General Robert Kennedy made it his objective to disrupt, if not eradicate, organized crime. Unlike its companions, however, the Travel Act is not targeted exclusively at gambling. Instead, the act has broader applications to any illegal activity that is conducted across state lines.

Key Aspects of Legislation

The Travel Act was designed to prosecute anyone who travels across state lines or uses the mail or any interstate facility with the intent to: "(1) distribute the proceeds of any unlawful activity; or (2) commit any crime of violence to further any unlawful activity; or (3) otherwise promote, manage, establish, carry on, or facilitate the promotion, management, establishment, or carrying on, of any unlawful activity." As with the Wagering Paraphernalia Act, the government need not prove that defendants intended to break the law; it only needs to show that a breach occurred.

Impact

Federal prosecutors utilize the Travel Act to take action against businesses that use the mail, the telephone, the newspapers, or the nation's roadways to conduct illegal activities. In relation to gambling, the Travel Act is most often employed in conjunction with the Wire Act and Interstate Transportation of Wagering Paraphernalia Act to maintain the outlaw status of Internet gambling. In *United States v. Smith* (1962), a federal court decided that Congress did not intend to restrict the application of the Travel Act "to cases in which there was an actual physical transportation of substantive materials in interstate commerce." Instead, using the telephone to transact illegal business was tantamount to transporting prohibited materials across state lines. Indeed, in a January 2004 case involving a violation of the Travel Act, the accused were found to have used the phone to set up dates between clients in Chicago and prostitutes in Miami. Thus, running an online casino that has a customer base outside the home state is considered illegal under the Travel Act. Finally, it is important to note that the objective of the

Travel Act is to punish the operators of illegal activities and not the clients, so it is unlikely that the act will be used to prosecute individuals who gamble online.

ILLEGAL GAMBLING BUSINESS ACT OF 1970

Background

Despite the legal measures established during the Kennedy administration, the federal government in the late 1960s maintained that large-scale gambling operations still constituted the financial backbone of organized crime. And because organized crime affected lawful interstate commerce, the federal government felt compelled to enact more laws to crack down on and eradicate criminal syndicates. Congress, therefore, passed a comprehensive Organized Crime Control Act in 1970. One part of that legislation package was the Illegal Gambling Business Act.

Key Aspects of Legislation

The Illegal Gambling Business Act was created to give a specific definition to an illegal gaming venture so that federal prosecutors could take action to shut it down—especially in cases in which the state may be reluctant to do so. For instance, the federal government since the Kennedy years had suspected that Nevada authorities were receiving payments from the big casinos and therefore were either slow or unwilling to take action against the criminals who ostensibly ran Las Vegas. The Illegal Gambling Business Act was meant to remedy that.

The act stipulates that to incur federal involvement, a gambling operation must first be in violation of a state or local law. Second, the gambling enterprise must be comprised of at least five individuals, and third, it must have been in operation for more than 30 days or have taken in $2,000 on any given day of business. In regard to the second requirement, federal prosecutors only have to show that five individuals were employed in any function in the business end of the enterprise. Bettors, therefore, are excluded from prosecution under this law.

Impact

Although the act may help quash small illegal gambling rackets whenever and wherever they are found, legal scholars expect that its biggest impact may come in the fight against Internet gambling enterprises. The application to online casino operators, however, is controversial. Since entire Internet gaming sites may be operated by one or two individuals, prosecutors would have to interpret the second restriction of the law to include ancillary personnel such as accountants or any computer maintenance service as being part of the requisite five-member staff. Because the law is vague in this respect, it is entirely possible that this broad definition may be employed. Even with this qualification, the act still only applies to domestic gambling operations. It is not clear how it could be used against operators who use foreign Internet hosts for their online casinos.

RACKETEER INFLUENCED AND CORRUPT ORGANIZATIONS ACT OF 1970 (RICO)

Background

Another piece of legislation enacted as part of the Organized Crime Control Act of 1970 was the Racketeer Influenced and Corrupt Organizations Act (RICO). This act painted gambling and other racketeering operations as harmful to interstate commerce and therefore requiring federal intervention.

Key Aspects of Legislation

RICO does not specifically target gambling, but its intent is to disrupt any business enterprise that utilizes funds derived from illegal means. The various subsections of the act indict investors, operators, and employees of any venture that is funded by ill-gotten money. To utilize the law, prosecutors must show that the business is connected to a continuous racketeering operation and that the operation affects interstate commerce. RICO defines racketeering operations as any of those outlawed by the Wire Act, the Travel Act, the Interstate Transportation of Wagering Paraphernalia Act, or the Illegal Gambling Business Act, or any activity that is in violation of state law (such as gambling).

Impact

RICO imposes both a criminal punishment (20 years to life imprisonment) and a civil fine (triple the damages and payment of litigation costs), so conviction is quite punitive. One gambling operator tried to escape from being prosecuted by the law as applied in Michigan and Ohio by claiming his poker games were rigged and therefore constituted larceny instead of illegal gambling. The courts did not agree. Others, enticed by triple damages, have tried to use the act for their own profit. An unlucky and vengeful Internet gambler, for example, tried to sue MasterCard International under RICO by claiming that the credit card company was part of an illegal gambling operation since it aided in wagering transactions. The attempt to win a payout after gambling away his money failed, however; the court ruled that MasterCard was not an investor, operator, or employee of the illegal enterprise as defined by the law. Still, legal experts anticipate that because RICO's penalties are harsh, the act will be called into play when and if the federal government begins a full-scale crackdown on Internet gambling operators.

The Interstate Horseracing Act of 1978

Background

When off-track betting (OTB) took off in the 1970s, gambling advocates immediately recognized the need for some regulation of simulcasting and cross-country wagering. After all, the gambling parlors in New York, the first state to legalize OTB, were already taking bets on the Kentucky Derby without concern for horse racing authorities in Kentucky. To keep OTB alive without alienating any group within the sport, various interest groups convinced the horse racing industry of the benefits of OTB regulation, and in 1978, the industry asked Congress to pass the Interstate Horseracing Act.

Key Aspects of Legislation

The Interstate Horseracing Act is a federal act because of the interstate nature of some off-track betting. The act stipulates that simulcasting of races cannot take place at a track without the consent of the track and local industry authorities. Furthermore, all off-track betting facilities have to meet the approval of every track within a 60-mile radius. OTB sites are not allowed to operate beyond that range in order to safeguard against any one firm monopolizing the market.

Impact

Although initially many in the racing industry predicted that OTB would spell doom for tracks by stealing away the patrons, it is now more commonly believed that OTB saved the sport. Horsemen and racing authorities credit the Interstate Horseracing Act with efficiently regulating OTB practices and enforcing the cooperation of the states where OTB is legal. The act has survived with only minor amendments to take into account changes in technology. The most recent amendment was in 2000, to make off-track pari-mutuel wagering legal across phone lines.

Indian Gaming Regulatory Act of 1988 (IGRA)

Background

In 1980, the state of Florida sued the Seminole Nation of Florida for running high-stakes bingo games on reservation land. The Seminole insisted they had a right to operate such games because charity bingo games were legal under state law. The state, however, argued that the big-money events were beyond the pale of charity games, and, therefore, the tribe's contests fell within the definition of illegal gambling. A Florida court decided the matter by declaring that since bingo was legal in the state, the Seminole had a right to operate the games. The court also maintained that even if the cash prizes were excessive and illegal under state law, the state government had no jurisdiction to regulate games operated on sovereign Indian land. The state appealed to the U.S. Supreme Court, but that judicial body refused to hear the case since it considered the matter to be an infraction of civil law and therefore within the purview of the state judiciary, which had already rendered a ruling.

In 1987, the Supreme Court, however, did hear an identical case involving the Cabazon Indians of California. The Court ruled that the Indians had not broken any criminal law by operating high-stakes bingo games since California law only concerned the regulation of such games. Therefore, the bingo games could not be prohibited; at best, they could be regulated through civil law. Yet, as the Florida court had previously noted, the state of California did not have the authority to enforce civil law on reservation land; only the federal government had the power to do so. In essence, the Supreme Court decreed that the state's hands were tied. Given this pronouncement, other Native American tribes began considering gambling enterprises to raise much-needed money for their mostly impoverished populations.

Fearing a widespread growth of unregulated gambling, the states pushed Congress to enact some kind of law to control Indian gaming. Knowing that they had the upper hand but still needed the goodwill of the states, many Native American tribes agreed to help shape and endorse this legislation. The result was the Indian Gaming Regulation Act (IGRA), which passed Congress in 1988. It was swiftly signed into law by President Ronald Reagan, who believed Indian gaming would decrease the need for federal handouts and propel Native Americans towards self-sufficiency.

Key Aspects of Legislation

The IGRA is a comprehensive set of guidelines that identifies what forms of gaming can be operated on tribal land, how these games are to be regulated, and who shall have regulatory control over them.

The IGRA divides Indian games into three classes:

- Class I: small-stakes traditional games that are subject only to tribal regulation.
- Class II: bingo and some card games that are nonbanking (that is, not played against a casino bank but only among individual players). These games are regulated by tribal authorities and the National Indian Gaming Commission.

- Class III: games not covered in the other classes. These include most casino games, such as roulette, craps, and slots, in addition to blackjack, poker, and other card games that are banked by a casino.

For a tribe to operate any Class II game, the same type of game must be legal (in any form) within the state where the tribe resides. The running of such games is subject to oversight by the National Indian Gaming Commission, a three-member panel that establishes guidelines and standards of operation. In Michigan, North Dakota, South Dakota, and Washington, casino-banked blackjack is considered a Class II game because reservations in these states legally ran blackjack games before the IGRA took effect. In all other states, banked blackjack is considered a Class III game.

To operate Class III games, a tribe must: (1) make sure the games are legal elsewhere within the state, (2) pass an ordinance authorizing the games, and (3) enter into a compact, or binding agreement, with the state government that will define how the games will be conducted, whether the state will have any say in the gaming operation, and what, if any, fees and assessments will be paid to the states. The IGRA also asserts federal authority over any criminal prosecutions that arise over the violation of state gambling laws at reservation gaming facilities.

Impact

The Indian Gaming Regulatory Act is without a doubt the most significant federal law on gambling in recent years. The rather loose terminology of the act opened the door to widespread Indian gaming in the 1990s. For example, if a state permitted charities to run occasional "Las Vegas nights" in which casino-type games were trotted out to give atmosphere and an element of risk to the act of donation, then by the strictures of the IGRA, Native American tribes in that state could (and did) insist they had a right to open full-fledged, 24-hour casinos on Indian land. And if a state resisted this type of demand, then the tribes could sue the state and bring federal authorities to force a compact, usually with the state losing out on any advantages it could have gained if it had been a willing partner. Fearing these consequences, many states in the 1990s willingly entered into Class III compacts with their tribes in order to gain some concessions out of a deal-making process in which the outcome—the inauguration of casino gambling—was seemingly inevitable. Coupled with riverboat gambling and some state-authorized land-based casinos, Indian casinos that sprang up in many parts of the country helped define the casino boom of the late 20th century.

Despite the apparent open-door policy of the IGRA, several states balked at permitting Indian gaming. Some states maintained that specific Class III games were not legal elsewhere in their jurisdictions; others simply insisted that the IGRA was not drafted to give license to the proliferation of casino gambling. In 1996, the states won an important victory when Florida's attorney general convinced the U.S. Supreme Court that the clause in the IGRA that permitted tribes to sue the states over stalled negotiations was unconstitutional. With this avenue blocked, the tribes could no longer count on the federal government to compel states to enter into compacts, and some states halted negotiations. Other states continued to grant compacts in the hopes that they could leverage many concessions out of the tribes that had now lost their bargaining advantage.

In 1998, the government adopted a revised Indian Gaming Regulatory Act that permitted the secretary of the Interior the power to mediate and, if necessary, force stalled negotiations between states and tribes. This appeared to return power to the tribes, but the Senate immediately barred the secretary from forcing compacts until federal courts could decide the legality of this method.

PROFESSIONAL AND AMATEUR SPORTS PROHIBITION ACT OF 1992 (PASPA)

Background

In 1970, Delaware's state lottery began taking bets on the outcome of professional football games. Dismayed that they might be tied to the promotion of gambling, the National Football League (NFL) sued the state. The courts, however, deemed that Delaware's actions were legal under its own laws. Given this green light, Oregon began tying its lottery to the outcome of professional football and basketball games later that year. At that point, licensed sports wagering was only operating out of Delaware, Oregon, and Nevada, where casinos had been running sports pools for some time.

For 20 years, the federal government left the matter of sports wagering in the hands of the states. Then in 1991, Congress decided to investigate the impact of sports gambling beyond the borders of the states in which it had been made legal. Senators such as John McCain of Arizona charged that sports wagering was harmful to individuals and to the nation as a whole and therefore required federal intervention. According to McCain and his supporters, many college students across the country were placing bets on school games through the Nevada pools and often losing sums they could not afford. These politicians, along with various sports leagues, also hoped to stop more state lotteries from being connected to sports games for fear that this would impact the integrity of the games. Spurred by McCain's crusade, Congress voted the following year to enact the Professional and Amateur Sports Protection Act (PASPA) to make it a federal violation to take bets on sporting events in the United States, except in those states in which state law had already deemed it legal.

Key Aspects of Legislation

PASPA makes it illegal for state governments, businesses, or individuals to conduct or promote any gambling venture that is based "directly or indirectly" on any professional and amateur sports contest (except horse racing, dog racing, and jai alai). Delaware, Oregon, and Nevada are exempt from the legislation, and, because of its tolerance of legalized gambling, New Jersey was given a year to decide if it wished to legalize sports betting before the act would go into effect in that state. New Jersey declined. With PASPA in effect, no state could henceforth make any provisions for legalizing sports gambling within its borders.

Impact

Because the act usurps state authority over this form of gambling, PASPA is one of the more controversial laws ever enacted. Prior to passage of the act, the U.S. Justice Department related its concerns about the abridgement of states' rights. It was also troubled about a section of the act that permitted sports organizations to enforce the law through civil injunctions—a role usually reserved for the U.S. Attorney General. Despite these concerns, Congress passed the act in hopes of limiting the spread of sports gambling.

In 1999, the National Gambling Impact Study Commission (NGISC) singled out sports gambling in Nevada as the most problematic and uncontrolled form of gambling in America. Therefore, regardless of the law, sports wagering continued to be the most popular form of gambling in America. The commission even conjectured that most Americans were "unaware of the risks and impacts of sports wagering and about the potential for legal consequences." In addition, the commission feared that the population most detrimentally affected was that of college students who wagered unreasonably and often developed the habits of problem gamblers at an early age. The National Collegiate Athletic Association (NCAA) then weighed in with its continuing concerns over the damaging affects of sports wagering upon the integrity of college sports. In 2000, the NCAA proposed to ban all betting related to college sports in America. Since gambling on college sports is already illegal in all but one state, the proposal was obviously aimed at closing Nevada's college sports gambling books. The new act failed to pass Congress in 2001, however, and wagering on all sports remains legal within Nevada's jurisdiction.

STATE LEGISLATION

Each of the 50 states in the Union has laws regarding gambling. Hawaii and Utah are the only states that ban all forms of gambling, so their laws are strictly prohibitory. The other 48 states tolerate some types of gambling and outlaw other types, so their laws are a mix of regulatory and prohibitory. The various legal codes adopted by the states that permit gambling, however, are remarkably similar. Only a few noteworthy distinctions can be made, and these include what forms of gambling are legal, the age that one can legally gamble, whether gambling in a social setting (that is, when players compete only with each other and not a casino bank) is considered a crime, and whether a violation of the gambling code constitutes a misdemeanor or a felony for players and promoters (those who operate or help promote gaming ventures). Given the uniformity of most state laws, then, the following list outlines the aforementioned distinctions and makes note of any special laws that are inherent to specific states.

Note: Throughout "none" means that a state does not have that form of gambling. "Indian gaming" means that a state has tribal gaming within its borders.

ALABAMA

Lottery: none
Non-tribal casinos: none
Racing: dog racing, dog and horse simulcasting (minimum gambling age is 19)
Other forms of legalized gambling: bingo (no minimum gambling age specified)
Infraction of gambling laws: misdemeanor for both players and promoters
Is social gambling tolerated? yes
Indian gaming: one bingo hall offering some video gaming machines (minimum gambling age is 18)

ALASKA

Lottery: none
Non-tribal casinos: none
Racing: none
Other forms of legalized gambling: bingo (minimum gambling age is 19)
Infraction of gambling laws: misdemeanor for players, felony for promoters
Is social gambling tolerated? yes
Indian gaming: five gaming halls offering bingo and pull-tabs (a paper ticket game in which players pull perforated windows on their tickets to reveal winning combinations of symbols) (minimum gambling age is 18)

ARIZONA

Lottery: yes (minimum gambling age is 21)
Non-tribal casinos: none
Racing: dog and horse racing and simulcasting (minimum gambling age is 21)

Other forms of legalized gambling: bingo (minimum gambling age is 21)

Infraction of gambling laws: misdemeanor for players, felony for promoters

Is social gambling tolerated? yes

Indian gaming: 22 casinos (minimum gambling age is 21)

Arkansas

Lottery: none

Non-tribal casinos: none

Racing: dog and horse racing and simulcasting, and Instant Racing video machines (minimum gambling age is 18)

Other forms of legalized gambling: bingo (no minimum age specified)

Infraction of gambling laws: petty fine for players, misdemeanor for promoters

Is social gambling tolerated? no

Indian gaming: none

California

Lottery: yes (minimum gambling age is 18)

Non-tribal casinos: none

Racing: horse racing and simulcasting (minimum gambling age is 18)

Other forms of legalized gambling: bingo and card rooms (minimum gambling age is 18)

Infraction of gambling laws: misdemeanor for both players and promoters

Is social gambling tolerated? yes

Indian gaming: 53 casinos (minimum gambling age is 18, or 21 if alcohol is served on the premises)

Colorado

Lottery: yes (minimum gambling age is 18)

Non-tribal casinos: 45 land-based, low-stakes casinos (minimum gambling age is 21)

Racing: dog and horse racing and simulcasting (minimum gambling age is 18)

Other forms of legalized gambling: bingo (minimum gambling age is 18)

Infraction of gambling laws: petty fine for players, misdemeanor to felony for promoters

Is social gambling tolerated? yes

Indian gaming: two low-stakes casinos (minimum gambling age is 21)

CONNECTICUT

Lottery: yes (minimum gambling age is 18)
Non-tribal casinos: none
Racing: dog racing and simulcasting (minimum gambling age is 18)
Other forms of legalized gambling: bingo (minimum gambling age is 18)
Infraction of gambling laws: misdemeanor for both players and promoters
Is social gambling tolerated? yes
Indian gaming: two casinos (minimum gambling age is 21)

DELAWARE

Lottery: yes (minimum gambling age is 18)
Non-tribal casinos: part of racetracks
Racing: three racinos offering horse racing, simulcasting, and video slot machines (minimum gambling age is 18)
Other forms of legalized gambling: bingo (minimum gambling age is 16)
Infraction of gambling laws: misdemeanor for both players and promoters
Is social gambling tolerated? yes
Indian gaming: none

DISTRICT OF COLUMBIA

Lottery: yes (minimum gambling age is 18)
Non-tribal casinos: none
Racing: none
Other forms of legalized gambling: bingo (minimum gambling age is 18)
Infraction of gambling laws: felony for both players and promoters
Is social gambling tolerated? the law is not specific
Indian gaming: none

FLORIDA

Lottery: yes (minimum gambling age is 18)
Non-tribal casinos: none (but day cruises permit casino gambling outside state jurisdiction)
Racing: dog and horse racing and simulcasting (minimum gambling age is 18)
Other forms of legalized gambling: bingo, card rooms at some pari-mutuel facilities (minimum gambling age is 18)
Infraction of gambling laws: misdemeanor for players, felony for promoters
Is social gambling tolerated? yes
Indian gaming: six gaming halls offering poker, high-stakes bingo, and video gaming machines (minimum gambling age is 18)

GEORGIA

Lottery: yes (minimum gambling age is 18)
Non-tribal casinos: none (but day cruises permit casino gambling outside state jurisdiction)
Racing: none
Other forms of legalized gambling: bingo (no minimum gambling age specified)
Infraction of gambling laws: misdemeanor for players, felony for promoters
Is social gambling tolerated? no
Indian gaming: none

HAWAII

Lottery: none
Non-tribal casinos: none
Racing: none
Other forms of legalized gambling: none
Infraction of gambling laws: misdemeanor for players, misdemeanor to felony for promoters
Is social gambling tolerated? yes
Indian gaming: none

IDAHO

Lottery: yes (minimum gambling age is 18)
Non-tribal casinos: none
Racing: horse racing and simulcasting (minimum gambling age is 18)
Other forms of legalized gambling: bingo (no minimum gambling age specified)
Infraction of gambling laws: misdemeanor for both players and promoters
Is social gambling tolerated? no
Indian gaming: six gaming halls offering bingo and video gaming machines (minimum gambling age is 18)

ILLINOIS

Lottery: yes (minimum gambling age is 18)
Non-tribal casinos: nine riverboat casinos (minimum gambling age is 21)
Racing: horse racing and simulcasting (minimum gambling age is 18)
Other forms of legalized gambling: bingo (minimum gambling age is 18)
Infraction of gambling laws: misdemeanor for players, misdemeanor to felony for promoters
Is social gambling tolerated? no
Indian gaming: none

INDIANA

Lottery: yes (minimum gambling age is 18)
Non-tribal casinos: 10 riverboat casinos (minimum gambling age is 21)
Racing: horse racing and simulcasting (minimum gambling age is 18)
Other forms of legalized gambling: bingo (minimum gambling age is 18)
Infraction of gambling laws: misdemeanor for players, felony for promoters
Is social gambling tolerated? yes
Indian gaming: none

IOWA

Lottery: yes (minimum gambling age is 21)
Non-tribal casinos: 10 riverboat casinos (minimum gambling age is 21)
Racing: three racinos offering dog and horse racing and simulcasting, and video slot machines (minimum gambling age is 21)
Other forms of legalized gambling: bingo (no minimum gambling age specified)
Infraction of gambling laws: misdemeanor to felony for both players and promoters
Is social gambling tolerated? no
Indian gaming: three casinos (minimum gambling age is 21)

KANSAS

Lottery: yes (minimum gambling age is 18)
Non-tribal casinos: none
Racing: dog and horse racing and simulcasting (minimum gambling age is 18)
Other forms of legalized gambling: bingo (no minimum gambling age specified)
Infraction of gambling laws: misdemeanor for players, felony for promoters
Is social gambling tolerated? no
Indian gaming: four casinos (minimum gambling age is 21)

KENTUCKY

Lottery: yes (minimum gambling age is 18)
Non-tribal casinos: none
Racing: horse racing and simulcasting (minimum gambling age is 18)
Other forms of legalized gambling: bingo (no minimum gambling age specified)
Infraction of gambling laws: misdemeanor for players, felony for promoters
Is social gambling tolerated? yes
Indian gaming: none

LOUISIANA

Lottery: yes (minimum gambling age is 21)

Non-tribal casinos: 13 riverboat casinos, one land-based casino (minimum gambling age is 21)

Racing: three racinos offering horse racing, simulcasting, and video slot machines (minimum gambling age is 18)

Other forms of legalized gambling: bingo (minimum gambling age is 18)

Infraction of gambling laws: misdemeanor for players, felony for promoters

Is social gambling tolerated? yes

Indian gaming: three casinos (minimum gambling age is 21)

MAINE

Lottery: yes (minimum gambling age is 18)

Non-tribal casinos: none (but cruises to Canada permit casino gambling outside state jurisdiction)

Racing: horse racing (minimum gambling age is 18)

Other forms of legalized gambling: bingo (minimum gambling age is 18)

Infraction of gambling laws: misdemeanor for players, felony for promoters

Is social gambling tolerated? yes

Indian gaming: none

MARYLAND

Lottery: yes (minimum gambling age is 18)

Non-tribal casinos: none

Racing: horse racing and simulcasting (minimum gambling age is 18)

Other forms of legalized gambling: bingo (minimum gambling age is 16)

Infraction of gambling laws: misdemeanor for players, felony for promoters

Is social gambling tolerated? no

Indian gaming: none

MASSACHUSETTS

Lottery: yes (minimum gambling age is 18)

Non-tribal casinos: none (but day cruises permit gambling outside state jurisdiction)

Racing: dog and horse racing and simulcasting (minimum gambling age is 18)

Other forms of legalized gambling: bingo (minimum gambling age is 18)

Infraction of gambling laws: misdemeanor for players, misdemeanor to felony for promoters

Is social gambling tolerated? the law is not specific

Indian gaming: none

MICHIGAN

Lottery: yes (minimum gambling age is 18)

Non-tribal casinos: three land-based casinos (minimum gambling age is 21)

Racing: horse racing and simulcasting (minimum gambling age is 18)

Other forms of legalized gambling: bingo (minimum gambling age is 18)

Infraction of gambling laws: misdemeanor for players and promoters

Is social gambling tolerated? no (with exceptions for senior-citizen homes and state fairs)

Indian gaming: 17 casinos (minimum gambling age varies between 18 and 21)

MINNESOTA

Lottery: yes (minimum gambling age is 18)

Non-tribal casinos: none

Racing: one track offering horse racing, simulcasting, and a card room (minimum gambling age is 18)

Other forms of legalized gambling: bingo (minimum gambling age is 18)

Infraction of gambling laws: misdemeanor for players and promoters

Is social gambling tolerated? yes

Indian gaming: 19 casinos (minimum gambling age is 18, or 21 if alcohol is served on the premises)

MISSISSIPPI

Lottery: no

Non-tribal casinos: 29 riverboat casinos (minimum gambling age is 21)

Racing: none

Other forms of legalized gambling: bingo (no minimum gambling age specified)

Infraction of gambling laws: misdemeanor for players and promoters

Is social gambling tolerated? no

Indian gaming: one casino (minimum gambling age is 21)

MISSOURI

Lottery: yes (minimum gambling age is 18)
Non-tribal casinos: 11 riverboat casinos (minimum gambling age is 21)
Racing: none
Other forms of legalized gambling: bingo (minimum gambling age is 16)
Infraction of gambling laws: misdemeanor for players, felony for promoters
Is social gambling tolerated? no
Indian gaming: none

MONTANA

Lottery: yes (minimum gambling age is 18)
Non-tribal casinos: none
Racing: horse racing and simulcasting (minimum gambling age is 18)
Other forms of legalized gambling: bingo, card rooms, various establishments throughout the state offer video gaming machines (minimum gambling age 18)
Infraction of gambling laws: misdemeanor for players and promoters
Is social gambling tolerated? yes
Indian gaming: five gaming halls offering video gaming machines, sports pools, simulcasting, and other small-stakes games (minimum gambling age is 18)

NEBRASKA

Lottery: yes (minimum gambling age is 19)
Non-tribal casinos: none
Racing: horse racing and simulcasting (minimum gambling age is 19)
Other forms of legalized gambling: bingo (minimum gambling age is 18)
Infraction of gambling laws: misdemeanor for players and promoters
Is social gambling tolerated? no
Indian gaming: two gaming halls offering bingo and pull-tabs (minimum gambling age is 18)

NEVADA

Lottery: no
Non-tribal casinos: 249 land-based casinos that gross more than $1 million (minimum gambling age is 21)
Racing: horse racing (minimum gambling age is 21)
Other forms of legalized gambling: bingo, sports betting in casinos (minimum gambling age is 21)

Infraction of gambling laws: misdemeanor for players, felony for promoters

Is social gambling tolerated? yes

Indian gaming: two casinos (minimum gambling age is 21)

NEW HAMPSHIRE

Lottery: yes (minimum gambling age is 18)

Non-tribal casinos: none

Racing: dog racing and simulcasting (minimum gambling age is 18)

Other forms of legalized gambling: bingo (minimum gambling age is 18)

Infraction of gambling laws: misdemeanor for players, misdemeanor to felony for promoters

Is social gambling tolerated? no

Indian gaming: none

NEW JERSEY

Lottery: yes (minimum gambling age is 18)

Non-tribal casinos: 12 land-based casinos (minimum gambling age is 21)

Racing: horse racing and simulcasting (minimum gambling age is 18)

Other forms of legalized gambling: bingo (minimum gambling age is 18)

Infraction of gambling laws: misdemeanor for players and promoters

Is social gambling tolerated? yes

Indian gaming: none

NEW MEXICO

Lottery: yes (minimum gambling age is 18)

Non-tribal casinos: none

Racing: four racinos offering horse racing and simulcasting and video slot machines (minimum gambling age is 18)

Other forms of legalized gambling: bingo, some veteran's clubs, fraternal orders, and pari-mutuel sites offer slot machines (minimum gambling age is 18)

Infraction of gambling laws: misdemeanor for players, felony for promoters

Is social gambling tolerated? yes

Indian gaming: 13 casinos (minimum gambling age is 21)

NEW YORK

Lottery: yes (minimum gambling age is 18)

Non-tribal casinos: none (but cruises to Europe permit casino gambling outside state jurisdiction)

Racing: four racinos offering horse racing and simulcasting, and video slot machines; seven other tracks offer horse racing and simulcasting (minimum gambling age is 18)

Other forms of legalized gambling: bingo (no minimum gambling age specified)

Infraction of gambling laws: misdemeanor for players, felony for promoters

Is social gambling tolerated? yes

Indian gaming: three casinos (minimum gambling age varies between 18 and 21), and three high-stakes bingo halls

North Carolina

Lottery: none

Non-tribal casinos: none

Racing: none

Other forms of legalized gambling: bingo (no minimum gambling age specified)

Infraction of gambling laws: misdemeanor for players and promoters

Is social gambling tolerated? no

Indian gaming: one casino offering video gaming machines and digital table games (minimum gambling age is 21)

North Dakota

Lottery: none

Non-tribal casinos: none

Racing: horse racing (minimum gambling age is 18)

Other forms of legalized gambling: bingo, charitable limited-stakes blackjack (minimum gambling age is 21; no minimum gambling age specified for bingo)

Infraction of gambling laws: misdemeanor for players, felony for promoters

Is social gambling tolerated? yes (a bet on an individual hand cannot exceed $25)

Indian gaming: five limited-stakes casinos, one of which has only video gaming machines, pull-tabs, and bingo (minimum gambling age is 21)

Ohio

Lottery: yes (minimum gambling age is 18)

Non-tribal casinos: none

Racing: horse racing and simulcasting (minimum gambling age 18)

Other forms of legalized gambling: bingo (minimum gambling age is 18)
Infraction of gambling laws: misdemeanor for players, felony for promoters
Is social gambling tolerated? yes
Indian gaming: none

OKLAHOMA

Lottery: none
Non-tribal casinos: none
Racing: horse racing and simulcasting (minimum gambling age is 18)
Other forms of legalized gambling: bingo (no minimum gambling age)
Infraction of gambling laws: misdemeanor for players, felony for promoters
Is social gambling tolerated? no
Indian gaming: 70 casinos and gaming halls offering a mix of video gaming machines, pull-tabs, high-stakes bingo, and other games (minimum gambling age varies between 18 and 21)

OREGON

Lottery: yes (minimum gambling age is 18)
Non-tribal casinos: none
Racing: dog and horse racing and simulcasting; Instant Racing video machines are legal, but an experiment in their use failed to elicit confidence and no machines are currently operational (minimum gambling age is 18)
Other forms of legalized gambling: bingo; bars may have limited-stakes video gaming machines (minimum gambling age is 18)
Infraction of gambling laws: misdemeanor for players, felony for promoters
Is social gambling tolerated? yes
Indian gaming: eight casinos (minimum gambling age is 21)

PENNSYLVANIA

Lottery: yes (minimum gambling age is 18)
Non-tribal casinos: none
Racing: horse racing and simulcasting (minimum gambling age is 18)
Other forms of legalized gambling: bingo (no minimum gambling age specified)
Infraction of gambling laws: misdemeanor for players and promoters
Is social gambling tolerated? the law is not specific
Indian gaming: none

Rhode Island

Lottery: yes (minimum gambling age is 18)
Non-tribal casinos: none
Racing: one racino offering dog racing, dog and horse race simulcasting, and video slot machines (minimum gambling age is 18)
Other forms of legalized gambling: bingo (minimum gambling age is 18)
Infraction of gambling laws: misdemeanor for players, felony for promoters
Is social gambling tolerated? no
Indian gaming: none

South Carolina

Lottery: yes (minimum gambling age is 18)
Non-tribal casinos: none (but day cruises permit gambling outside state jurisdiction)
Racing: none
Other forms of legalized gambling: bingo (no minimum gambling age specified)
Infraction of gambling laws: misdemeanor for players and promoters
Is social gambling tolerated? yes
Indian gaming: one high-stakes bingo hall

South Dakota

Lottery: yes (minimum gambling age is 18)
Non-tribal casinos: 41 limited-stakes casinos (minimum gambling age is 21)
Racing: horse racing and dog and horse race simulcasting (minimum gambling age is 18)
Other forms of legalized gambling: bingo, bars may have video gaming machines (minimum gambling age is 21; no minimum gambling age specified for bingo)
Infraction of gambling laws: misdemeanor for players, felony for promoters
Is social gambling tolerated? no
Indian gaming: nine casinos (minimum gambling age is 21)

Tennessee

Lottery: yes (minimum gambling age is 18)
Non-tribal casinos: none
Racing: none
Other forms of legalized gambling: bingo (no minimum gambling age specified)

Infraction of gambling laws: misdemeanor for players, felony for promoters

Is social gambling tolerated? no

Indian gaming: none

TEXAS

Lottery: yes (minimum gambling age is 18)

Non-tribal casinos: none (but day cruises permit gambling outside state jurisdiction)

Racing: dog and horse racing and simulcasting (minimum gambling age is 21)

Other forms of legalized gambling: none

Infraction of gambling laws: misdemeanor for players and promoters

Is social gambling tolerated? yes

Indian gaming: two gaming halls offering bingo, card games, and video gaming machines (minimum gambling age is 21)

UTAH

Lottery: none

Non-tribal casinos: none

Racing: none

Other forms of legalized gambling: bingo

Infraction of gambling laws: misdemeanor for players, felony for promoters

Is social gambling tolerated? no

Indian gaming: none

VERMONT

Lottery: yes (minimum gambling age is 18)

Non-tribal casinos: none

Racing: none

Other forms of legalized gambling: bingo (minimum gambling age is 18)

Infraction of gambling laws: misdemeanor for players and promoters

Is social gambling tolerated? no

Indian gaming: none

VIRGINIA

Lottery: yes (minimum gambling age is 18)

Non-tribal casinos: none

Racing: horse racing and simulcasting (minimum gambling age is 18)

Other forms of legalized gambling: bingo (no minimum gambling age specified)

Infraction of gambling laws: misdemeanor for players, felony for promoters

Is social gambling tolerated? no

Indian gaming: none

WASHINGTON

Lottery: yes (minimum gambling age is 18)

Non-tribal casinos: none

Racing: horse racing and simulcasting (minimum gambling age is 18)

Other forms of legalized gambling: bingo, card rooms (minimum gambling age is 18; no minimum gambling age specified for bingo)

Infraction of gambling laws: misdemeanor for players, felony for promoters

Is social gambling tolerated? yes

Indian gaming: 26 casinos (minimum gambling age is 18, 21 if alcohol is served on the premises)

WEST VIRGINIA

Lottery: yes (minimum gambling age is 18)

Non-tribal casinos: none

Racing: four racinos offering dog and horse racing, simulcasting, and video slots (minimum gambling age is 18)

Other forms of legalized gambling: bingo (minimum gambling age is 18)

Infraction of gambling laws: misdemeanor for players and promoters

Is social gambling tolerated? no

Indian gaming: none

WISCONSIN

Lottery: yes (minimum gambling age is 18)

Non-tribal casinos: none

Racing: dog racing and simulcasting (minimum gambling age is 18)

Other forms of legalized gambling: bingo (no minimum gambling age specified)

Infraction of gambling laws: misdemeanor for players, felony for promoters

Is social gambling tolerated? no

Indian gaming: 14 casinos (minimum gambling age is 21)

WYOMING

Lottery: none

Non-tribal casinos: none

Racing: horse racing and simulcasting and Instant Racing video machines (minimum gambling age is 18)

Other forms of legalized gambling: bingo (minimum gambling age is 18)

Infraction of gambling laws: misdemeanor for players, felony for promoters

Is social gambling tolerated? yes

Indian gaming: one bingo hall

COURT CASES

Since the 1800s, hundreds of court cases relating to gambling have passed through the American judicial system. More than 300 have been submitted to the U.S. Supreme Court alone. The majority of cases that have come before the state and federal courts involve infractions of gambling laws. Some of these concern the nonpayment of taxes on gambling profits; others entail the operation of illegal gambling rackets. Most are relatively minor legal matters that have not significantly impacted the progress or scope of legalized gambling. The court cases presented in the following section, however, have had more significance in shaping the definition of legalized gambling in America and the ways in which it may be operated, advertised, and regulated. These federal and state cases are listed chronologically to follow the evolution of judicial rulings as they have tried to keep abreast of the changing times.

HORNER V. UNITED STATES, 147 U.S. 449 (1893)

Background

Amid the end-of-the-century backlash against lotteries in America, the states and the federal government enacted many anti-lottery statutes. The Anti-Lottery Act of 1890 was the most debilitating of the federal regulations, since it outlawed the use of the mail for the dissemination or transport of any material that was related to the operation of a lottery. Lacking other methods of advertisement, the mail had become the lifeline of most lotteries because it provided a means of reaching customers and receiving their entry payments. The new law crippled the remaining lotteries by choking off their source of income.

In 1891, a banker named Edward H. Horner mailed a circular from New York to a patron in Chicago. The circular advertised the selling of bonds issued by the Austrian Empire. The bonds were part of a revenue-raising scheme in which the Austrian government would stage drawings each year that determined the amount the bearer of specific bonds would receive upon their surrender. Most of these annual repayments were small increases over the bond's initial cost, but a few select bonds would receive huge cash prizes. In May 1892, Horner was charged in a federal circuit court with using the mail to further a lottery scheme as defined by the Anti-Lottery Act. Although he was convicted of the crime and charged a $100 fine, Horner appealed his case the following year. In 1893, the appellate court sided with Horner but asked the Supreme Court to review the circuit court's decision to convict.

Legal Issues

In staging Horner's appeal to the Supreme Court, the defense counsel argued that the selling or purchasing of government bonds does not fall under the definition of a lottery as outlined by the Anti-Lottery Act. Despite the element of chance involved in the drawing of prizes, the defense insisted that the issuing of bonds cannot be construed as, in the words of the act, "a lottery, so-called gift concert, or similar enterprise offering prizes depending upon lot or chance." Horner's lawyers pointed out that since the bonds do meet such a criterion, their client could not have been guilty of any crime.

Decision

In deciding the case, the Court noted that the wording of the recent Anti-Lottery Act was an amendment over previous acts that condemned only "illegal" lotteries. Since the Austrian bonds could not be considered illegal, the defense would have been within their rights to have the case dismissed under such a definition. But the 1890 act struck the word "illegal" and thereby prohibited any lottery or similar enterprise from using the U.S. mail. According to the justices, the fact that the Austrian bond scheme involved the chance drawing of prizes brought it within the regulatory scope of the revised Anti-Lottery Act.

Impact

The Court's ruling was significant for two reasons. First, it made clear that the Anti-Lottery Act would be used to vigorously stamp out lotteries. Second, it demonstrated that the definition of a lottery under the act was broad enough to apply to almost any similar scheme, thus forewarning anyone bent on trying to circumvent the law.

STATE V. ROSENTHAL, 93 NEV. 36 (1977)

Background

From the 1960s through the late 1970s, Frank "Lefty" Rosenthal was an advisory executive for a company that ran three Las Vegas casinos. Nevada gaming authorities suspected that Rosenthal was connected to organized crime, so they tried to oust him from his position by denying him a gaming license. Rosenthal previously had been denied a Nevada gaming license, but he had held on to his right to work for the casinos. In 1975, the gaming commission proved that Rosenthal not only worked in the Nevada casinos but had a say in their management, thus making him liable to obtaining a gaming license. When he petitioned for a license in 1976, the commission voted to deny him that privilege because of previous convictions for bribery and fixing the outcome of a sports event (both of which were committed in other states).

Rosenthal contested the decision in a district court. He argued that he had already paid for his crimes and had earned the right to obtain a license. He claimed the commission had unfairly targeted him and was not applying the same standards to his petition as to other lawful petitions. The judge agreed and ordered the commission to strike Rosenthal's name from its infamous "Black Book" of people banned from Las Vegas casinos. The gaming commission appealed the case to the Nevada Supreme Court in 1977.

Legal Issues

Since Rosenthal's complaint was based on a claim that the Nevada Gaming Commission was using unfair and unregulated standards, he was compelled to show that his treatment was in violation of the commission's guidelines. The commission's regulatory code stated that the petitioner for a gaming license had to be (a) a person of good character, (b) a person who would not, by past associations or reputation, bring adverse publicity to Nevada, and (c) a person with sufficient business experience. Given these criteria, the commission has the power to deny a license "for any cause deemed reasonable." Rosenthal maintained that these standards were arbitrary and vague and could be used to unfairly deny a license out of capricious whim or even spite.

Decision

In passing its unanimous decision, the Nevada Supreme Court maintained that the gaming commission is invested with the duty to issue and revoke gaming licenses as it sees fit. The commission is expected to be made up of competent individuals who have the needed capacity to determine a candidate's suitability to hold a license. Although the criteria for acceptance or denial may be broad, the justices affirmed, they are understandable and were not unfairly applied in this case, since Rosenthal's background reasonably suggested past behaviors that conflicted with the given standards. Rosenthal, therefore, could gain no relief by appealing to the court. In fact, no license applicant or license holder could seek redress in court unless the commission had taken some disciplinary action against the licensee.

Impact

Rosenthal's argument that his right to hold a license had been infringed was also dismissed by the court. As Justice Gordon Rufus Thompson's opinion states, "gaming is a privilege conferred by the state and does not carry with it the rights inherent in useful trades and occupations." Therefore, as the court upheld the gaming commission's right to deny Rosenthal a gaming license, it also set a legal precedent stipulating that operating a gaming enterprise is a privilege granted by the state and ultimately controlled by the state's regulations.

Seminole Tribe of Florida v. Butterworth, 658 F. 2d 310 (1981)

Background

In the late 1970s, the State of Florida placed a limit of $100 on the amount of charity bingo jackpots. In 1978, Florida's Seminole Indians decided to raise the stakes of their charity bingo games as high as $10,000. They defended their decision by arguing that the host of local bingo games run by other charities offered too much competition. The result, the tribe claimed, was that tourists and game players who might have visited the Seminole reservation to play bingo were now spending their money elsewhere. Of course, when the Seminole jackpots became popular knowledge, hundreds of visitors streamed into the reservation and left outside charities in want of players.

Robert Butterworth, the sheriff of Broward County, Florida, had previously warned the Seminole that if they decided to run their high-stakes bingo hall, he would enforce the state's charity gaming laws and make appropriate arrests. When the Seminole went ahead with their plans, Butterworth performed his duty. In an effort to find relief from the sheriff, the Seminole sued Butterworth in 1979. The state, in turn, countersued the tribe for unlawful gaming.

Legal Issues

The case was first heard in district court, where both parties asked for a summary judgment. The state argued simply that the tribe had violated the prize limits set by Florida statutes. Therefore, the state wished to prosecute the Seminole for breach of its public law. In determining the legality of this, the district court judge examined the public law in question. The law spelled out the prize limits as well as other restrictions placed upon charitable bingo games, and it imposed a criminal punishment upon violators. This last provision was significant to Florida's argument, since the state insisted that because the law granted criminal punishment, the state had the right to take action against the tribes (because states had jurisdiction over Indian land when criminal law was brought to bear).

Decision

The district judge, however, ruled that laws providing for criminal punishment are not necessarily criminal laws. In this case, the judge believed that the Florida statute was regulatory in nature because it explained how bingo was to be regulated instead of criminalizing the act of playing bingo. If the law had been one that banned bingo statewide, then the Seminole could have been accused of a criminal violation. In this case, however, the infraction was a civil matter about how the games were played, and the state thus had no authority to enforce civil regulatory law on Indian land. The district court's summary judgment was for the Seminole. The state appealed the case, but the 5th Circuit Court of Appeals upheld the district court's decision. Undeterred, the state tried to appeal the case to the U.S. Supreme Court. That august body declined to hear the case, but in its denial, the Court supported the view that the Seminole were not operating an illegal game; they were merely changing the way it was played. The Supreme Court maintained that such civic matters could best be decided by the lower courts.

Impact

Seminole v. Butterworth was the first case to test the sovereign right of a Native American tribe to run gaming operations without state intervention. The decision applied only to Florida's Seminole, but it had a nationwide impact. Other tribes in other states decided to challenge their own state's regulatory authority. The most important of these challenges would come in *California v. Cabazon Band of Mission Indians*, a case which reached the U.S. Supreme Court and ultimately opened the doors to a massive expansion in Indian gaming across the country.

Posadas de Puerto Rico Associates v. Tourism Company of Puerto Rico, 478 U.S. 328 (1986)

Background

The Commonwealth of Puerto Rico tolerates some forms of casino gambling, but a statute, administered by the island's Tourism Company (a public organization), prohibits casinos from advertising to the public. The Condado Holiday Inn, a hotel casino, had consistently violated the law over the years and had willingly paid fines for its numerous infractions. But in 1986, the casino decided to challenge the Tourism Company's restriction on the grounds that it violated commercial free speech.

Legal Issues

A Puerto Rican superior court heard the case and ruled that the government did have the power to limit free speech in this case. The court stated that advertisements meant to invite tourists to a casino were legal, and therefore a casino could not be held liable if the advertisements were accidentally viewed by citizens of the commonwealth. But any direct promotion to the Puerto Rican people was illegal. In summation, the court implied that past action against the casino might have violated commercial free speech rights as defined by this judgment, but the Tourism Company's code was not unconstitutional as the casino claimed. The casino appealed its case to the Puerto Rican Supreme Court (which dismissed the case) and then to the U.S Supreme Court.

Decision

In the U.S. Supreme Court, four of the seven justices upheld the ruling of the Puerto Rican court, stating that the commonwealth had an interest in restricting gambling among its own citizens. Three justices, however, dissented. They argued that since gambling was legal in Puerto Rico, the legislature there had no right to infringe on commercial speech. Furthermore, by selectively banning casino advertisements, the government was not adhering to the concept of equal protection under the law.

Impact

In deciding for the commonwealth, the Supreme Court affirmed that the legislature of Puerto Rico is empowered to enact laws based on the democratic will of its people. In this case, the legislature had a right to limit some forms of speech provided that it was done in the interest of protecting its citizens from what the majority perceived as a socially harmful activity.

CALIFORNIA V. CABAZON BAND OF MISSION INDIANS, 480 U.S. 202 (1987)

Background

The Cabazon and Morongo Indians ran bingo games on their reservation land for some years under the auspices of California's charitable gaming provisions. According to these provisions, all charitable organizations are allowed to operate bingo games if the money is used for charity (in this case, the betterment of the impoverished tribes) and the prizes do not exceed $250. The Cabazon, however, emboldened by the *Seminole v. Butterworth* Supreme Court case, raised the stakes of their bingo games beyond the $250 limit. The local county authorities tried to force the tribes to comply with the charity laws and sought to apply these laws to a card room that the Cabazon also operated. The Cabazon and Morengo decided to bring federal suit against their parent counties in 1985 after the door to the Cabazon card room (a trailer) had been repeatedly padlocked by the county. The state immediately intervened and took charge of its case in district court.

Legal Issues

The district court granted a summary judgment in favor of the Cabazon and Morengo. The judge contended that state and local regulatory laws had no power on Indian reservations, which were sovereign entities according to the federal government. The state appealed the case, and the 9th Circuit Court of Appeals upheld the district court's summary judgment. Still unsatisfied, the state appealed to the U.S. Supreme Court, which agreed to hear the case in December 1986.

In weighing the matter, the Supreme Court considered whether California had any authority to regulate Indian gaming. The state pointed to a 1953 public law statute in which California and six other states were granted jurisdiction over criminal offenses committed by or against Indians within all Indian territories located in those states. To determine if this law was applicable, the Court looked to the case of *Bryan v. Itasca County*, 426 U.S. 373 (1976), which had previously interpreted the public statute to apply to civil litigation involving private matters between Indians and the states, and not to issues of civil regulation. If civil regulatory laws were meant to be encompassed under the public law, the Court reasoned in *Bryan v. Itasca County*, then the sovereignty of Indian tribes would be seriously impaired.

Decision

In reaching a decision, the Supreme Court maintained that *Bryan v. Itasca County* set a precedent that gave California some authority to intervene in tribal affairs in cases in which there was a breach of criminal law. Six of the nine justices asserted that in the case before them, the Cabazon and Morengo had not broken criminal laws because bingo and card rooms were tolerated forms of gambling in all California. The only disagreement between the state and the Indians was the method in which these games were operated (specifically, the value of the prizes awarded). Therefore, the majority of the Court concluded that the case concerned regulation of the games, making the issue a civil law dispute. Civil legislation is within the jurisdiction of the state, the Court agreed, but the state's power to enforce civil legislation does not extend onto Native American land, which is sovereign according to federal law. California was thus caught in a bind, and could not hope to limit the stakes of the Cabazon and Morengo bingo games unless the Indians abridged their own sovereignty and invited them to do so.

Impact

The *Cabazon* decision is, perhaps, the most significant gambling ruling of the 20th century. Though the justices were divided, the Supreme Court's verdict made clear that Native Americans had the authority as sovereign entities to run gaming operations on their own land free of any state regulations. Only an amendment to the U.S. Constitution, the Court asserted, could change the relationship between Indian tribes and state authorities.

The affirmation of their sovereignty bolstered Indian pride and self-determination. It also led other Indians to consider gaming enterprises as a remedy to the poverty that gripped the majority of the nation's reservations. The landslide of Native American groups that did turn to gaming after the *Cabazon* decision was predictable, and the onrush worried state and federal authorities. Fearing that widespread and untouchable gambling would incur a host of social problems and invite organized crime to infiltrate the tribal operations, Congress hurried to pass the Indian Gaming Regulatory Act (IGRA) in 1988. This stopgap measure was enacted to standardize tribal gaming ventures, encourage states and tribes to work together to monitor gambling, and ensure that criminal elements could not hijack tribal enterprises for their own profit.

GNOC Corp. v. Shmuel Aboud, U.S. District Court, New Jersey; 715 Fed. Supp. 644 (1989)

Background

In February 1985, Shmuel Aboud was staying at the Golden Nugget Casino in Atlantic City, New Jersey, where his rooms, meals, and drinks had been provided for free of charge at the discretion of the hotel's customer service representative. The hotel representative is granted the privilege to determine whether patrons qualify for complimentary room and board by assessing the patron's duration on the gaming floor and the amount of the patron's average bet. According to Aboud, the casino representative assured him that his complimentary service would be maintained as long as Aboud continued to gamble. Aboud insisted that although he did gamble frequently, it did not seem to satisfy the representative, who supposedly woke Aboud up at 4 A.M. one morning to request that he immediately visit the gambling tables so that he could continue his complimentary stay. Aboud further claimed that throughout his stay he was brought free alcoholic beverages even if he had not asked for them, and over time, he became visibly drunk. He also suffered various bodily pains for which he was prescribed a narcotic by physicians procured by the casino. After his extended visit, Aboud left the casino owing $28,000. On June 19, the casino sued Aboud to recover its debt. Aboud immediately countersued for $250,000 in damages, alleging that the casino had committed fraud, malicious conduct, unjust enrichment, and negligence.

Legal Issues

Aboud's counterclaim argued that the casino had intentionally plied him with alcohol to force him to gamble unreasonably. In addition, Aboud alleged that the prescription of the narcotic Percodan was also part of the casino's orchestrated attempt to wrangle more money out of him while he was in an unfit state to gamble responsibly. He contended that several casino employees watched as he continued to gamble while drugged or intoxicated and did nothing to stop him. The Golden Nugget responded by arguing that even if its employees did try to compel Aboud to play while unfit, the casino could not be held responsible because such action was not part of the employees' duties. Aboud asserted that compelling patrons to gamble was a duty of the employees since it directly benefited the company they worked for and therefore would benefit them as well.

Decision

The court held that sufficient case evidence and New Jersey law suggested that the casino was responsible for the acts of its employees. Because of the state's strong alcohol impairment laws that, for example, prohibit tavern owners from serving alcoholic drinks to visibly inebriated customers, the casino's duty, in this similar instance, was to foresee the risk of its patron's intoxication and take steps to keep impaired patrons from unsound gambling. In this particular instance, however, the court sided with the Golden Nugget in dismissing Aboud's claim since he was unable to prove his case.

Impact

The court's decision, though favoring the Golden Nugget, warned that casinos could face punitive damages for encouraging intoxicated customers to continue gambling once the inebriation is visible to employees or other patrons. The legal implications prompted many casinos to institute measures—such as training their staff and security personnel to spot potentially impaired gamblers—to counter the possibility of similar lawsuits.

THERE TO CARE, INC. V. COMMISSIONER OF THE INDIANA DEPARTMENT OF REVENUE, 19 F. 3D 1195; 7TH CIR. (1994)

Background

In 1992, the state of Indiana ordered There to Care (TTC), a charitable gaming organization in Mishawaka, to cease running its bingo games. According to state authorities, the charity had not been in operation in Indiana for five years (as state law requires), it was holding bingo games too frequently (three events per week is acceptable under state law), and it rented gaming facilities that were too expensive (a statute stipulates that rented halls must not cost more than $200 per day). The state also claimed that TTC had a sister charity—managed by the same organization—that ran bingo out of the same halls in order to evade the three-event-per-week limit. Contending that the state's order to desist was a violation of First Amendment rights, There to Care filed suit in federal court.

Legal Issues

According to TTC lawyers, the charity proposed that bingo was free speech and therefore could not be abridged by the state. The plaintiffs also argued that since the charity halls are the site of fundraising and recruitment of volunteers and that posters on the walls relate the organization's mission to players, banning the games is also a violation of these means of free speech and expression. TTC lawyers used previous case law to show that legal interpretations of First Amendment rights had placed severe restraints on any state's power to regulate charitable organizations. TTC insisted that as long as it was using its bingo games to do charitable work, then it had the right to rent any hall and convene seven days a week if it so chose. The state believed that its laws were clear, generous, and equitable to all charities. Suddenly granting charities an unregulated power to conduct bingo in the manner they wished would be equivalent to legalizing gambling.

Decision

A circuit court agreed with the state. In the judge's view, Indiana already was giving charities a special privilege in conducting bingo games. No commercial organization in the state, for example, had this privilege. By setting limits on bingo games or other fundraising endeavors, the court maintained that the state had not violated First Amendment rights because it had in no way infringed upon what the charity could say or express during its games.

Impact

The Indiana decision cautioned all charitable organizations from interpreting their gaming privileges as gaming rights. In this manner, the case ensured that charitable gaming would remain on a relatively small scale and not blossom into an unmanageable industry of debatable moral and social worth.

Seminole Tribe of Florida v. Florida, 517 U.S. 44 (1996)

Background

The 1988 Indian Gaming Regulatory Act (IGRA) gave Native American tribes the right to enter into compact negotiations with their respective states to legalize gambling on Indian land. Under the terms of the compact-making process, the states were compelled by law to negotiate in good faith to ensure that the tribes could legalize whatever form of gambling was already permissible in the states. If the states stonewalled the process or refused to negotiate, the tribes had the power, under the auspices of the act, to bring suit in federal court. Although many states were still reluctant to abide more gambling within their borders, the threat of suit convinced many states to conclude compacts with petitioning tribes.

In 1991, the Seminole Indians of Florida sued the state of Florida and its governor, Lawton Chiles, for failing to negotiate a compact that would allow the tribe to institute casino gambling on its reservations. The state responded by asking that the district court dismiss the suit on the grounds that the Eleventh Amendment protected the states against this type of legal redress. The district court denied the defendant's move for dismissal, and the state appealed that decision. A court of appeals subsequently sustained the state's motion and reversed the district court's denial. The Seminole, then, asked the U.S. Supreme Court to review the appellate court's conclusion.

Legal Issues

The Eleventh Amendment stipulates: "The Judicial power of the United States shall not be construed to extend to any suit in law or equity, commenced or prosecuted against one of the United States by Citizens of another State, or by Citizens or Subjects of any Foreign State." In interpreting the amendment, the Supreme Court examined previous cases to conclude that each state is a sovereign entity and that sovereignty ensures that the states cannot be sued without their consent. Since in the present case Florida was not consenting to be sued by the Seminole, it was therefore claiming immunity from judicial recourse. The Supreme Court, however, also had to weigh the Eleventh Amendment's protection against the IGRA's intent to abrogate states' rights to compel them to negotiate compacts with Indian tribes.

Decision

In making its decision, the Supreme Court looked to the Indian Commerce Clause, the constitutional clause under which the IGRA was passed. According to the Court, this clause did strip power from the states and therefore seem to nullify any claims for immunity from suit. The majority of the justices, however, argued that this divesting of state power was not what the Constitution intends; therefore, the Court held that the Eleventh Amendment superceded any powers granted under the IGRA. Florida was indeed immune from lawsuit.

The Court's decision was not unanimous. Four of the nine justices dissented, stating that the Court had for the first time found that states were not subject to federal jurisdiction when sued by an individual exercising a federal right.

Impact

From the near split decision, it was obvious that the Supreme Court's verdict was monumental. The Native Americans who were hoping to bring states to the negotiating table over gambling issues now lacked the power to force the states to act. In the wake of the decision, many states ceased negotiations or ignored tribal requests for gaming privileges, and the rapid expansion of Indian gaming slowed considerably. Some states continued to negotiate but now with increased demands (higher fees and more state involvement, for example). Some tribes tried to circumvent the provisions for lawsuits and go directly to the secretary of the Interior to force the states to negotiate. This method of recourse is outlined in the IGRA and seemed a worthwhile option. Congress, though, checked the secretary's decision-making powers until the constitutionality of this option could be verified. Congress is still considering the question.

GREATER NEW ORLEANS BROADCASTING ASSOCIATION, INC., V. UNITED STATES, 527 U.S. 173 (1999)

Background

Radio and television broadcasters in the New Orleans metropolitan region intended to air advertisements for casinos in the area. Their broadcast range covered Louisiana and extended into neighboring Mississippi. Both states had legalized gambling. The stations knew, however, that the Federal Communications Commission (FCC) and U.S. broadcasting codes forbid the transmission of gambling information and advertisements over the airwaves. The broadcasters decided to sue the FCC to show that the restrictions were a violation of First Amendment rights.

Legal Issues

A district court and a federal court of appeals ruled in favor of the FCC, the latter stating that since gambling was an activity that could be banned itself, the promotion of gambling had no just claim to First Amendment protection. When the case was remanded to the Supreme Court, that body suspended the lower court's decision until the issues of another case—*44 Liquormart, Inc. v. Rhode Island*, 517 U.S. 484 (1996)—might be brought to bear. In the *Liquormart* decision, the Supreme Court had ruled that the power to ban speech was not as broad as the power to ban the related activity. In response, the appellate court argued that its rulings were based on the belief that the prohibition of gambling advertisements adequately demonstrated the government's regulatory powers without broadening those powers unjustly. The Court maintained, for instance, that the FCC's banning of the ads was not tantamount to restricting participation in legalized gambling.

Decision

The Supreme Court ultimately reversed the lower court's decision. The justices asserted that banning the advertisements was a breach of the right to commercial free speech since the broadcasted information was not misleading nor did it concern an illegal activity (since both states tolerated gambling). In drafting their opinion, the justices maintained that although helping states regulate casino gambling within their own borders demanded some federal action, Congress had not yet created a consistent, national plan to do so unequivocally. Therefore the courts should be wary of curbing free speech without compelling reason.

Impact

The Supreme Court's decision made it clear that if legalized gambling was tolerated as an industry in specific jurisdictions, then that industry had the right to promote itself within those jurisdictions. To abridge or deny that right was to infringe upon the industry's ability to conduct lawful business and to limit customers' choice in the marketplace.

People v. World Interactive Gaming Corporation, 714 N.Y.S. 2d 844 (1999)

Background

In February 1998, the New York attorney general began investigating World Interactive Gaming Corporation (WIGC) after receiving word that the company was cold-calling U.S. residents and selling them shares of WIGC stock. WIGC, which has offices in New York, is the owner of a casino in Antigua. The casino has an Internet site that grants clients a means to gamble over the World Wide Web. The casino's Internet software asks players to enter their home address as part of the admission requirements; the software is configured to deny access to players who enter a U.S. state address where casino gambling is illegal. However, members of the attorney general's staff, posing as players, were easily able to circumvent this control by entering a Nevada address (where casino gambling is legal) while still physically residing in New York. The attorney general then launched a suit against WIGC for failing to register with New York in order to do business within the state. Since Internet gambling in the United States is deemed unlawful by the Justice Department, the attorney general hoped that either failing to register or registering an illegal form of business would shut down the company's American operations.

Legal Issues

At issue in the case was whether the state had the power to force a foreign company that had a license to operate a casino legally in Antigua to refrain from offering its Internet gambling opportunities to citizens of New York. The attorney general expected that because WIGC had its business offices in New York, had created and implemented its Internet gambling software in the state, and had conducted its cold-calling stock-selling campaign from its stateside offices, the courts would determine that the company executes its business from America and therefore was under state jurisdiction. WIGC anticipated that the laws regarding Internet gambling were sufficiently vague to make such a claim impossible. They also pointed to the fact that because the company's casino resides in Antigua, the gambling—even over the Internet—occurs there and is thus outside New York jurisdiction.

Decision

The New York Superior Court maintained that although an Internet casino may be a technological innovation, it was not unlike a traditional brick-and-mortar business in terms of regulation. According to the court, WIGC possessed enough interests in New York to make it susceptible to state business laws. The court also dismissed the company's notion that the actual gambling was transpiring in Antigua when it was obvious that players in New York placed bets, paid debts, and reaped winnings while residing within the state's borders. Without these actions, no gambling could have taken place. The court therefore concluded that WIGC had violated state gambling laws, which outlaw any form of gambling not expressly approved by the legislature, and the federal Wire Act, which makes it illegal to use the phone lines to make gambling transactions.

Impact

The decision served as a warning to other Internet gambling companies that they were not immune to lawsuits simply because of their unique ability to trace transactions to offshore locations. If a company in any way operated in the United States, it could be prosecuted for applicable state and federal violations.

UNITED STATES V. COHEN, 260 F. 3D 68 (2001)

Background

In 1996, Jay Cohen, a former stock trader, left America and moved to the island nation of Antigua to set up shop as a bookmaker. There, along with some friends (all of whom were also U.S. citizens), he founded the World Sports Exchange (WSE), a betting agency that took wagers by phone or through an Internet web site. WSE's customers were primarily Americans, since Cohen and his organization advertised their service over U.S. radio and television airwaves and through select newspapers. By November 1998, the WSE had received 60,000 phone wagers from U.S. clients (6,100 of whom were residents of New York). Some of the New York bets were placed by FBI agents investigating offshore bookmakers. After collecting enough evidence in this manner, the FBI arrested Cohen in March 1998, while he was back in America, and charged him with violating the U.S. Wire Act, which prohibits the use of wire communications (namely phone lines in this case) for the purpose of gambling. It was the first trial of a U.S. citizen for Internet gambling—an area of case law that had few precedents, and a topic whose legality was (and is) still highly debated in legal circles.

Legal Issues

After a ten-day trial in 2000, a district court found Cohen guilty of eight different counts of violating the clauses of the Wire Act. Cohen was subsequently sentenced to 21 months' imprisonment. He immediately appealed his conviction on the basis that the district court judge had ordered the jury to ignore Cohen's plea that he earnestly believed in the legality of his business and his actions. He also argued, among other complaints, that he was protected by the Wire Act's "safe harbor" provision, which afforded immunity if (1) betting was legal both in the place of origin and the destination of the wager and (2) the wire transmission contained only information that would assist in the placing of bets and not the bets themselves.

Decision

The 2nd Circuit Court of Appeals, which reviewed Cohen's case, rejected his entire defense. In denying the safe harbor provision, the court agreed with the district judge's ruling that wagering, though legal in Antigua, is not legal in New York. Despite the state's tolerance of off-track betting and some Indian gambling, New York's constitution prohibits any bookmaking or gambling not specifically authorized by the legislature. While Cohen argued that betting of some kind was legal in New York and thus safe harbor applied, both courts insisted that legalization meant that this type of bookmaking would have to be specifically permitted by law, which it was not.

As for the second requirement of the safe harbor provision, the courts also dismissed Cohen's claim that the information in the Internet and phone wagers only assisted WSE in placing the bets for its clients. The courts agreed that since the customers authorized the company to take their wagers on certain sporting events, WSE agents were taking bets and not merely assisting in the process.

Finally, both courts ruled that Cohen knew that his company was taking wagers and knew that these acts violated New York law. His beliefs about the unjustness or illegality of the New York laws were immaterial in his defense. Consciously flouting the laws was enough to ensure his arrest and trial.

Impact

Cohen was the first U.S. citizen to be tried for operating an Internet gambling business. Previous operators had been arrested but had pled guilty without trial. Cohen's case thus set a precedent in which federal law was shown to be broad enough and suitable enough to apply to a new, hitherto untested area of law. By securing a conviction, the government proved that law enforcement and the courts would pursue gambling operators with available laws even if the legality of Internet gaming was still a subject of debate among scholars and politicians.

CHAPTER 3

CHRONOLOGY

This chapter provides a chronology of important events in the history of legalized gambling in the United States. The focus of this time line will be on the latter half of the 20th century, when gambling's greatest expansion occurred.

Prior to European Colonization

- In precolonial America, Native Americans enjoy various games of chance. When the first Europeans arrive, they are surprised to see eastern tribes wagering on the throw of dice (made of smoothed rocks) and other identifiable forms of gambling.

1612

- Five years after landing in North America, Captain John Smith of the Jamestown colony petitions England's King James I to let the Virginia Company hold a lottery to assist with finances. Over the next three years, four drawings are held to help the colonists obtain needed supplies.

1620

- After a boatload of 20 horses arrives in the Virginia colony, the English settlers make horse racing a regular diversion from their daily toils.

1630

- In the newly founded Massachusetts Bay Colony, Puritan zeal clamps down on dice and card playing. As a result, religious authorities in the town of Boston enact the first American law against gambling. The law, in part, insists that "All persons . . . that have cards, dice, or tables in their houses, shall make away with them . . . under pain of punishment." Citing Scripture, clerics like Cotton Mather would continue to condemn gambling as sinful and contrary to the Puritan ideal of industriousness.

Legalized Gambling

1665

- The first permanent racetrack in America is set up on Long Island. Other colonies will follow New York's lead and establish their own tracks in coming years.

1721

- The New Hampshire colonial government passes an antigambling act based on the impoverishment this vice brings upon gamblers and their families.

1737

- Massachusetts's colonial government revises the Bay Colony's gambling law. The amended code stipulates that games of chance may be played in moderation but not plied as a trade or a means to take advantage of others.

1747

- Yale College uses a lottery to fund construction needs. Harvard will do likewise in 1765.

1776

- The newly organized Continental Congress institutes a national lottery in hopes of raising $1 million to help fight for independence against Great Britain. The lottery fails and Congress is unable to return ticket buyers' money. The individual colonies copy the idea to raise and pay for local armies. These colonial lotteries are largely successful and last until war's end in 1783.

1780s and 1790s

- Lotteries are used at the local level throughout the United States to finance civic works, church building, and educational institutions. In 1793, the federal government holds Federal Lottery #1 to pay for the new capital city, to be located in the District of Columbia.

1815

- New Orleans begins issuing gaming licenses as a means to control the already widespread gambling activities in the city.

1820

- Shady operators and a flurry of scandals prompt New York to become the first state to ban lotteries.

Chronology

1823

- The Grand National Lottery is held in Washington, D.C., to pay for civic improvements to the capital. The lottery contractor, however, absconds with the proceeds of the ticket sales. The winner of the grand prize sues the government and eventually receives his prize money after the Supreme Court rules in his favor.

1830s

- As lottery scandals continue to make news, the country experiences a gambling backlash. Reformist groups eventually succeed in closing down gambling halls in New Orleans and in other communities along the Mississippi River. In 1835, five gamblers are lynched in the state of Mississippi, though they were ostensibly murdered for their abolitionist leanings. By the beginning of the Civil War, reform-minded governments have instituted lottery bans in every state.

1848

- The beginning of the gold rush in California brings gamblers and thieves to the territory. Reformers in San Francisco get several laws passed to curtail gambling, but the statutes are unpopular and difficult to enforce. Unable to halt the vice, California's legislature makes gambling a legal profession (until 1855), thereby allowing the government to tax gambling profits.

1863

- A mile-long track is first laid down at the New York resort town of Saratoga Springs. Within a few years, the Saratoga Club House caters to the political and social elite, a clientele that helps the racing club weather the post–Civil War gambling backlash.

1868

- After the ravages of the Civil War, the Northern states are reluctant to pay for Reconstruction in the South. Southern states reinstitute lotteries to pay for rebuilding. The most famous of these is the Serpent, a national lottery run in Louisiana. The first drawing in 1868 is extremely popular and successful. The lottery organizers continue to run the operation for the next three decades, well after the civic need for the lottery's income. Charges of corruption plague the Serpent, and it is eventually shut down in another nationwide backlash against lotteries.

Legalized Gambling

1887

- In San Francisco, Charles Fey invents the slot machine.

1890

- The U.S. Congress prohibits the transfer of lottery tickets and payments through the mail. This action is primarily responsible for the downfall of Louisiana's Serpent lottery.

1894

- In response to tales of unscrupulous bookmakers and dishonest competitors, New York racetrack operators and horse owners form the Jockey Club. The club lays out racing guidelines and licensing rules in an attempt to standardize the racing scene nationwide.

1895

- The U.S. Congress bans any form of interstate commerce that relates to lottery operations.

1906

- Despite the clean image promoted by the Jockey Club, horse racing suffers from a national antigambling fervor. Kentucky keeps racing alive by forming a government commission to oversee racing operations. Most other states, including New York, close their tracks by 1911.

1908

- After bookmaking is outlawed in Kentucky, Colonel Matt Winn, the owner of Churchill Downs racetrack, installs pari-mutuel machines to take patrons' wagers. The machines rake in a large sum during that year's run of the Kentucky Derby and change the face of racetrack gambling from then on.

1910

- After all other states, one by one, have instituted bans against gambling, Nevada finally closes its casinos. Besides the operation of a few racetracks in the South, legalized gambling is effectively prohibited throughout the nation.

1929

- The Great Depression descends upon America. Lacking sources of revenue, the states begin rethinking their bans on gambling.

Chronology

1931

- Nevada reinstates casino gambling as a means of generating tax revenue and sparking tourism (primarily from neighboring California). Nevada's counties are responsible for regulating gaming enterprises, and they share in the tax proceeds. Las Vegas begins its history as a modern gaming center when the Meadows Club opens.

1933

- To counter the effects of the depression, Michigan, New Hampshire, and Ohio legalize pari-mutuel betting at racetracks. Other states such as Illinois, Kentucky, and Louisiana continue to have success with their pari-mutuel systems.
- Prohibition of alcohol in the United States ends with the repeal of the Eighteenth Amendment. Without the steady flow of money from bootlegging, organized crime looks to expand other operations, such as gambling rackets.

1935

- With the rise of pari-mutuel betting, Delaware, Florida, Illinois, Louisiana, Massachusetts, Michigan, New Hampshire, Ohio, Rhode Island, and West Virginia pass new racetrack-betting legislation.

1941

- The El Rancho Vegas is the first casino to open on the Las Vegas Strip. The El Rancho is the first of a new breed of Las Vegas casinos to offer hotel accommodations and some tourist services for guests. The next year, the Last Frontier opens on the Strip and continues the trend.

1945

- Nevada begins licensing its casinos. As part of the licensing contract, the casinos agree to pay taxes on earnings as well as set fees on the games offered.

1946

- New York mobster Benjamin "Bugsy" Siegel opens the Flamingo Casino on the Las Vegas Strip. The Flamingo was the first of the huge hotel/casinos to offer a wide array of guest services, including a golf course, gift shops, and stage shows. Siegel's vision was to add glamour to the Vegas Strip and turn the small-time gambling operations into a grand resort community. Trying to realize his grand dream meant spending a lot of mob money, and the Flamingo's first-year profits never covered its expenses.

1947

- Unnerved by Bugsy Siegel's mismanagement of the Flamingo (coupled with accusations that he was lining his own pockets with part of the casino's proceeds), the New York mob has Siegel murdered.

1950

- The Senate Special Committee on Organized Crime in Interstate Commerce holds investigative hearings in Las Vegas. Headed by Senator Carey Estes Kefauver, the committee believes that Las Vegas casinos are plagued by mobsters and that the gambling culture is morally and economically damaging to American society. The investigative committee's conclusions possess no legal ramifications, but they do contribute to a popular backlash against gambling.

1955

- In response to public outcry against organized crime's involvement in Las Vegas, Nevada establishes a Gaming Control Board. This body is given the power to license casino operators and enforce state gambling regulations.

1959

- Grant Sawyer wins election as Nevada's governor on a platform that promises to rid the state's casinos of connections to organized crime. In one of his first acts as governor, Sawyer creates a Gaming Commission to oversee the decisions of the Gaming Control Board, which many have accused of being in the pay of casino mobsters.

1961

- The 1961 Federal Interstate Wireline Act is adopted. The act declares that bookmakers who use phone lines (or any other wire communication) across states or between a state and another country to take bets are guilty of a felony. Three decades later, this controversial piece of legislation will serve as the foundation for the Justice Department's argument that Internet gambling violates U.S. law and is therefore illegal.

Chronology

1963

- Weary of increased tax burdens, the voters of New Hampshire approve an initiative to let the state government run a lottery to pay for some education expenses. This lottery—the first lottery operated since the close of the Serpent in Louisiana—is designed to attract players from neighboring states. Tickets are first sold in 1964, but at $3 apiece, ticket sales do not meet expectations. Just over half the $10 million projected earnings are realized, and ticket sales steadily fall over subsequent years due to lack of public interest.

1966

- Billionaire Howard Hughes begins buying up casinos from mob owners.
- Mob front man Jay Sarno opens Caesar's Palace on the Las Vegas Strip. This hotel/casino, designed to reflect the architecture and times of ancient Rome, was the first of the "themed" casinos that would come to dominate the Strip over the next few decades.

1967

- Aware that a percentage of the state's income was funding the New Hampshire lottery, New York authorizes a lottery of its own. Tickets are sold at $1 and $2, but like New Hampshire, New York is unable to generate sufficient public interest with a single monthly drawing. Expected revenues fall far short of predictions.

1969

- Spurred by Howard Hughes's success at buying mobsters out of the legalized gambling business, the Nevada legislature passes the Corporate Gaming Act that allows public corporations to invest in casinos. The move is instrumental in driving organized crime out of Las Vegas because the management of casinos is now answerable to a board of directors and the Securities and Exchange Commission. Ironically, Hughes is forced to stop purchasing casinos because his growing number of them violates standing antitrust laws.

1970

- Aware of the failures of the New Hampshire and New York lotteries, New Jersey launches a state lottery that is designed to succeed. The lottery commission uses mass advertising to broadcast lottery drawings that are to be held weekly instead of monthly. In addition, tickets are sold at only

50 cents apiece. The combination of frequent drawings and low-priced tickets prove a winning formula and bring in $78 million in the first six months of the lottery's operation.

- New York governor Nelson Rockefeller adds a proposal to legalize off-track betting (OTB) to a packet of legislative bills designed to help close the state's budget deficit. Hurried through the legislature, the governor's proposal passes with little time for debate. Any opposition is quelled, however, when OTB proves a windfall for the state treasury. New York, thus, becomes the first state to offer off-track betting.

1972

- New Jersey inaugurates the first daily drawing lottery, which increases the frequency of lottery play.
- The federal government organizes the Commission on the Review of National Policy Toward Gambling to assess the impact of the industry on the United States.

1974

- Massachusetts markets the first "instant game" lottery. This extremely popular lottery works by dispensing scratch-off tickets to customers via machine.

1975

- Federal law is amended to permit the states to advertise lotteries on television and radio.
- New Jersey creates a new "Pick-it" lottery that allows customers to choose their own daily winning numbers. This format is so successful that New Jersey drops its other daily drawing game within a year, and other states immediately start their own "daily numbers" games.

1976

- After three years of study, the Commission on the Review of National Policy Toward Gambling issues its final report. According to its findings, the commission insists that casino gambling will be difficult to introduce to areas with dense populations because the social costs of legalized casino gambling will likely outweigh its economic benefits. Despite this, the report concludes that gambling should be available to those who want it and that the states should maintain their control over its legalization.
- Improving on the "daily numbers" lottery format, New York State introduces Lotto, a weekly game that entails picking the right combination of six numbers to win the grand prize. Since there is a good chance that no

player will pick the right sequence of numbers, unclaimed jackpots are carried over from week to week, eventually creating multimillion-dollar awards that attract even more players.

- By a slim margin, New Jersey voters pass legislation that would permit casino gambling in Atlantic City. The purported motive is to resurrect the once-popular Jersey Shore, which had suffered a decline in tourism since the end of World War II. The first casino in Atlantic City, however, would not open for another two years.

1978

- The Seminole Nation in Florida begins running bingo games with prizes reaching $10,000. The Seminole argue that the high stakes are necessary because charity games on non-Indian land have drawn visitors away from the reservations. Backed by irate citizens and religious charities that sponsored the competing bingo games, Broward County Sheriff Robert Butterworth brings a lawsuit against the Seminole operation.

1980

- The American Psychiatric Association recognizes pathological gambling as a disorder.

1981

- ***October 5:*** In *Seminole Tribe of Florida v. Butterworth*, a federal court of appeals declares that because bingo is legal in the state of Florida, Seminole gaming is not a criminal offense but a matter of civil regulation. At the same time, the court finds that even if gambling was a civil matter, the state had no authority to prohibit Indian gaming because Native American land is sovereign. Sheriff Butterworth appeals to the U.S. Supreme Court, which dismisses the case in the following year on grounds that a civil violation does not merit federal involvement.

1984

- New York begins running its Lotto drawings twice a week, and ticket sales peak at more than $900 million.

1987

- Faced with large and popular lotteries hosted in states such as New York and California, the less-populous states of Iowa, Kansas, Missouri, Oregon, Rhode Island, and West Virginia, and the District of Columbia band together at various points throughout the year to form the Multi-State Lottery Association (MUSL). The new entity operates Lotto America, which can now offer multimillion-dollar cash prizes. Delaware, Idaho, Indiana, Kentucky, Maine, Minnesota, Montana, South Dakota, and Wisconsin join MUSL over the next four years.

- ***February 25:*** In *California v. Cabazon Band of Mission Indians*, the U.S. Supreme Court avers that Native Americans have the right to operate gambling operations in any state that tolerates gaming on non-tribal land. Furthermore, the Court declares that no state authority has the right to regulate Indian gaming unless empowered to do so by an act of Congress.

1988

- ***October 17:*** As a result of pressure from the states over the open-door ruling in *California v. Cabazon*, Congress passes the Indian Gaming Regulatory Act (IGRA). The act allows the federal government to regulate Indian bingo games while forcing the states and the tribes to negotiate via compacts how larger-stakes games and casino gambling will be regulated. Instrumental in this application of this new law is the establishment of the National Indian Gaming Commission (NIGC), a three-member panel that creates guidelines and standards for Indian gaming nationwide.

1989

- ***July 1:*** Because its agricultural-based economy is slowing, Iowa approves limited-stakes casino gambling on board riverboats. The first of Iowa's riverboat casinos launches in 1991.
- ***October 16:*** South Dakota also becomes the first state to operate video lottery terminals (VLTs). Placed in restaurants, bars, and convenience stores, the machines run a variety of wagering games (such as video poker), and proceeds are, in part, sent to the state's lottery pool.
- ***November 1:*** South Dakota voters agree to allow limited-stakes gambling in the historic community of Deadwood. The legislature's plan is to use gaming proceeds to revitalize the town and bring tourism back to the Black Hills region. The success of the operation is quickly apparent, and in the following year, South Dakota adopts an amendment to its constitution that makes limited-stakes casino gambling legal in the state. Three Rocky Mountain mining towns are granted casinos to bring income to their failing economies. Voters throughout the rest of the state, however, are reluctant to let casinos spread into their communities.
- ***November 15:*** Oregon is the first state to tolerate a lottery tied to the outcome of sporting events.

1990

- ***June 3:*** Native Americans lose a federal lawsuit in which they charge that the Indian Gaming Regulatory Act is a violation of tribal sovereignty. The U.S. Supreme Court refuses to hear an appeal.

- *June 9:* West Virginia allows video poker terminals to be installed at its Mountaineer Park racetrack (slot machines would come to the track in 1997). The combination of racetrack and casino ushers in the era of the "racino." Six other states have since opened racinos to increase revenues from racing venues.

1991

- *April 1:* Iowa launches its first riverboat casinos. Illinois follows suit in September. In subsequent years, Mississippi (1992), Louisiana (1993), Missouri (1994), and Indiana (1995) legalize riverboat gambling. The legislatures of all these states argue that gambling is a means of bringing revenue to their troubled economies.
- *November:* Massachusetts becomes the first state to allow its citizens to play the lottery by phone.
- *October:* The Minnesota lottery partners with Nintendo to make online wagering available through specific versions of the at-home Nintendo game machine. Public protest quickly puts an end to the experiment.

1992

- Greyhound racing reaches its peak. The sport slowly declines as animal rights organizations declare the sport inhumane.
- *April 22:* The Multi-State Lottery Association holds the first drawing for Powerball, a new lottery based on picking six numbers from a field of 45. The chances of winning Powerball are extremely remote, so cash jackpots soar quickly. Ticket sales over the next couple of years reach more than $1 billion.
- *June 18:* Without consulting state voters, the legislature of Louisiana passes and the governor signs the Louisiana Economic Development and Gaming Corporation Act. This act permits the creation of a single land-based casino in downtown New Orleans. Control of this unique casino is given to a private corporation, but a majority of the proceeds are channeled to the state and, in part, to the Compulsive and Problem Gaming Fund. Over the next several years, the project suffers under poor management and slow construction. The facility is not fully operational until 1999.
- *October 28:* President George H. W. Bush signs the Professional and Amateur Sports Protection Act, which effectively bans wagering on team sports in every state except Nevada.

1994

- *March 31:* Iowa dispenses with its riverboat gambling laws that had restricted maximum bets to $5 and limited hours of operation.

- *May:* Riding the wave of backlash against massive expansion of the casino industry, the National Coalition Against Legalized Gambling is formed. The lobbying powers of the organization help defeat many gambling bills across the country.

1996

- *December 5:* After winning the approval of voters in November, the Michigan Gaming Control and Revenue Act becomes law. The act permits casino gambling in a restricted area of the state, namely the region around Detroit. Three casinos open their doors in 1999. Michigan is the most recent state (as of early 2005) to legalize land-based casino gambling on non-tribal land.
- *March 17:* Florida's attorney general argues before the U.S. Supreme Court that the clause in the Indian Gaming Regulatory Act that grants tribes the right to sue their home state (if the state fails to negotiate a gambling compact with a tribe in good faith) is unconstitutional. In *Seminole Tribe of Florida v. State of Florida*, the Court sides with Florida and grants immunity to all states from suits brought against them under such circumstances.
- *August 3:* Congress creates the National Gambling Impact Study Commission (NGISC) to examine the social and economic impact of legal and illegal gambling on America.

1998

- *January 26:* The Department of the Interior adopts an amended version of the Indian Gaming Regulatory Act to counter any stalemates that might arise from broken negotiations between tribes and the states. The new act empowers the secretary of the Interior to mediate (and ultimately force) a compact between tribal and state governments that cannot reach a gaming agreement on their own. But before this channel can be exploited, the Senate immediately bars the secretary of the Interior from forcing compacts until federal courts can decide the legality of this amendment.

1999

- *June 18:* The National Gambling Impact Study Commission releases its report on the state of gambling in America. As part of its assessment, the commission maintains that, with the notable exception of Internet gambling, most gaming operations should continue to be the purview of the state and tribal governments. In addition, because of the need for closer scrutiny of the impact of gaming on individual communities, the commission recommends "a pause in the expansion of gambling in order to allow time for an assessment of the costs and benefits already visible, as well as those which remain to be identified."

2000

- ***January 14:*** Instant Racing video terminals are unveiled at Arkansas racetracks. The machines, which allow patrons to bet on previously run races, prove popular and successful.

2002

- ***June 14:*** The New York attorney general convinces Citibank—one of the largest issuers of credit in the country—to ban its customers from using credit cards to pay for cybergambling. Citibank and other credit card companies bow to state and federal government pressure after the Justice Department suggests that credit corporations could be charged with "aiding and abetting" anyone convicted of patronizing a gambling web site.

2003

- ***June 1:*** Illinois raises its gambling tax to 70 percent, the highest in the nation. As a result, gambling revenues in Illinois total $719.9 million in this year.
- ***June 10:*** The House of Representatives passes the Unlawful Internet Gambling Funding Prohibition Act, a piece of legislation that would make it illegal for credit institutions to allow their customers to pay for Internet gambling with credit cards. The bill enters the Senate but does not come up for vote before the congressional session ends.

2004

- ***March 25:*** After filing a complaint with the World Trade Organization (WTO) in 2003, the Caribbean nation that comprises the islands of Antigua and Barbuda wins a verdict, which states that U.S. bans on Internet gambling are unfair and harmful to the tiny island nation's economy. Many Internet casinos are hosted by computer servers in Antigua that rent space to American operators. By intimidating service providers and credit card institutions, the U.S. government has crippled some of the online casinos and thus deprived the struggling nation of needed revenue. By its agreements with the WTO, the United States is bound to repeal its laws, but most analysts argue that this will not happen because America is an integral trade partner in the organization and will likely appeal the decision.
- ***April 5:*** After a grand jury investigation begins subpoenaing select online service providers, Google and Yahoo!, two of the Internet's largest search

engines and web hosts, agree to pull advertisements for gambling web sites.

- ***July 1:*** Iowa lifts its cruising requirements for its riverboat casinos. It is the last of the riverboat gambling states to disband its cruising mandates, and now all six of the riverboat states have their casinos moored to docks year-round.

2005

- ***May 19:*** Although California governor Arnold Schwarzenegger supports the Lytton Band of Pomo Indians in their bid to build an urban casino in San Pablo, he publicly opposes the placing of any other American Indian casino near the state's urban area.
- ***June 22:*** California becomes the 12th state to join the Mega Millions Lottery. With California's inclusion, jackpots are estimated to reach $400 million.

CHAPTER 4

BIOGRAPHICAL LISTING

This chapter profiles significant individuals and groups of persons who are part of the history of legalized gambling in the United States. This controversial issue has touched many sectors of the American public, and therefore the list includes prominent politicians, spokespersons, business leaders, mobsters, and Native American tribes. Given the focus of legalized gambling, the individual sketches are purposefully brief and are not meant to provide a comprehensive biography.

Spencer Bachus, Alabama representative since 1992. The chairman of the Subcommittee on Financial Institutions and Consumer Credit, Bachus, a Republican, is the sponsor of the Unlawful Internet Gambling Funding Prohibition Act (H.R. 2143), which prohibits credit card institutions from allowing their customers to use credit cards to transact with Internet casinos. The bill passed the House in June 2003 but was not voted on in the senate before the congressional term ended.

William Bennett, casino operator. Along with partner William Pennington, Bennett bought the failing Circus Circus hotel and casino in Las Vegas in 1974. The two men redesigned the operation to cater to families instead of just gamblers. The new focus proved successful and helped retool the image of Las Vegas in the 1980s from "Sin City" to a family-friendly vacation spot. Bennett and Pennington were able to use the proceeds from Circus Circus to open the Excalibur and Luxor hotel-casinos, two other family-friendly destinations also located on the Las Vegas Strip.

Marshall Caifano, Chicago mob boss also known as Johnny Marshall. In 1960, Caifano was the first gangster to have his name put in the Nevada Gaming Commission's "Black Book." This list, started by Governor Grant Sawyer, contains the names of crime figures to be excluded from setting foot within any Nevada casino. In 1962, Caifano sued in court to have his name removed. After four years of appeals, a federal court upheld the state's authority to regulate casinos as it saw fit.

Richard Canfield, gambling hall operator. After touring the gambling houses of Europe, Canfield set up his own operations in New York City in the 1880s. With a partner, he ran the Madison Square Club, one of the most respected gambling halls in the city, and earned a reputation as an honest operator. He then bought out the Club House at the Saratoga racetrack in 1893. Canfield catered the Club House to wealthy gamblers, and the establishment became known for big-stakes card games.

William Clinton, 42nd president of the United States from 1993 to 2001. Clinton presided over the era of gambling's greatest expansion. Unsure of how to handle the new behemoth, the president created the National Gambling Impact Study Commission (NGISC) in 1997 to assess the impact of gambling on the nation. After the commission issued its recommendations in 1999, little was done to change the industry. Given the economic success of American gaming, however, Clinton sought to reap some of the rewards. In 1994, he considered instituting a 4 percent "sin tax" on gambling, but the matter was soon dropped. In response to the threat, the casino industry organized the American Gaming Association in the following year to become its lobbying arm in government. In 1999, Clinton proposed a gambler's tax that would appropriate 28 percent of monies won at bingo and keno. That bill was killed by Congress.

Jay Cohen, former operator of the World Sports Exchange web site. In 2000, Cohen was the first person to be convicted of violating U.S. laws regarding the use of the Internet to take wagers on sporting events from gamblers in America. Citing criminal violations of the Wire Act of 1961, the Justice Department prosecuted Cohen in a New York federal court, which sentenced him to 21 months in prison. Although he served 17 months of his term and was released, he continues to appeal his conviction.

Tony Cornero, gambling hall operator. After state authorities clamped down on his gambling operations in California in the late 1920s, Tony Cornero was the first gambling hall operator to move to Las Vegas. There he opened the Meadows Club in 1931. The Meadows offered roulette, craps, and card games under one roof—a unique combination that would be imitated by subsequent casino operators.

James Crosby, businessman and land developer. After buying out the Mary Carter Paint Company, Crosby diversified the corporation by opening a casino in the Bahamas. With capital from this business, he started Resorts International and helped persuade New Jersey voters to legalize gambling in Atlantic City. There he opened the city's first casino in 1978.

Morris Dalitz (Moe Dalitz), mobster and casino operator. A midwestern bootlegger during Prohibition, Dalitz moved into casino operations in the 1940s. He set up shop in Las Vegas and ran the Desert Inn as a source for mob funds. Dalitz is also remembered for bringing Hollywood-style entertainment to Las Vegas, giving the city of vice an atmosphere of glamour in its 1950s and 1960s heyday.

Gray Davis, governor of California from 1999 to 2003. Unlike his predecessor Pete Wilson, Gray Davis offered to allow "limited" expansion of Indian gaming in his state. He renegotiated tribal compacts, allowing more slot machines and Vegas-style games in exchange for a higher percentage of Indian gaming revenues.

John Davis, gambling hall operator. Thought to be the first casino operator in America, John Davis is credited with opening the first high-class 24-hour casino in New Orleans in 1827. He catered to rich gamblers and plied them with fine food and wine in addition to the pleasures of the betting tables.

George Devol, riverboat gambler. Author of *Forty Years as a Gambler on the Mississippi,* Devol was perhaps the most famous of the riverboat gamblers. Devol mastered three-card monte and used it to fleece many travelers in the 1850s and 1860s. He also spent time managing a racetrack in New Orleans and gambling houses in Mobile, Alabama.

Frank Fahrenkopf, Jr. president and CEO of the American Gaming Association (AGA). A lawyer and former chairman of the Republican Party from 1983 to 1989, Fahrenkopf became president of the AGA at its inception in 1995. In this capacity, he is the chief spokesman for the casino industry and has made many speeches, broadcasts, and written arguments on regulatory and policy issues.

Charles Fey, inventor of the modern slot machine. Although other inventors had created slot machines before Fey, the common three-drum machine with an automatic payout is his unique creation. Fey was a mechanic in San Francisco in 1899 when he built his first machine, which he dubbed the Liberty Bell.

Jonathan F. Green, gambler and reformer. A proficient gambler in the early 19th century, Green changed his ways and became an antigambling spokesman by mid-century. Known as "Green, the Reformed Gambler," he published books on gambler's tricks and their loathsome lives, and he lectured on the evils of gambling through the Midwest and parts of the East Coast. Professional gamblers insisted that Green was a fraud and was merely playing upon the credulity of his audiences who paid handsomely for his books and lecture tours.

Tom Grey, United Methodist minister and executive director of the National Coalition Against Legalized Gambling (NCALG). When a riverboat docked in his hometown of Galena, Illinois, in 1992, Grey began his antigambling crusade. He started organizing his home state and eventually spread NCALG across Illinois's borders. His growing involvement in the organization, however, forced Grey to step down as a community pastor, and he continues to devote his time exclusively to NCALG.

William Harrah, casino operator and industry magnate. From Reno, Nevada, in the 1930s, Harrah built a casino empire over the next four decades. He believed the strength of his business was in providing top-notch service to his customers, and thus he was the first casino operator to provide bus transportation from California to his Nevada resorts.

Richard Hayward (Skip Hayward), tribal chairman. A former pipe fitter, Hayward was instrumental in reorganizing the Pequot Indian reservation in the mid-1970s after only two members of the tribe remained on ancestral land in Mashantucket, Connecticut. Locating dispersed members, Hayward brought them back to the reservation with a promise of revitalizing the tribe through economic development. When Hayward's initial moneymaking schemes failed, he turned to high-stakes bingo in 1986. Then in 1990, Hayward found a backer who would finance a casino venture so the tribe could begin Vegas-style gambling. The Pequot built Foxwoods, the largest casino in the world, and began operating it after a lengthy contest with state authorities.

Barron Hilton, hotel magnate. Using the wealth and power of his family's hotel business, Hilton bought up many Las Vegas hotels and casinos once the Corporate Gaming Act was passed in 1969. He also owns other casinos in Reno and Laughlin, Nevada. The gambling revenues from these properties now make up the lion's share of the Hilton Hotel Corporation's income.

Howard Hughes, investor and business tycoon. Once the prime owner and stockholder of TWA, Hughes was forced to sell out when antitrust suits were brought against the company in 1966. He took his stock money and bought out six casino operations in Las Vegas and one in Reno. His presence brought other investors who eventually forced mob owners out of Las Vegas as the casinos became corporatized.

Leonard W. Jerome, investor and racetrack owner. With investor August Belmont, Jerome bought property in Long Island, New York, in order to build a racetrack. In 1866, Jerome Park was opened. Besides its opulent feel, Jerome and Belmont's enterprise was attractive to the well-to-do because of its newly formed jockey club that held 1,300 members of the social elite in its register.

Carey Estes Kefauver, Kentucky senator from 1949 to 1963. As chairman of the Senate Special Committee on Organized Crime in Interstate Commerce in 1950 and 1951, Kefauver and his colleagues examined the extent to which organized crime dominated legalized gambling and other business networks. After holding hearings in Las Vegas, the Kefauver Committee concluded that legalized gambling was a social detriment. The pronouncement had no legal ramifications, but it did inspire voters to defeat legalized gambling measures in several states. In addition, the hearings—which were televised—made the nation aware of the pervasiveness of organized crime in America.

Robert Kennedy, U.S. attorney general from 1961 to 1964. Believing that Nevada's casinos would not voluntarily purge themselves of ties to organized crime, Kennedy suggested in 1961 that Nevada governor Grant Sawyer deputize federal agents to round up the criminals. Although Kennedy felt that legalized gambling would be best regulated by the federal government, he backed down when Sawyer promised to step up enforcement efforts at the state level.

Kirk Kerkorian, casino executive and developer. A former airline executive, Kerkorian became interested in Las Vegas casinos in the 1960s. His preference for building the biggest and the best hotel-casinos started with the Las Vegas International in 1969. After selling that to the Hilton Corporation, he opened the MGM Grand in 1973 and then sold it to Bally's in 1986. He currently is a board member of the new MGM Grand, the largest hotel-casino in the world.

Jon Kyl, Arizona senator since 1994. Chairman of the Republican Policy Committee, Kyl has been a vocal opponent of gambling in the United States. In March 13, 2003, he sponsored Senate bill 627 that seeks to outlaw Internet gambling by targeting both operators and credit institutions that allow their customers to use credit cards to pay for Internet gambling. A similar bill passed in the House of Representatives in June 2003, but unlike Kyl's bill, the House bill lacks criminal penalties for Internet casino operators. The Senate bill was read twice before the Committee on Banking, Housing, and Urban Affairs, but no action was taken before the congressional session ended.

Don Laughlin, casino operator. After being expelled from high school for running a slot machine operation, Laughlin moved to Las Vegas, where he ran a small gaming establishment in the early 1950s. In 1964, he relocated operations to a then-unknown motel and casino on the Nevada-Arizona border. Catering mainly to senior citizens who spent the winter in the Southwest, the establishment prospered, and eventually a whole new gambling town—Laughlin, Nevada—sprang up from Laughlin's vision.

Cotton Mather, Puritan clergyman. As a New England minister in the late 1600s, Mather lectured against the sins of gambling. Unlike some of his clerical brethren, Mather did not argue that dice or other games of chance promoted idleness; instead, he maintained that "casting lots" was a serious act of divination and therefore should not be equated with money or sport.

Jim Morrissey, racetrack and gambling resort operator and U.S. congressman (1866 to 1870). A gambling hall operator in New York City, Morrissey took an interest in nearby Saratoga Springs as an opportune location to open a racetrack. The resort town already had a wealthy clientele, and it boasted a few gaming halls. In 1861, Morrissey and associates opened their first gambling hall, and two years later laid down a racetrack in Saratoga.

Then, in 1867, Morrissey opened the Saratoga Club House, a ritzy pleasure palace and gambling hall that rivaled the gaming salons of Europe.

Francis Nicholls, governor of Louisiana from 1877 to 1880 and 1888 to 1892. Under Nicholls's second tenure as governor, Louisiana's Serpent Lottery came to a close. Pressured by the federal authorities, who argued that the lottery illegally accepted payments through the mail, Nicholls let the lottery's charter lapse in 1892. When lottery operators tried to persuade Nicholls to renew the charter with promised donations to worthy state projects, Nicholls declared the attempt a bribe and ensured the Serpent's downfall.

Richard Nicolls, first English governor of New York from 1664 to 1668. Appointed colonial governor when the English took over New Amsterdam from the Dutch, Nicolls gave the city and state its current name. An ardent horseman, Governor Nicolls had the colony's first horse track laid out on Long Island. The first colonial prize race was run there in 1666.

Donald O'Callaghan (Mike O'Callaghan), newspaper editor and former governor of Nevada from 1971 to 1979. Until his death in 2004, O'Callaghan was the managing editor of the *Las Vegas Sun*, but he is better remembered as the two-term governor of Nevada. In that capacity, he oversaw the initial years of corporate gaming in Las Vegas and helped establish big companies like Hilton Hotels in their new ventures.

Henry Pankhurst, reform preacher. A Presbyterian pastor in New York City, Pankhurst gained fame in 1892 when he delivered a sermon that painted the mayor and the police as corrupt and tolerant of criminal gambling. Shown to be lacking proof for these charges, Pankhurst went through New York's seedy gambling establishments and other dens of vice and recorded what he saw. His evidence eventually brought about newspaper exposés and a state senate investigation that caused the downfall of the city government in 1895. Unfortunately for Pankhurst, the subsequent administration was just as corrupt.

Edward Pendleton, gambling hall operator. In 1832, Pendleton opened a gambling hall in Washington, D.C. The popular establishment was frequented by the social elite and high-ranking politicians (including President James Buchanan). From his connections, Pendleton became quite influential in politics in the pre–Civil War era.

Steven Perskie, Atlantic City civic leader. As a member of the Committee to Rebuild Atlantic City (an advocacy group that pushed for legalized gambling in New Jersey), Perskie fought to get the Atlantic County Community College to adopt a curriculum that would train local residents in casino operation. In 1977, the state approved this curriculum, and the school became the first in the United States to offer a gaming-based education. Perskie went on to chair the New Jersey Casino Control Commission and author the state's gaming law.

Leonard Prescott, tribal gaming executive. In 1987, Prescott became chairman of the Shakopee Mdewakanton Dakota's Little Six gaming enterprise in Minnesota. He was voted out of office in the early 1990s after helping build the tribe's Mystic Lake casino. He was also a founding member of the National Indian Gaming Association.

Ronald Reagan, 40th president of the United States from 1981 to 1989. As president, Reagan was an advocate of Native American self-reliance. He slashed government aid to Native American tribes while supporting tribal casinos as an answer to poverty and joblessness on reservations. He signed the Indian Gaming Regulatory Act (IGRA) in 1988, which empowered American Indians to start gaming operations with the willing or forced complicity of the states.

Si Redd, game manufacturer and entrepreneur. Redd was a slot machine distributor for Bally's before developing the first video gaming machine in the 1970s. He then started up his own company, International Gaming Technologies, which is an industry leader in the manufacture of slots and other gaming devices. In 1995, he opened the Oasis Resort and Casino in Mesquite, Nevada, and ran it until his death in 2003.

Jay Sarno, casino operator. To save the flagging gambling industry in Las Vegas, Sarno built Caesar's Palace with mob money in 1966 and single-handedly began the theme-based casino-resort craze. The subsequent glut of themed resorts resurrected Las Vegas by bringing in more and more tourists as well as gamblers.

Grant Sawyer, governor of Nevada from 1958 to 1966. Serving two terms in office, Governor Sawyer tried to rid Las Vegas of mob connections by pushing the ineffectual Gaming Commission to enforce tough regulations. The strategy didn't work, and the mob bosses ended up driving Sawyer from office by contributing huge sums to his competitor's election campaign. Still, Sawyer's attempt at enforcement deterred the federal government from stepping in and taking over the regulation of Nevada's casinos.

Arnold Schwarzenegger, elected governor of California in 2004. As governor, Schwarzenegger has agreed to allow Native American bands in California an increase in the number of casinos they can operate and the number of slot machines they can run. In return, Schwarzenegger expects each gaming tribe to pay $1 billion to the state to keep their monopoly on slots and a fee for slot machines in excess of the previous limit of 2,000 per tribe.

Benjamin Siegel, mob associate and casino operator. Working with the financial backing of mob boss Meyer Lansky, "Bugsy" Siegel was the visionary behind the Las Vegas Strip. In 1946, Siegel built the luxurious Flamingo hotel and casino as the first step in creating a gambling mecca in the desert that would lure Hollywood elites and high-rollers. Lansky, however, was not fond of Siegel's overspending or his reported skimming from the business profits. Siegel was murdered in 1947, most likely by hit men representing displeased mob interests. His death gave Las Vegas a nefarious reputation, which ironically drew in many tourists.

Ed Thorp, mathematician and author. In 1962, Thorp penned *Beat the Dealer*, a guide to improving one's odds in playing blackjack against a casino. Thorp's strategy involves a form of card counting that gives players an advantage during protracted games. The book became very popular and helped make blackjack one of the most played table games in casinos thereafter. It also gave rise to casino surveillance teams whose duty it was to spot and oust card counters or other devious players.

Donald Trump, investor and business tycoon. A hotel developer in the 1970s, Trump turned to hotel-casinos in the mid-1980s. In Atlantic City, he built Trump Plaza, Trump Marina, and the Trump Taj Mahal. The last of these was the largest casino in the world when it opened in 1989. Fighting against Steve Wynn and other competitors, Trump has always seemed to come from the brink of bankruptcy back to a position of power in Atlantic City. Trump Hotels and Casinos, a small part of Trump's business empire, now owns casinos in New Jersey and Indiana.

Lowell Weicker, governor of Connecticut from 1991 to 1995. A congressman who won federal recognition for the Pequot Indians in 1983, Weicker, as governor, fought against the tribe in its bid to run a Vegas-style casino in 1990. When the Pequot sued the governor for failing to enter into a compact, Weicker unsuccessfully tried to repeal the state's law that permitted charities to run "Las Vegas nights," since the Indians used this as the basis for their claim to operate table games. Finally, when a federal mediator compelled Weicker to negotiate, he submitted a plan that was ironically more permissive than the tribe's original proposal. The state, realizing its error, tried to get the mediator to reject its own offer. The federal agent ignored this entreaty and made the governor's plan the official compact that brought Vegas-style gambling to Connecticut.

Pete Wilson, governor of California from 1991 to 1999. Through his career as governor, Wilson was an obstacle to expanded Indian gaming in California. One of his particular targets was tribal casinos' use of video slot machines, which he called illegal because normal slots were outlawed in the state. Wilson refused to negotiate contracts with tribes that operated the machines against state law.

Matt Winn, racetrack operator. Under pressure to close down Churchill Downs racetrack due to a 1908 law against bookmaking in Kentucky, Colonel Matt Winn, the park's manager, figured out a way to continue to take bets without the need for bookmakers. Winn unearthed a forgotten statute that allowed pool betting and then installed pari-mutuel machines at his track. The machines created the odds and took the bets for the racetrack, and, to make them more enticing, Winn had a slice of their profits donated to the state. For outwitting the antigambling fervor of the times, Winn is considered the savior of Kentucky horse racing.

Steve Wynn, casino operator. After taking over the run-down Golden Nugget in 1973, Wynn transformed the casino into one of the most elegant in downtown Las Vegas. With this success, he found a backer to finance another Golden Nugget casino in Atlantic City. In 1987, he sold this latter property to Bally's and returned to Las Vegas to build the highly successful Mirage hotel-casino and, later, the themed Treasure Island.

CHAPTER 5

GLOSSARY

This chapter presents definitions of many of the most salient terms that might appear in any discussion of the social or political aspects of legalized gambling. It therefore does not include any definitions of gambling terminology narrowly related to the components or play of specific games of chance.

bingo A game usually played on cards containing a five-by-five grid of squares, of which 24 of the 25 spaces are occupied by numbers ranging from 1 to 75. When the numbers are called by a dealer, players cover up the corresponding squares on their cards. Winners declare "bingo" when they have successfully filled in required patterns of squares (usually a complete row or column or the four corners). Bingo is a game often conducted by charitable organizations, including Native American tribes.

blackjack A card game in which players continually accept cards on a voluntary basis until they achieve a point total of 21 or a sum that they feel is close enough to it to beat the point totals of other players. A value of 21 or the highest point total wins each hand. Blackjack, also known as twenty-one, is a popular game in many casinos and can also be played in a video format.

compulsive gambling See **problem gambling**.

bookmaking The act of accepting the bets of other gamblers who wish to wager on the outcome of a race or other sporting event. Illegal bookmaking is a common problem in most states, especially as it relates to sports wagering.

brick-and-mortar casino The common term for a land-based (and sometimes riverboat) casino. The adjectival phrase "brick-and-mortar" is used to draw a distinction between casinos that have a physical site and Internet casinos, which exist only in cyberspace.

casino A building or room of a gaming establishment where patrons can sit at game tables and partake of roulette, craps, poker, blackjack, and other high-stakes games, or visit gambling devices such as slot machines, which typically return lower payouts. Common state-sanctioned casinos are private enterprises that are heavily taxed by the federal and state governments. Casinos on Native American land return their profits to tribal welfare funds.

compact A binding agreement between a state government and a Native American tribe that wishes to start Class III (casino-type) gaming enterprises on reservation land. A compact spells out what types of gambling will be legal on the reservation and what fees the specific tribe will pay to the host state. These agreements are required under the Indian Gaming Regulatory Act (IGRA) as a condition for tribes to begin gaming ventures. A few tribes, however, have argued that compacts abridge their sovereign rights, and therefore these tribes have started "uncompacted" gaming on their lands.

craps A common casino game in which gamblers wager on the outcome of a dice roll. Specific combinations outlined in the game will earn the players a return on their wagers based on the probability that that combination will occur in the throw of the dice. The term "craps" refers to losing combinations that also commonly occur.

cybergambling See **Internet gambling**.

day cruise An oceangoing cruise that usually departs from and returns to the same port. Some day cruises operate casinos onboard once the ship passes beyond the three-mile, territorial-water limit of a state's legal jurisdiction.

dog racing A sport in which dogs (typically greyhounds) are run in competition along a preset track. Wagers are usually placed on which dogs will come in first, second, or third, sometimes on pari-mutuel machines.

faro A card game in which players place bets on the order in which cards will be dealt from a deck. The game enjoyed popularity during the 19th century and was one of many games played by professional gamblers along the Western frontier.

gaming A word often employed in place of *gambling* because of the latter term's negative connotation in public usage. Gaming and gambling, however, are equivalent and have the same legal definition.

horse racing A sport involving the racing of horses around a predetermined track. Horse racing today includes the running of thoroughbreds and quarter horses. It also encompasses harness racing, in which a small two-wheeled chariot—occupied by a driver—is attached to each horse. Wagers on horse racing typically involve guessing which horses will come in first, second, or third in each race, though other, more complex wagers can be made. Bets may also be made on pari-mutuel machines.

Indian gaming Any form of gaming enterprise—such as casino gaming or bingo—taking place on Native American land. In order for Indian tribes to host gaming on their land, the specific type of gambling being requested must already be legal in some form in the parent state. Once this is established, the tribe and the state government typically enter into a compact to determine how the game will be regulated and what fees will be proffered to the state from the game's proceeds.

instant-game lottery A game in which players purchase tickets (often dispensed from a vending machine) that have concealed numbers or images on them. In "scratchers" players scratch off coated areas of a ticket in hopes of revealing a winning combination of the numbers or images. In pull-tab tickets, a paper coating is pulled back to reveal the pictures or numbers underneath. Instant lotteries are usually connected to state lotteries, but charitable organizations—including Indian tribes—also may offer instant games.

Instant Racing A video gaming machine that replays images of already-run races and allows players to wager on their outcome. Instant Racing was first unveiled at racetracks in Arkansas in 2000; it has since proven quite popular and profitable.

Internet casino A web site that offers cybergambling in many forms, the most common of which are video poker, blackjack, and other card games. Players log on to Internet casinos and play the games by using credit sources (such as credit cards) to pay for their virtual gambling credits. Running an Internet casino is illegal in the United States, so many American operators host their web sites from foreign soil in hopes of evading U.S. laws.

Internet gambling A term coined within the last decade of the 20th century to denote wagering that is conducted through the Internet. It is also referred to as cybergambling and electronic gambling (or e-gambling).

jai alai A team sport that resembles handball, only the players use scooped rackets (instead of their hands) to hurl a ball against a wall. In states where it is legal to bet on the sport (usually through pari-mutuel facilities), gamblers place wagers on the team that they expect to win the game.

jockey club An association of horse breeders, riders, and track officials that regulate and maintain fair play at a racetrack or group of tracks. The American Jockey Club, a national collective of such horse experts and aficionados, was formed in 1894 and devised the rules by which all licensed tracks operate.

limited-stakes casino A casino that limits the amount of money that each gambler can wager on every play of a game (each hand of poker, for example). Colorado casinos limit their players' bets to $5 per hand. South Dakota's casinos had $5 limits for some time but raised the limit to $100 in November 2000 to attract more customers. Some Native American casinos also have limited stakes set by their tribal compacts.

lottery A gambling enterprise in which winning numbers are randomly drawn from a common pool of lots. State lotteries today operate many types of these games, from weekly lotto drawings, to daily numbers games, to instant-game lotteries. The odds of winning state lottery games are very low, and states have been accused of immorally banking on the desperation of the poorest members of society to risk their earnings on the slim chance of winning big. Lottery states have also been criticized for blurring the distinction between the business of government and the commercial enterprise of gambling.

monte A card game played with a deck of 40 cards. Two sets of two cards are drawn from the deck and displayed. Players then bet on whether the next card drawn will match one of the suits in one of the two sets. The game is also sometimes referred to as monte bank.

off-track betting (OTB) Legally wagering on the outcome of racing events without having to visit the track. OTB parlors, operating on pari-mutuel wagering systems, were first opened in New York in 1970. The experiment proved so lucrative and popular that, throughout the next two decades, other states followed New York's lead. The majority of tracks in the United States now have authorized off-track betting locations.

pari-mutuel machine A device that determines the true odds of a horse race or other sporting event by basing the ration on how many players wager on each horse or team in the contest. Gamblers place their bets with the machine, which in turn prints out tickets that indicate the players' choices. Winners redeem these tickets at the track or off-track betting facility. Pari-mutuels were the salvation of horse racing at the turn of the century because they allowed tracks to dispense with the need of bookmakers to take patrons' bets.

poker A card game in which players compete against each other to win a pot (usually an amount of money that grows as each player wagers on the strength of his or her set of cards, called a hand). Each hand is made up of five cards that, when arranged, form specific combinations that have a ranked value. The highest ranked hand of cards in a round wins the pot, and money from that pot may be used again to wager in subsequent rounds. Various forms of this table game stipulate how players select their cards, and a video version is as popular as the table game in many casinos.

problem gambling A pattern of behavior that indicates an individual's pathological abuse of or dependence on gambling at the expense of work, family, and personal interests. The term *compulsive gambling* is often used interchangeably with problem gambling, but the American Psychiatric Association maintains that the problem is a mental dependence, not a compulsive behavior. Problem gambling has a host of symptomatic behaviors that include lying about gambling losses, "chasing" losses by gambling more, and irritability when gamblers are forced to withdraw from gambling. Conservative estimates place the number of pathological gamblers in the United States at more than 7.5 million.

pull-tab See **instant game lottery**.

riverboat casino A casino operated onboard a riverboat. Riverboat casinos were inaugurated in modern times to bring casino gambling to states that didn't want the stigma of corruption and crime that seemed to be part of the Las Vegas casino image. As part of the planned attraction to voters in the 1980s and 1990s, gambling on riverboats was only to be conducted while the vessels were moving. By the 21st century, however, all six states that have riverboat casinos have allowed them to operate without cruising requirements.

roulette A typical casino game in which a small ball is spun around a slotted wheel placed horizontally on a table or stand. As the wheel slows, the ball will randomly come to rest in one of the slots, each of which is marked with a color and number. Winners of the game are determined from bets placed previously on the expected winning color/number combination.

slot machine A mechanical gambling device in which players place coins or tokens in a slot and then pull a handle to activate three drums spinning behind a viewing window. Pictures on each drum must match a certain combination when the drums stop spinning for a player to win a payout. Slots, as they are sometimes abbreviated, are so popular with gamblers that casinos reap half their total profits from these machines. Computerized versions of the game are now also commonly installed in casinos. These digital devices typically do not have handles but rely on the press of a button to start game play. Video poker variants are also hugely popular.

video lottery terminal (VLT) A type of slot machine or a video variant that is run by state lottery associations. Some detractors maintain that such devices are slots and thus should be illegal in states where casino gaming is not tolerated. The states that run VLTs, however, draw a distinction by noting that slots are coin-in, coin-out machines that are banked by a casino. Video lottery terminals, on the other hand, are banked by the lottery fund and usually dispense tickets, not coins, that are redeemable at a cashier's desk.

PART II

GUIDE TO FURTHER RESEARCH

CHAPTER 6

How to Research Legalized Gambling Issues

Legalized gambling is a highly controversial issue that engenders continuous debate. The social and economic impact of casinos, the expansion of Indian gaming, and the uncertain future of Internet gambling are just a few of the hot-button topics that have set gambling proponents and detractors at odds at the dawn of the new millennium. Thankfully for researchers, all the debate has been captured in books, magazine articles, congressional testimony, and Internet news articles. There are even whole web sites devoted to the views of gambling's defenders, and similar sites are dedicated to the words and attitudes of gambling's critics. With the wealth of information available, the researcher's job becomes one of sifting and sorting through the excess rather than tracking down the elusive tidbit. Therefore, this chapter is designed to provide those who are interested in researching legalized gambling with the tools necessary to approach the topic effectively.

BOOK SOURCES

While much of the controversy concerning issues of legalized gambling is best captured in timely periodical articles, newspaper editorials, and up-to-the-minute Internet news wire services, the background and historical context that informs such pieces has been more thoroughly expounded in books. Obviously, the most recent works possess information on the more current topics (such as Internet gambling), but there are a few older histories of gambling that are still referenced in contemporary studies. For example, both Herbert Asbury's *Sucker's Progress: An Informal History of Gambling in America from the Colonies to Canfield* and Henry Chafetz's *Play the Devil: A History of Gambling in the United States from 1492 to 1955* (see chapter 7 for bibliographic citations) are valuable resources for understanding the changing moral and social climate that has, at various times, encouraged and discouraged the growth of gambling in the United States. The two books are also extremely useful for detailing the colorful characters and the public and political attitudes that defined American gambling history prior to the rise of Las Vegas and the resort casino. Few modern resources ever contend with the pageantry of the early years of American gambling, preferring instead to rely on the history as presented in Asbury's and Chafetz's works.

Other, more recent book resources are touchstones for various gambling-related issues—from state governments' involvement in lotteries to the transformation of Las Vegas from a gambler's paradise to a family vacation spot and back again. Each of these sources is ideal for drawing together information from disparate resources (e.g., speeches, legal documents, periodical articles) into a composite whole that can give readers a detailed examination of a topic area. However, researchers delving into books should be aware of two factors that will impact the way in which the information can be utilized.

First, like all media, book authors have a point of view—a bias—that will affect what sources they consult for their data and how they arrange that data in order to draw their conclusions. While this may seem an obvious caution to make, researchers should seek out reviews or critiques of the books they read to find out how other gambling scholars—especially those with opposing views—have appraised the work. Reviews and critiques of recently published book sources are often available on book merchant web sites such as Amazon.com (http://www.amazon.com) and Barnes and Noble.com (http://www.bn.com). If the book is older or has not been reviewed on merchant sites, appraisals can often be found by simply typing the book's name into an Internet search engine.

The second factor that will impact a book's usefulness is its publication date. Several key aspects of legalized gambling are continually evolving: Indian tribes gain federal recognition (and thus the sanction to institute gaming enterprises) almost daily, states debate the authorization of lotteries during various election periods, and the U.S. Congress considers new and old gambling measures at various sessions throughout each year. Thus, the state of some topical issues may change greatly from how they are presented in even the most recently published book. Similarly, the information within a book is never contemporaneous with its publication date. A book printed in 2004 may have research extending only until 2001, depending on the time it took the author to write the book and secure a publisher to release it. Such factors do not make the book obsolete, since book authors still provide excellent analyses of events of the recent past, and they often make insightful conjectures about future trends. However, researchers should extend and even test an author's analysis by bringing the topic up-to-date through more timely periodicals and Internet resources that address the same subject.

The more recent books on the topic of legalized gambling may be available at local libraries, though many smaller community libraries often have limited storage capacity and therefore tend to sell off or dispense with older, damaged, or unpopular titles. Researchers are more apt to find the book resources they need at university libraries. There, whole shelves are commonly devoted to this topic, and any book resource unavailable can usually be requested from other university libraries in the area. Students and instructors have the broadest privileges at university libraries (especially in terms of how many books can be checked out over extended periods), but most university libraries currently permit nonstudents in the community to purchase or otherwise acquire library cards to check out materials from the general stacks.

PERIODICAL AND NEWSPAPER DATABASES

Besides acting as a storehouse of useful books, libraries typically provide patrons with access to periodical and newspaper databases. In researching the topic of legalized gambling, these databases are essential reference tools. Both university and public libraries commonly subscribe to a database service such as InfoTrac or EBSCO that index articles from various periodical and newspaper resources (both national and international). By typing in key search terms (such as legalized gambling or Indian gaming), one can pull up an array of article entries that match the search terms. Some of the entries that result from a search will link to computerized reproductions of the articles as they appear in their original print sources; other entries are merely abstracts that give a hint of what topics the original articles cover. These latter entries will require the researcher to track down the hardcopy originals. Libraries will often store hardbound volumes or microfilm versions of original print sources for those publications that do not provide full text reproductions on the periodical databases. A reference librarian can help one determine how to obtain these stored periodicals.

Many of the publications available on periodical databases will have articles from the most recent print-source copies as well as archives of articles from previous issues. Depending on the periodical, the archives may extend two decades into the past. A researcher should take the time to ascertain the scope of the archive for each relevant periodical. Additionally, periodical and newspaper databases give their users the ability to limit searches by time period. Thus, one can choose to pull up articles that were published in a specific year or between a span of years. This power to limit searches is an excellent means to find articles on Indian gaming in the 1980s, for example, or editorials on the influence of gambling lobbies in the election year 2000.

Since articles written prior to the 1980s will not typically show up on periodical databases, students of the subject may have to be more creative in locating information pertaining to earlier decades. One useful method is to examine the bibliographies of books on legalized gambling. Many times the authors of well-researched books will provide citations for (and, sometimes, summaries of the content of) pertinent periodical resources published prior to the time periods covered by magazine and newspaper databases.

While library databases offer the convenience of collecting scattered articles into one easy-to-examine format, those researching legalized gambling (or any topic) should be aware that individual databases draw from a limited number of periodical sources. That is, even though a database may have hundreds of journals, newspapers, and magazines within its archive, not all extant print sources will be referenced. Furthermore, each database commonly draws from a different pool of resources, so conducting searches on more than one database is a good way of ensuring broader coverage of print resources.

Even by casting this larger net, some useful publications may not fall within the purview of database search engines. Some of these publications have simply not licensed their content to be used or accessed by any database. Tracking down articles on legalized gambling in these overlooked print resources can be more challenging. If one is looking for a specific journal or newspaper that is not represented in a database, then it may be possible to track down the periodical through the Internet. Several publications—from academic journals to local newspapers—have their own web sites, and some offer archives of previously published articles. By typing in a known author, article title, or even subject (such as gambling) into the search field commonly provided on these web sites, one may be able to locate the full text of a desired article. Researchers should be aware, however, that while some publications provide access to their archives free of charge, others do not. A few of the latter offer the lead-in text of an article and charge a fee to view the full text, and others require that a subscription rate be paid up front for unlimited access.

GOVERNMENT SURVEY ARCHIVES

In the late 1990s, two national surveys were conducted on the impact of gambling on the United States. Although the commissions responsible for these monumental reports have since disbanded, the repositories of their work are housed on the Internet. Both of these surveys continue to influence the debates over the potential good and possible ills of gambling in America.

National Gambling Impact Study Commission (NGISC)

The National Gambling Impact Study Commission (NGISC) is a defunct government body that was charged by President Bill Clinton to assess the state of gambling in America and determine the gaming industry's national impact. The commission was chartered in 1996 and completed its duties in 1999 when it issued its Final Report. According to the Final Report, the commission recommended that the expansion of gambling in the United States be halted while further assessment of its social and economic impacts could be studied. Since the commission had no legal power, the recommendations were largely ignored. However, given the scope of the research, the commission's findings and conclusions have continued to inform both sides of the legalized gambling debate in America.

All of the papers and research related to the National Gambling Impact Study Commission are now housed in the University of North Texas Libraries' Cyber Cemetery (URL: http://govinfo.library.unt.edu/ngisc), a repository for documents issued by defunct government commissions.

Public Sector Gaming Study Commission (PSGSC)

Organized in 1999, the Public Sector Gaming Study Commission (PSGSC) was a body of state and local leaders commissioned by the National Council of Legislators from Gaming States to investigate the impact of gaming on host states and make a report. Although the federal government had already conducted its own survey through the National Gambling Impact Study Commission, the PSGSC was suspicious of that commission's findings since it had not received any data or input from the public sector.

The Gaming Study Commission's report was issued in 2000, and its conclusions regarding the gaming industry's national impact were more optimistic than the dire predictions of the federal study. The text of the report is now housed in the electronic archives of Florida State University (URL: http://iog.fsu.edu/research/psgcs.html), the co-sponsor of the Gaming Study Commission.

INTERNET RESOURCES

The Internet is a vast storehouse of information waiting to be tapped by computer users. For those interested in the topic of legalized gambling, the World Wide Web is probably the best place to start research because of the variety of resources that can be found there. In addition to housing the web pages of specific magazines or newspapers that may cover gambling news, the Internet overflows with sites devoted to both pro- and anti-gambling advocacy, government regulation of gaming, legal issues pertaining to gambling, and personal views and academic assessments of various gambling topics. These types of sites provide news, analysis, and opinions on gaming issues, and they often contain gateways, or links, to other sites that might be of further use.

Navigating and accessing the wealth of information from the various web sites that contend with gambling topics is the first challenge to Internet researchers. Some research information may be readily accessed in the most basic search of the Web; other topics of interest may take time to locate by following a complex chain of links. Thus, patience and determination are the bywords of the most fruitful Internet searches. And once useful web sites are found, bookmarking each site and cataloging the information there will facilitate researchers in retrieving that data for future reference. Knowing how to conduct efficient searches and store the found information, then, are two basic keys to using the Web to research legalized gambling.

USING SEARCH ENGINES

To help glean information from the World Wide Web, there are many search engines and web directories available. Search engines are specific web sites that specialize in scouring the Internet for information and then indexing that information for a user. A search engine operates via keywords, or search terms, that tell the engine what information to look for and retrieve. For example, a researcher looking for information on the Indian Gaming Regulation Act (IGRA) might enter that title in the search field on a search engine web page. After pressing the "search" key near the search field, the engine will pull up and organize a list of web sites and web documents that contain the given terms. The list, or index, will be structured in a hierarchy of relevance. That is, the retrieved documents that contain all the words *Indian*, *Gaming*, *Regulation*, and *Act* will be listed at the top, and the documents that contain only some of the words will be arranged toward the bottom of the list. Sometimes it can be fruitful to search in this unrestricted manner, since occasionally sites that contain only a few of the terms—such as "Gaming" and "Regulation," for example—might be unexpectedly useful. However, if only sites and documents on the IGRA are desired, then it is more efficient to enclose the search terms in quotation marks. Thus, a search for "*Indian Gaming Regulation Act*" will limit a search engine to pull up only those sites that have text in which all four words are grouped in that order.

The use of search engines is typically very straightforward and relies almost exclusively on entering the keyword search terms. Each search engine may have its own quirks, but any problems or queries that arise can usually be answered by the "help" link provided on each engine's Internet home page. This link may also give users more specific guidelines on how to limit or expand their searches to produce the desired results in a more efficient manner. Thankfully for researchers, the operating instructions for search engines are nearly identical, and therefore the manner in which searches can be narrowed or broadened in scope are nearly universal. The following is a list of some of the most general methods by which search field keywords can be manipulated:

- To conduct broad searches, enter a few general terms that convey the desired topic. Simply typing *gambling*, for example, will result in a list of any document or site that includes the word *gambling* somewhere in its text. This is an ineffective approach, since the index will include gambling information sites, as well as Internet gambling halls and any other web document that uses the word in any context—not necessarily in relation to legalized gambling. Typing such keywords *legalized gambling*, *Indian gaming*, or *problem gambling*, for example, will be more limiting because the first resources listed in the index should contain both terms (though not necessarily as a single phrase unless the user encloses them in quotation marks).
- To perform narrow searches on specific topics, add as many relevant terms to the search field as possible. Thus, entering *California Indian gaming* will prompt a search engine to first list those sites that have text that matches all three terms. Adding quotes to a specific phrase will instruct the engine to find sites where all three words are aligned as a single phrase. In this way, very specific search prompts can cut through the millions of entries on somewhat related topics to bring forth those sites that match specifically the terms entered. Obviously, though, this operation has the drawback of excluding potentially useful sites that may not contain the exact wording of the search terms. Thus, searching for "*Treatments for Problem Gambling*" may unfortunately exclude web sites that use terms such as "*Compulsive Gambling*". To conduct more thorough research, then, may require multiple searches using different keywords and, perhaps, the implementation of Boolean limiters (explained hereafter).
- To further limit searches, use the Boolean term "AND" between two or more desired terms in the search field. For example, typing *Casinos AND Connecticut* will instruct a search engine to find documents and web pages that contain both terms. A plus sign can also be used to indicate an AND limiter. Thus, "*Las Vegas*" + *casinos* + "*organized crime*" will yield an index that contains documents having all three terms.
- To limit searches by excluding unwanted results, utilize the Boolean term "NOT" before undesired terms in a search field. *Riverboat casinos NOT Illinois*, for instance, will bring up web sites and documents that in some way relate to riverboat casinos but not ones that mention Illinois by

name. A minus sign (–) can also be used in place of the NOT term to achieve the same results.

- Finally, to broaden a search, use the Boolean "OR" term between two or more search terms. For example, typing *gambling OR gaming* will result in a massive index of entries that contain either term (used in any context). The OR function is, perhaps, the least useful of the Boolean terms because the lists generated will likely be exceedingly long and unfocused. It is typically more beneficial to conduct multiple focused searches rather than blanket searches on broad topics.

Currently, there are many search engines available on the Internet, all of which are managed by distinct companies. While each may have its own method of searching and ranking results, the indexes generated by one engine will be similar to those generated by any other. Among the most popular search engines on the Internet are:

Alta Vista (http://www.altavista.com)
Excite (http://www.excite.com)
Google (http://www.google.com)
HotBot (http://www.hotbot.com)
Lycos (http:// www.lycos.com)
WebCrawler (http://www.webcrawler.com)

Because search engines are designed with specific subject orientations and ranking criteria, however, each does have its strengths and weaknesses. In an effort to compensate for this, some companies have created metasearch engines that plug search field queries into several of the web's search engines at once and then compile the results into a single index. Some of the most commonly used metasearch sites are:

AskJeeves (http://www.ask.com)
Dogpile (http://www.dogpile.com)
Metacrawler (http://www.metacrawler.com)
Search (http://www.search.com)

Many Internet researchers find these metasearch sites useful because they cast a wide net and therefore provide an excellent place to begin a thorough examination of a topic.

USING WEB DIRECTORIES

Since search engines begin scanning the Internet from the ground up (that is, by looking for keyword search terms wherever they may exist in web site names, web documents, and other web-related text), researchers may find it more useful to approach the topic of legalized gambling from the top down by utilizing a web directory. Like search engines, web directories provide entries that link to specific sites and documents of interest, but instead of randomly ranging through the billions of sites on the Internet, web directories use preset categories that lead users to the most popular sites that relate to a given topic.

One of the most popular web directories is available from Yahoo!, an indexing web site that offers both directory and search engine capabilities. On the site's home page (http://www.yahoo.com) is a section for its web directory. By following the link, a user can pull up a categorical list of popular subject areas (such as Business & Economy, Entertainment, Science, and Arts & Humanities). Gambling information falls under the Recreation & Sports heading, and the subject title Gambling will appear in a subsidiary list of topics when that initial Recreation & Sports link is selected. Following the Gambling link will lead to site listings for specific topics such as Casinos or Video Poker. Most of these site links will connect a user to an organization or web service provider that is related to the specific topic. Following the Casino and Gaming Industry category link, for example, will lead one to a list that includes Organizations. That link, in turn, connects to a list of several site links that include, among others, the American Gaming Association web site and the National Indian Gaming Association web site.

Because web services like Yahoo! have done some of the research work and created lists of what they consider the more valuable resources on a topic, users often feel secure in the belief that the information on these sites is more credible than that on unlisted sites. While this may be true to a degree—since the resource sites typically listed in a web directory include the web sites of major organizations and government agencies—not all useful web resources are represented. Web documents from scholarly journals and common periodicals are usually excluded from web directories. More thorough searching using a search engine is advisable. Still, the organizations that are accessible through web directories are commonly the preeminent sites that relate to a specific field of research. To begin Internet research on the topic of legalized gambling, one can do no better than to start with the main organizations and government agencies that are already grouped for convenience in a web directory.

USEFUL GAMBLING WEB SITES

Many of the legalized gambling web sites that are accessible through web directory catalogs are those of prominent advocacy organizations and government regulatory bureaus (which are all listed in chapter 8 of this book). While these sites are extremely useful—especially for partisan analysis and statistics, there are other particularly relevant sites that may or may not be represented on web directories. A few of these helpful but often unlisted Internet sites are arranged hereafter:

- **Casino Man** (http://www.casinoman.net) is a web service that provides information on various aspects of gambling. It has categorized links to historical overviews of the industry, discussions of gambling ethics, and chat forums on topical gambling issues. Most importantly for gambling researchers, though, Casino Man has a news link that leads to an archive of many gambling-related news stories and press releases culled from Internet news sources.
- **Gamble Tribune** (http://www.gambletribune.org) is a nonpartisan site that gathers together Internet news articles on topical gambling issues. The web site's main page is broken into subcategories such as Gambling News, Games Rules, and History of Games, and each subcategory offers a few recent news items that are relevant to the topic.
- **Gambling and the Law** (http://www.gamblingandthe law.com) is a web site run by Professor I. Nelson Rose, one of the foremost legal authorities on gambling in America. On his web site, Rose has compiled many of the articles he has written over the past few years, as well as provided useful links to other sites that contend with the legal issues that relate to gambling.
- **Indian Gaming News** (http://www.pechanga.net/IndianGamingNews.html) is another Internet news service that collects various stories from national publications (with an online presence) and displays them in one, convenient listing. All the articles on this site, however, pertain specifically to Indian gaming.

FINDING ORGANIZATIONS AND INDIVIDUALS ON THE WEB

Poring through articles and web documents may lead students of legalized gambling to seek out more information on specific individuals or relevant organizations that are referenced in these sources. Many web directories can provide links to prominent and popular organizations, and chapter 8 of this book also contains a fairly thorough catalog of government agencies and independent advocacy groups, but neither of these resource lists is exhaustive. If web contact information for an organization does not appear in this book or in web directories, then Internet users should try typing the name of the desired organization into a search engine.

While it may be tempting to simply insert an organization's name into a web address and see if the right web site responds to a query command, it is more productive to enter the full name of the organization into a search field of a search engine. This is because some organizations' web addresses utilize abbreviated forms of their official names. For example, the home page of the National Indian Gaming Association is located on the web at http://www.indiangaming.org, while the California Nations Indian Gaming Association relies on its initials and can be found at http://www.cniga.com. By entering the entire name of the organization into a search engine, the organization's official web site and web address should rank among the first listings in the index created and will thereby eliminate the guesswork of randomly typing in hypothetical addresses.

Furthermore, as these two examples above indicate, organizations on the web use different address suffixes to delineate what type of site they are. Governmental departments use the *.gov* suffix, educational institutions employ the *.edu* suffix, most (but not all) advocacy groups favor the *.org* suffix to distinguish themselves as organizations, and corporate as well as some personal web sites rely on the ubiquitous *.com* suffix. Again, by merely typing an organization's name into a search engine, one can avoid guessing which suffix applies.

Finally, when searching for individuals on the Internet, the same strategies apply. Typing a person's name into a search engine (leaving out any middle initial unless more than one individual is likely to have the same name) should lead to any web pages and documents that mention that individual. Some individuals have personal web pages with contact information. Others may be organization spokespeople or staff writers for specific periodicals, and their contact information will probably reside on the web site of the respective organization or news source. In addition, the names of journalists, commentators, and researchers will often accompany articles that they have written. Therefore, those looking for more information on legalized gambling may be able to use a search engine to pull up several topical articles written by the same individual.

BOOKMARKING ONLINE SOURCES

Searching through the endless amount of online data can be made easier by following the aforementioned strategies, but once relevant web sources are located, another task of the researcher is to organize the useful material so it can be handily recalled. Unlike hardbound reference materials, Internet resources cannot be picked up from a pile and scanned when pertinent information is needed. Instead, the key to effectively utilizing web sites and web documents for reference is to create a virtual "folder" in which these resources are stored.

Web browsers (such as Netscape and Microsoft's Internet Explorer) as well as Internet service providers (such as America Online) commonly provide users with a "Favorites" (or "Bookmarks") menu among their Internet tools. This menu allows users to create and name folders where, with the click of a button, web site addresses can be "bookmarked" or cataloged. The process for compiling these folders is nearly identical from one browser to the next. Typically, researchers who find a useful web page can open their Favorites menu from the browser toolbar and then select the function "Add Top Window to Favorites" (or a similar phrase). The name and web address of the given site should then be accessible when the Favorites menu is reopened. Users need only click on the web site name (which can be manually altered for convenience) in the menu listing to have the browser locate and open that site.

Students of legalized gambling will likely have sites for organizations such as the American Gaming Association, gambling news services such as Casino Man, and tribal agencies such as the National Indian Gaming Association bookmarked in the Favorites folder. If the list of these resources remains manageable, keeping them all within one Favorites folder should be sufficient. If the number of sites becomes unwieldy, however, then a researcher may wish to create separate Favorites folders for advocacy groups, government agencies, news groups, and the like.

The bookmarking and storage features of web browsers, coupled with the versatility of search engines, will make the vast resources of the Internet into an extremely useful asset for those researching the subject of legalized gambling. By following some of the tips in this chapter, one should be able to put together a valuable and up-to-date library of reference materials on legalized gambling that will benefit any investigation of the topic.

CONDUCTING LEGAL RESEARCH

While legalized gambling in the United States is the subject of ethical debate in the public arena, its name attests that it is also a matter of legislative and judicial concern. Tolerance for various forms of gambling has fluctuated over the nation's history, and the legalization or outlawing of games of chance has always been marked by the passing of a state or federal law. These laws are often challenged or repealed as the whims of the public or an appointed governing body change to suit the moral temper of the times. Researchers, then, will need to be aware not only of the formative legal history of gambling in America but also of the most current battles waged in the chambers of state houses as well as in the nation's capital.

In addition, both federal and state laws have been challenged in the courts, and various rulings have contributed to the way in which legal strictures are interpreted and applied. Students of legalized gambling will undoubtedly run across many references to court cases that have impacted gambling in the United States. The more significant cases are often thoroughly discussed in various books and articles, but some of the lesser-known cases may escape detailed description and analysis. Thankfully for researchers, the Internet has made it unnecessary to pore through voluminous law books to find the statutes and legal cases that bear upon legalized gambling issues. Locating and navigating the web's legal resources, however, is not always a straightforward task for those unaccustomed to legal research. Here are few helpful tools.

FINDING LAWS

There are several web sites on the Internet that lay out the text of state and federal gambling laws. The U.S. Code (the compilation of all federal laws), for example, can be reached through the House of Representatives Office of the Law Revision Council web site (http://uscode.house.gov). This database can be searched by code title, section number, or even subject. Thus, the law entitled "Gambling Ships" is 18 USC Sec. 1082, and it can be reached by searching under the law's title, its section number, or even by typing *gaming* in the web site's keyword search field.

The federal code can also be searched through the Cornell Law School web site (http://www4.law.cornell.edu/uscode/). Cornell's site is, perhaps, more user-friendly because it provides a master list of the U.S. Code that can be navigated with ease. For example, by following the link to Title 18 (the federal criminal code), one can search through the "crimes" listing to find "chapter 50"—laws that pertain to the criminalization of some gambling activities.

While these federal databases are comprehensive, they are primarily helpful if a specific law code or title is known. Otherwise, users are required to sift through a lengthy list of laws that contain search terms such as "gambling" or "gaming." A more focused method of conducting Internet research on gambling laws is available from the archives of the National Gambling Impact Study Commission (http://govinfo.library.unt.edu/ngisc/reports/statutes.html). On this web site, the commission has organized a Gambling Statutes Database that is conveniently broken down into a list of federal laws (searchable by topic) and a list of state laws (searchable by state) that relate specifically to gambling. Researchers should be aware, however, that the information on this database was last updated in 1999, so any more recent laws will be beyond its scope.

Another useful legal resource is the U.S. Federal Gambling Laws web site (http://www.gambling-law-us.com). This site, created and managed by lawyer Chuck Humphrey, has easy-to-navigate pages that provide basic information on state and federal gambling laws. The handful of federal laws that Humphrey explicates are the most commonly referenced in litigation and debates, and the state codes that he includes define the basic gambling laws of each state.

KEEPING UP WITH LEGISLATION

The U.S. Congress regularly addresses gambling legislation that is proposed by one or more of its members. Some of these bills, such as the 2003 Unlawful Internet Gambling Funding Prohibition Act, pass one chamber of Congress while failing or stalling in the second. Keeping abreast of the progress of legislation can be a daunting task. News services may keep readers current on the status of topical bills, but the Library of Congress maintains the most comprehensive list of all legislation that has been proposed, voted upon, and signed into law.

Accessing the legal resources of the Library of Congress requires logging onto its THOMAS database (http://thomas.loc.gov). This web catalog can be used in many ways, but there are two features that are most helpful in researching legislation that relates to legalized gambling.

First, the records of the current session of Congress can be searched by specific bill numbers or by keywords (such as *gaming*). Each session of Congress is designated by a number that changes consecutively every two years (the 108th Congress, for example, was in session from 2003 through 2004; the 109th Congress will be in session from 2005 through 2006). By searching for *gaming* or *gambling* in the current session's records, a user will be able to pull up a list of all the legislative action that relates to those terms respectively.

The second helpful function available on the THOMAS site is the ability to search the Bill Summary & Status catalog of both current and past congressional sessions (as far back as the 93rd session). Users can choose a session of Congress and search its records by means of keywords, bill numbers, bill sponsors, relevant committees, and other focused criteria. Conducting such a search will yield brief entries, each of which will include a bill number, its sponsors and cosponsors (if any), the committees it has been referred to, and any action that Congress has taken on the bill. Following the link given for the bill number will lead to another list through which users can access the exact text of the legislation.

Although all federal legislation is available in one convenient database, the same is not true for bills addressed in state legislatures. Unfortunately, there is no single site that offers a thorough account of the legislative actions in all 50 states. However, each state typically has its own legal database that is accessible through its government web site. For example, the home page for the government of Alabama (http://www.alabama.gov) has links that will eventually connect interested visitors to its ALISON (Alabama Legislative Information System Online) web site. Such sites can then be examined and manipulated in much the same way as the federal government's THOMAS site.

FINDING COURT DECISIONS

Legislative databases are excellent resources for locating specific bills and noting how they have been amended over time. These databases, however, do not cover the ways in which the legislation has been utilized or challenged after being signed into law. This facet of the legal process is partially documented on judicial databases, where researchers can learn how various courts have interpreted laws, ruled on cases that involve infractions of laws, and even upheld or abolished the very legal authority of specific laws.

The most far-reaching legal cases are commonly those that garner the attention of the U.S. Supreme Court, the highest authority of judicial review and decision making in America. Many cases involving legal and illegal gambling have come before this august body (several of the most significant are detailed in chapter 2 of this book). To seek out the arguments before, and the judicial decisions of, the Supreme Court, researchers should consult the Cornell Law School Legal Information Institute web site (http://www.law.cornell.edu). This legal resource has records of all Supreme Court decisions rendered since 1990. The site also maintains an archive of 600 other influential Supreme Court decisions that predate the contemporary record.

Some federal lower court decisions can be found on the Legal Information Institute site (of primary interest are the listing for the federal court of appeals), but these records often don't extend very far back in time. A better resource for a variety of federal lower-court records (including circuit and appellate court decisions) is the Washburn School of Law web site (http://www.washlaw.edu).

Both the Cornell and Washburn web sites also have listings for state court cases. These listings are actually links that lead to the government web sites of each individual state. Every state's archive of court cases, though, varies in scope and detail.

Searching through the legal documents found on the above sites (or any other web site) can be a daunting task. Legal citation is a language all its own, and navigating the host of briefs, cases, decisions, and opinions requires a rudimentary understanding of legal terminology. The first aspect of legal citation that researchers should become familiar with is the way in which cases are titled.

In most newspaper or magazine articles, the titles of court cases are often abbreviated to the names of the plaintiff and the defendant. Thus, the first California case to challenge the state's authority over Indian gaming rights is commonly referred to as *California v. Cabazon.* The full citation of this case, however, reads *California v. Cabazon Band of Mission Indians*, 480 U.S. 202 (1987). This citation first spells out the plaintiff and defendant and then notes that the case can be found in volume 480 of the U.S. Supreme Court Reports, beginning on page 202. It also indicates that the case was decided in 1987. The citation for a lower court case will replace the "U.S." marker in a Supreme Court reference with another notation that indicates the district or circuit in which the given case was heard.

Beyond the unique titling of court cases, the jargon within the formal complaints and the judicial decisions can also be somewhat inscrutable. While a close reading of the relevant court documents should convey the basic progress and conclusion of a case, any confusing language can be cleared up by consulting legal resources. Both the Legal Information Institute and the Washburn web sites, for example, have helpful pages devoted to clarifying difficult terminology for users who are not legal scholars.

CHAPTER 7

ANNOTATED BIBLIOGRAPHY

This chapter provides a representative bibliography of works relating to the topic of legalized gambling in America. The collection of references includes books, periodicals, Internet documents, and other media resources—most of which have been published after 1980, during the era of legalized gambling's greatest expansion in the United States. Besides being selected for their timeliness, some of the resources in this bibliography have been chosen for their clear examination of the history of gambling in America; others have been included because they offer valuable opinions about the effects of legalized gambling on the nation.

BOOKS

Aasved, Mikal J. *The Psychodynamics and Psychology of Gambling: The Gambler's Mind.* Springfield, Ill.: Charles C. Thomas, 2002. The first of a proposed four-volume set on gambling theory, this book sets out to explain why people gamble. To answer this question, Aasved draws on a host of psychological theorists (Sigmund Freud, B. F. Skinner, and others) that offer some insight into gambling behavior. Of particular interest is the author's examination of why some players are able to control their gambling while others drift into the dangerous realm of problem gambling.

Abt, Vicki, James F. Smith, and Eugene Martin Christiansen. *The Business of Risk: Commercial Gambling in Mainstream America.* Lawrence: University Press of Kansas, 1985. This work is one of the earlier (now seminal) attempts to outline the history and economic and social impact of legalized gambling in America. Abt and her colleagues are quick to dispense with the notion of gambling as a romanticized vice and focus instead on gambling as an industry. In this respect, the authors examine the forms of commercial gambling in America and how these various venues have become an institutionalized leisure activity with state sanction and public support.

Alvarez, A. *The Biggest Game in Town.* San Francisco: Chronicle, 2002. This reprint of a 1983 classic looks at the lifestyles and playing styles of many attendees of the World Series of Poker tournament in Las Vegas. Alvarez's portraits of the card sharps reveal obsession, superstition, psychological stamina, and other traits of the often eccentric big-stakes gamblers.

Asbury, Herbert. *Sucker's Progress: An Informal History of Gambling in America from the Colonies to Canfield.* New York: Dodd, Mead & Company, 1938. One of the few early histories of gambling in the United States, Asbury's work is a thorough and engaging project. His extensive tome covers gambling history from colonial days through the end of the 19th century. Major figures such as Mike McDonald, John Morrissey, and Robert Canfield each receive a full chapter, while other sections of the book detail the rise of riverboat gambling and gambling on the Western frontier.

Barker, Thomas, and Marjie Britz. *Jokers Wild: Legalized Gambling in the Twenty-first Century.* Westport, Conn.: Praeger, 2000. Barker and Britz look at the economic, political, and social legacy of legalized gambling on the eve of a new millennium. Recognizing that gambling is America's fastest growing industry, the authors set out to ascertain whether the expansion of gambling will continue into the 21st century or whether it will slow due to market saturation and public backlash.

Bellin, Andy. *Poker Nation: A High-Stakes, Low-Life Adventure into the Heart of a Gambling Country.* New York: HarperCollins, 2002. Picking up on the recent resurgence of poker in the public eye, Bellin, a card aficionado, discusses the role poker has played in American pop culture. While his book offers basic advice on playing the game, Bellin also details the lives of famous poker players and the spread of card rooms, tournaments, and other outlets for this favored pastime.

Benedict, Jeff. *Without Reservation: The Making of America's Most Powerful Indian Tribe and Foxwoods, the World's Largest Casino.* New York: HarperCollins, 2000. Benedict traces the struggle between the Mashantucket Pequot tribe and the Connecticut state government over tribal gaming in the 1990s—a contest that ultimately culminated in the opening of Foxwoods Casino on Indian land. The hugely successful gambling venture invigorated the tribe, but it angered local business owners and the general public, leaving relations between the Pequot and the state strained ever after.

Biracree, Tom, and Wendy Insinger. *The Complete Book of Thoroughbred Horse Racing.* Garden City, N.Y.: Dolphin Books, 1982. Though two decades old, this extensive volume covers all aspects of horse racing from breeding to wagering. For those interested in the latter topic, there are sections on how stakes are computed, how pari-mutuel betting works, and even a brief history of horse-race gambling. Charts and graphs accompany the insightful and engaging text.

Borg, Mary O., Paul M. Mason, and Stephen L. Shapiro. *The Economic Consequences of State Lotteries.* Westport, Conn.: Praeger, 1991. Written by three economics professors, this book examines the revenues generated by state lotteries and how they are allocated to specific state programs, such as education. By investigating state policies, the authors discuss other relevant issues such as how state governments promote lotteries and whether players are overspending on the purchase of lottery tickets.

Braidwaite, Larry. *Gambling: A Deadly Game.* Nashville, Tenn.: Broadman & Holman, 1985. Written from a moralistic viewpoint, Braidwaite's work examines the downside of legal gambling's expansion in the 1980s. Braidwaite emphasizes the problems of compulsive gambling, the crumbling of host communities, and the spread of illegal gambling in the wake of legalized gambling.

Brenner, Reuven, with Gabrielle A. Brenner. *Gambling and Speculation: A Theory, a History, and a Future of Some Human Decisions.* New York: Cambridge University Press, 1990. Setting out to discover why people gamble, the authors examine worldwide gambling behaviors and the attempts by governments and other interest groups to condemn these behaviors. The Brenners admit that their research has made them skeptical of prohibitionist arguments; therefore much of their book is a dissection of antigambling strategies.

Bridges, Tyler. *Bad Bet on the Bayou: The Rise of Gambling in Louisiana and the Fall of Governor Edwin Edwards.* New York: Farrar, Straus and Giroux, 2002. New Orleans reporter Tyler Bridges explores the gambling history of his home state from pre–Civil War days through the modern times. His focus, however, is on the popular governor Edwin Edwards, who was elected four times during the 1970s, 1980s, and 1990s. Edwards believed that legalized gambling could save Louisiana's economy when the state's oil boom dried up. He therefore sanctioned the riverboat industry and the creation of the only state-authorized casino. But as Bridges records, the governor became tied to corrupt businessmen and ultimately fell from grace when he was indicted for extorting money from the riverboats.

Burbank, Jeff. *License to Steal: Nevada's Gaming Control System in the Megaresort Age.* Reno: University of Nevada Press, 2000. Using interviews, newspaper accounts, and state documents, investigative reporter Burbank delves into the dark history of gambling in Nevada. He presents many of the cases that have come before the state's gaming commission to illustrate the seedy characters and corrupt business practices that have all helped shape Nevada's gambling industry.

Bybee, Shannon, et al. *Gaming Law: Cases and Materials.* New York: Matthew Bender, 2003. Aimed at law students, this compendium holds roughly 100 law cases relating to legalized gambling. Each entry is modified from the legal transcripts and includes some judicial opinion and case summary.

Chafetz, Henry. *Play the Devil: A History of Gambling in the United States from 1492 to 1955.* New York: Clarkson N. Potter, 1960. Chafetz's account of gambling in America before the advent of the Las Vegas Strip casino culture is thoroughly engaging. Chafetz uses historical vignettes to illustrate the ways in which the nation's gambling culture developed from colonial card playing to the genteel racetrack circuit to the respected wagering on the stock exchange. Along the way he reveals how individual enterprise, political influence, and business interests propelled the burgeoning industry forward and helped it become ingrained in American society.

Clotfelter, Charles T., and Philip J. Cook. *Selling Hope: State Lotteries in America.* Cambridge, Mass.: Harvard University Press, 1989. This examination of state lotteries throughout American history focuses on the controversies inherent in the government operation of a business enterprise. Clotfelter and Cook discuss the questionable ethics of state governments actively relying, if not preying, on the gambling propensities of their citizenry and the troubling statistics that suggest that much of lottery revenues come from the poorest ranks of the populace.

Collins, Peter. *Gambling and the Public Interest.* Westport, Conn.: Praeger, 2003. Collins examines the scholarly, public, and administrative debates on the legal status of gambling and how legalized gambling should be regulated. Instead of retelling what the state of legalized gambling has been in America, Collins prefers to investigate whether the government's relationship to the gambling industry is in the public interest.

Darian-Smith, Eve. *New Capitalists: Law, Politics, and Identity Surrounding Casino Gaming on Native American Land.* Florence, Ky.: Wadsworth, 2003. University of California professor Eve Darian-Smith examines how the relatively new phenomenon of Indian gaming has transformed many tribes and also changed the way that non-Indians view the new breed of venture capitalists.

Davies, Richard O., and Richard G. Abram. *Betting the Line: Sports Wagering in American Life.* Columbus: Ohio State University Press, 2001. Davies and Abram explain how the illegality of sports wagering in all but one state adds to the excitement of this form of gambling. The authors suggest, however, that the burgeoning semi-underground enterprise has ironically helped college and professional sports maintain their popularity in America.

DeArment, Robert K. *Knights of the Green Cloth: The Saga of the Frontier Gamblers.* Norman: University of Oklahoma Press, 1982. A historian of the Old West, DeArment discusses how frontier gamblers followed the nation's westward expansion from the cradle of New Orleans to the gold country around San Francisco.

Demaris, Ovid. *The Boardwalk Jungle.* New York: Bantam, 1986. After outlining the history of Atlantic City as a favored resort town, Demaris examines the transformation of the community once it legalized gambling in the 1970s. The author maintains that the push for legalization was manipulated by politicians and business interests, and that the immediate impact of gambling was detrimental to the citizens and the region.

Dement, Jeffrey W. *Going for Broke: The Depiction of Compulsive Gambling in Film.* Lanham, Md.: Scarecrow, 1999. Examining 20 films of the past 50 years that involve depictions of compulsive gamblers, Dement argues that Hollywood inaccurately portrays the severity of the problem and ends up glorifying the character by never contending with the destructive consequences of such pathological behavior.

Denton, Sally, and Roger Morris. *The Money and the Power: The Making of Las Vegas and Its Hold on America, 1947–2000.* New York: Knopf, 2001. Part history of Las Vegas's seedy past and part examination of the city's influence on American fascination with greed and artifice, this book investigates the connection between the Nevada gambling industry and crime, politics, and the nation's moral character. Particularly informative are the brief biographies of the major players who helped shape America's "Sin City."

Dombrink, John, and William N. Thompson. *The Last Resort: Success and Failure in Campaigns for Casinos.* Reno: University of Nevada Press, 1990. Dombrink and Thompson outline models for the successful implementation of casinos into states such as Nevada and New Jersey as well as the failed attempts to bring casinos to states such as Florida and Texas. Although some of the then-topical matters are now outdated, the value in this book lies in its clear analysis of the political and economic issues that surround the proposal of and subsequent debate over casino implementation in each state.

Eadington, William R., and Judy A. Cornelius, eds. *Indian Gaming and the Law.* 2nd ed. Reno: University of Nevada Press, 1998. This is an updated collection of essays and personal narratives presented at a 1989 symposium concerning the rise of tribal gaming after the passage of the Indian Gaming Regulatory Act. Included are discussions of the politics of Indian gaming and its impact on tribes. Eadington is also the editor of many other mid-1980s collections of papers on gambling topics. Those anthologies are also dated but useful for historical analysis.

Earley, Pete. *Super Casino: Inside the "New" Las Vegas.* New York: Bantam, 2000. *Washington Post* reporter Pete Earley writes that the "old" Las Vegas—with its connections to Elvis, Frank Sinatra, crime, and scandals—is a faded memory. Today's Vegas casino industry is big business. Earley discusses the corporate structure of Las Vegas casinos, but he cannot resist sprinkling in some anecdotal narratives from high rollers and other casino hangers-on that seem to recapture some of the old "Sin City" charm.

Eisler, Kim Isaac. *Revenge of the Pequots: How a Small Native American Tribe Created the World's Most Profitable Casino.* New York: Simon & Schuster,

2001. This is a political and legal history of the building of Foxwoods casino and the revitalization of the Pequot tribe of Connecticut. Eisler stresses the irony of how a formerly dispossessed people would eventually become a major economic powerhouse with enough political clout to affect the election of President Bill Clinton.

Ezell, John Samuel. *Fortune's Merry Wheel: The Lottery in America.* Cambridge, Mass.: Harvard University Press, 1960. Although written before the reintroduction of state lotteries in the 1960s, Ezell's account of the early history of lotteries in America is very thorough. He explains that while lotteries were popular with a gambling public, they fell victim to backlash movements when corruption and scandal made them the targets of progressive-era politics.

Findlay, John M. *People of Chance: Gambling in American Society from Jamestown to Las Vegas.* New York: Oxford University Press, 1986. Findlay astutely ties Americans' continual interest in gambling to the adventurous, risk-taking spirit that defined the character of the nation's first settlers. He then traces this ingrained attitude through other historical periods up through the realization of the gambling mecca of Las Vegas. To Findlay, Las Vegas is the embodiment of American gambling ideals because it hearkens back to the Western frontier while moving forward through venture capitalism.

Freeman, Bob, and Barbara Freeman, with Jim McKinley. *Wanta Bet? A Study of the Pari-Mutuels System in the United States, How It Works—And the Sports Involved.* Henderson, La.: Freeman Mutuels Management, 1982. A very thorough examination of how pari-mutuel betting works. The authors discuss the way the system is used in figuring the odds on horse racing, dog racing, and jai alai contests in the United States. Perhaps the most unusual chapter lists all the personnel needed to operate a pari-mutuel facility, including track nurses and the armored car service that delivers the facility's daily bankroll.

Frey, James H., and William R. Eadington, eds. *Gambling: Views from the Social Sciences.* Annals of the American Academy of Political and Social Science, vol. 474. Beverly Hills: Sage, 1984. This collection of studies and papers focuses on the sociologic impact of the gaming industry as well as the leisure activity of gambling. Although outdated, the analysis covers gambling psychology, the economic impact of lotteries, police enforcement of gambling laws, and urban development in gambling communities.

Fromson, Brett Duval. *Hitting the Jackpot: The Inside Story of the Richest Indian Tribe in History.* Boston: Atlantic Monthly, 2003. Journalist Fromson narrates the rags-to-riches story of the Pequot Indians of Connecticut and the building of Foxwoods casino. He highlights the shrewd legal wrangling that paved the way for the creation of Foxwoods, as well as the problems within the tribe and the local community after the casino became a huge success.

Goodman, Robert. *The Luck Business: The Devastating Consequences and Broken Promises of America's Gambling Explosion.* New York: The Free Press, 1995. According to Goodman, a former director of the United States Gambling Study, the gambling industry is out to maximize its profits, and therefore it is unconcerned about the social and economic consequences of its business practices. Perhaps more troubling to Goodman is the government's complicity—embracing and supporting gambling as a way of increasing revenues and spurring job growth without recognizing the costs of gambling's expansion.

Grinols, Earl L. *Gambling in America: Costs and Benefits.* New York: Cambridge University Press, 2004. This study maintains that the arguments used to support legalized gambling in America are often based on erroneous claims and exaggerated statistics. Grinols insists that a careful examination of the impact of gambling on society reveals that the costs outweigh the supposed benefits.

Haley, James, ed. *Gambling.* San Diego: Greenhaven Press, 2004. Part of the Examining Pop Culture series, this volume is a collection of previously published articles that cover various aspects of gambling history. The anthology is an approachable overview of the topic, and it introduces readers to several magazine writers and book authors who have written on gambling.

Hsu, Cathy H. C., ed. *Legalized Casino Gaming in the United States: The Economic and Social Impact.* New York: The Haworth Hospitality Press, 1999. This collection of concise essays contends with the history and impact of legalized gambling in America. Specific chapters examine various gambling venues from Las Vegas to riverboat casinos to Indian gaming. Charts and graphs are included, and each chapter appends a helpful bibliography for further research on the individual chapter topics.

Jeffries, James. *Book on Bookies: An Inside Look at a Successful Sports Gambling Operation.* Boulder, Colo.: Paladin, 2000. Although written as a "how-to" manual on establishing and running a sports book, this work does offer insights into how these illegitimate operations are organized, how odds are determined, and how the Internet is changing the nature of the game.

Johnson, Nelson. *Boardwalk Empire: The Birth, High Times, and Corruption of Atlantic City.* Medford, N.J.: Plexus, 2002. Johnson first looks at the economic reasons behind Atlantic City's decision to adopt legalized gambling as a way to revitalize its crumbling boardwalk. He then charts the meteoric rise of the city after corporate gambling ventures invested in the community. While Atlantic City's transformation was advertised as carefully orchestrated to avoid the crime and corruption of Las Vegas's evolution, Johnson points out that the New Jersey experiment was just as troubled as its Nevada counterpart.

Johnston, David. *Temples of Chance: How America Inc. Bought Out Murder Inc. to Win Control of the Casino Business.* New York: Doubleday, 1992. *Philadelphia Inquirer* reporter David Johnston suggests that corporate control of casinos is more sinister than the past influence of organized crime. According to Johnston, the gloss of respectability given by business leaders such as Donald Trump has made politicians less stringent in regulating gambling and even invited the greedy among them to share in the profits of this multimillion-dollar industry.

Kefauver, Estes. *Crime in America.* New York: Greenwood Press, 1968. Kefauver headed the Senate investigations into organized crime in the early 1950s. Part of those investigations targeted mob influence in gambling enterprises. This book is a reprint of his 1951 recollection of the Senate inquiries and relates Kefauver's lament of the pervasiveness of crime in many facets of American life.

Land, Barbara, and Myrick Land. *A Short History of Las Vegas.* Las Vegas: University of Nevada Press, 1999. Starting from primitive times, two journalists narrate the growth and development of the American gambling mecca. Their work is a good, concise introduction to Las Vegas history.

———. *A Short History of Reno.* Las Vegas: University of Nevada Press, 1995. The Lands provide an entertaining look at Las Vegas's often overlooked sister city. They chart Reno's frontier days as a haven for prostitution, its mid-20th century renown as the divorce capital, and its final rise to become a gambling destination and entertainment hot spot.

Lane, Ambrose I. *Return of the Buffalo: The Story behind America's Indian Gaming Explosion.* Westport, Conn.: Bergin & Garvey, 1995. Lane recounts the struggle of California's Cabazon band of Mission Indians to institute Indian gaming as a means of economic empowerment. The book reveals run-ins with law enforcement and political powers—contests that culminated in the U.S. Supreme Court's Cabazon ruling in 1987.

Lears, Jackson. *Something for Nothing: Luck in America.* New York: Viking, 2003. This book is a careful analysis of how Americans' love of gambling and dreams of instant wealth have run afoul of the traditional belief that hard work is the way to prosperity. While the former attitudes have been castigated as immoral and indolent, Lear suggests that risk taking and the desire for wealth have done much to expand the nation, build its industries, and inspire its people.

Mahon, Gigi. *The Company That Bought Boardwalk: A Reporter's Story of Resorts International.* New York: Random House, 1981. Mahon digs into the history of Resorts International, the one-time paint company that entered the casino business when it opened the Chalfonte-Haddon Hall in Atlantic City. Eschewing some detail, Mahon concentrates on the provocative and perhaps scandalous aspects of the company's dealings as it wrangled for its piece of the gambling industry.

Martinez, Andres. *24/7: Living It Up and Doubling Down in the New Las Vegas.* New York: Dell, 2000. Taking his $50,000 book advance, Martinez, a former Ivy League lawyer and ex–*Wall Street Journal* reporter, decides to visit 10 casino resorts in Las Vegas in an attempt to immerse himself in the new Vegas culture and learn the history of the Strip from those who live, work, and play there. While certainly a comic narrative, Martinez's view from the front lines of casino gambling is perceptive and riveting.

Mason, W. Dale. *Indian Gaming: Tribal Sovereignty and American Politics.* Norman: University of Oklahoma Press, 2000. A University of New Mexico professor argues that revenues from Indian casinos are turning once-overlooked tribes into powerful political forces. Mason notes how some tribes have contributed huge sums to election campaigns to make sure that Indian interests are protected by sympathetic candidates.

McGowan, Richard A. *Government and the Transformation of the Gaming Industry.* Northampton, Mass.: Edward Elgar, 2001. In this examination of the gambling industry, McGowan maintains that state lotteries (discussed in another of his books) have been eclipsed by casino gambling, sports betting, and video machines in terms of devouring the lion's share of gaming profits. This transformation, McGowan claims, has occurred because of the gaming industry's economic strategies and the tolerant political climate of the late 20th century.

———. *State Lotteries and Legalized Gambling: Painless Revenue or Painful Mirage.* Westport, Conn.: Quorum Books, 1994. Professor McGowan's work focuses on the public policy aspects of lotteries. Noting that state lotteries are government-run businesses in the field of entertainment, McGowan examines how the state governments must balance the need for revenue with the ethical concern of operating a gambling venture. His analysis also includes a history of lotteries in America and a discussion of foreign lotteries in relation to their U.S. counterparts.

McMillen, Jan, ed. *Gambling Cultures: Studies in History and Interpretation.* New York: Routledge, 1996. This anthology explores manifestations of gambling in various cultures of the world. The range of multidisciplinary essays includes political studies, social impact studies, and historical analyses. A few of the pieces contend with aspects of gambling culture in the United States—from charting the industry's expansion to discussing how gambling has been imagined in popular culture—but the other essays on foreign gambling cultures make interesting comparisons to the U.S. phenomenon.

Mullis, Angela, and David Kemper, eds. *Indian Gaming: Who Wins?* Los Angeles: UCLA American Indian Studies Center, 2001. This anthology covers various social and political aspects of Indian gaming in the wake of the 1988 Indian Gaming Regulatory Act. Essays include a discussion of the impact of gambling upon tribal culture, the growing power of gaming tribes, and the subsequent resistance by white Americans to expanding Indian gaming.

Nibert, Dennis. *Hitting the Lottery Jackpot: State Governments and the Taxing of Dreams.* New York: Monthly Review Press, 1999. In this critique of state lotteries, Nibert contends that this form of gambling preys on the poor and minorities who risk needed cash on the hopes of hitting it big. According to the author, lotteries are a questionable source of revenue for states because they require state governments to actively promote gambling.

O'Brien, Timothy L. *Bad Bet: The Inside Story of the Glamour, Glitz, and Danger of America's Gambling Industry.* New York: Times Books, 1998. Basing his chapters on locales in which gambling has taken root, O'Brien explores the evolving history of gaming in America. His overriding claim is that in order to keep patrons coming back, the industry has continually tried to increase the speed and excitement of its games. Since Americans are already attuned to a high-speed lifestyle in which instant gratification is the ideal for many, O'Brien acknowledges that the newest gaming platforms such as video gaming and Internet casinos will likely keep the public's interest while distracting them from the dangers of gambling's expansion.

Reith, Gerda. *The Age of Chance: Gambling in Western Culture.* New York: Routledge, 1999. Reith looks at the way in which games of chance have become embedded in the Western consciousness. For her, they represent play as well as risk and therefore capitalize on these two inherent fascinations of Western culture. In fact, Reith argues that the unpredictability of chance mirrors the unpredictability of life and that tapping into this seemingly randomized world of chance is equivalent to indulging in some sacred realm of belief where mundane, rational order does not hold sway. That brief sense of otherworldliness, according to Reith, is the true appeal of gambling.

Riconda, Andrew, ed. *Gambling* (The Reference Shelf). New York: H.W. Wilson, 1995. This anthology collects previously printed articles and book excerpts on various aspects of gambling. Some pieces cover aspects of gambling history, others contend with specific issues such as problem gambling. There is also a section of firsthand accounts from gamblers and others connected to the topic. A short bibliography is appended.

Rosecrance, John. *Gambling without Guilt: The Legitimization of an American Pastime.* Pacific Grov, Calif.: Brooks-Cole, 1988. Rosecrance denies that compulsive gambling is an obsessive, uncontrollable behavior. Instead, he argues that bad luck, poor money management, and a lack of gambling skill are the causes of problem gambling. He contends that as players gain more familiarity with gambling, they will learn how to avoid excessive losses.

Shaffer, Howard J., ed. *Futures at Stake: Youth, Gambling, and Society.* University of Nevada Press, 2003. Compiling essays from various clinicians, legal professionals, public servants, and industry insiders, this anthology discusses the rise of youth gambling in the United States. Chapters contend with the legal aspects of youth gambling, treatment options for underage gamblers, and other social and economic aspects of the problem.

Sheehan, Jack. *The Players: The Men Who Made Las Vegas*. Las Vegas: University of Nevada Press, 1997. This work devotes chapters to each of several Las Vegas visionaries and entrepreneurs who helped shape the gambling community in Las Vegas. Included are such legendary figures as Benny Binion, Howard Hughes, Kirk Kerkorian, Jay Sarno, and Steve Wynn.

Sifakis, Carl. *Encyclopedia of Gambling*. New York: Facts On File, 1990. This reference work primarily focuses on various gambling terms and games. A few token entries on noted gamblers and such prominent icons as Las Vegas are, however, included. Each entry is thoroughly annotated in straightforward language that makes difficult topics (such as the mechanics of specific games) easy to grasp. The book also contains a glossary and a useful bibliography.

Sternlieb, George, and James W. Hughes. *The Atlantic City Gamble*. Cambridge, Mass.: Harvard University Press, 1985. Detailing the first five years of gambling in Atlantic City, the authors illustrate the pros and cons of the industry's impact. They then show how legalization in New Jersey can be used as a model for other states that are contemplating gambling measures.

Thompson, William N. *Legalized Gambling: A Reference Handbook*. Santa Barbara, Calif.: ABC-CLIO, 1994. Thompson's handbook is a general overview of legalized gambling in America and Canada (as it existed in the early 1990s). Chapters include a short history of the issue, an annotated list of gaming laws, a selection of related organizations, and a discussion of major court cases. There is also a bibliography and a section devoted to charts and tables (with information that is now obsolete).

Torr, James D. *Gambling: Opposing Viewpoints*. San Diego: Greenhaven Press, 2002. This anthology collects pre-published articles and book excerpts that debate the pros and cons of legalized gambling in America. Topics include the regulation of gambling, the impact of gambling on host communities, and the morality of legalized gambling. Overall, it is a fine introduction to the basic opinions surrounding gambling's social and economic controversies.

Tronnes, Mike, ed. *Literary Las Vegas: The Best Writing about America's Most Fabulous City*. New York: Henry Holt, 1995. Twenty-six short pieces on the glitz, glamour, and sordid past of Las Vegas fill this anthology. There is an excerpt from Hunter S. Thompson's famed memoir *Fear and Loathing in Las Vegas* as well as writings by playwright Noel Coward (on his stint in Las Vegas), essayist Joan Didion (on the city's wedding chapels), and other lesser-known authors that offer interesting views on the city's gambling culture.

UNLV International Gaming Institute. *The Gaming Industry: Introduction and Perspectives.* New York: John Wiley & Sons, 1996. This introduction to gambling in the United States is aimed at those interested in working for the gaming industry. As such, it has chapters on casino organization, food service operations, and accounting. There are, however, introductory chapters on casino history and regulation that will appeal to both students and researchers.

Valley, David J., and Diana Lindsay. *Jackpot Trail: Indian Gaming in Southern California.* El Cajon, Calif.: Sunbelt, 2003. Valley's book is a tour guide that gives detailed information on the 21 tribes that currently have gaming enterprises. It also analyzes the quick growth of California tribal gaming and its impact on the state's economy.

Volberg, Rachel A. *When the Chips Are Down: Problem Gambling in America.* New York: Century Foundation, 2001. Volberg, a student of problem gambling and its impact on society, examines what studies and research have been done in the field and how these have influenced public policies. She also discusses how the industry has been affected by the issue and what steps both corporate and tribal casinos are taking to address it.

Von Herrmann, Denise. *The Big Gamble: The Politics of Lottery and Casino Expansion.* Westport, Conn.: Praeger, 2002. Von Herrmann's work analyzes public policy in light of new studies into the morality of politics. Under this rubric, the author examines how gambling measures are adopted and regulated, as well as the role of government in its support of and active participation in legalized gambling. She also addresses some of the social impacts that result from the implementation of gambling policies.

PERIODICALS

"All Bets Are On." *Economist,* vol. 372, no. 8395, October 2, 2004, p. 67. America's gambling industry is consolidating and setting its sights on the global market, but these overseas ventures could fail if the industry cannot eliminate competition from Internet casinos.

Angwin, Julia. "Could U.S. Bid to Curb Gambling on the Web Go the Way of Prohibition?" *Wall Street Journal* (Eastern Edition), August 2, 2004, p. B1. The U.S. Justice Department is hoping to close off all sources of Internet gambling from American patrons. Offshore operators are fighting this new prohibition.

Applebome, Peter. "Taste of Tahoe." *New York Times,* June 27, 2004, p. 23 (Metro section). Mighty M Gaming plans to reopen Monticello Raceway in New York and build a casino on the site.

Arnone, Michael. "New Courses in the Cards." *Chronicle of Higher Education,* vol. 50, no. 30, April 2, 2004, p. A6. The popularity of casino gaming and state-sponsored gaming has prompted universities to offer courses on casino management and other gaming professions.

Bagli, Charles V. "Major Step toward Casino in the Catskills." *New York Times*, June 11, 2004, p. B1. Governor George Pataki agrees to look into a Cayuga Indian claim to land in New York in exchange for a share of tribal gaming revenues.

Baker, Al. "New York Begins to Cash In with Video Lottery Terminals." *New York Times*, March 8, 2004, p. B1. Video gaming terminals at parlors near the Saratoga Springs Racetrack are turning profits, but detractors fear the spread of gambling ills.

Baker, Stephen, and Brian Grow. "Gambling Sites, This Is a Holdup." *Business Week*, vol. 3895, August 9, 2004, p. 60. Gangs of Internet racketeers are blocking access to gaming web sites if the operators don't pay extortion fees.

Bartlett, Donald L., and James B. Steele. "Wheel of Misfortune." *Time*, vol. 160, no. 25, December 16, 2002, p. 44. Indian gaming is creating a few wealthy Native Americans who wield enough power to flout federal laws. Most Native Americans are not seeing the benefits of gaming revenues.

———. "Who Gets the Money?" *Time*, vol. 160, no. 25, December 16, 2002, p. 48. Much of the profits of Indian gaming are going to outside, non-tribal investors. The money that stays within the tribes is being used to buy up land near metropolitan areas with the aim to building casinos beyond traditional reservation limits.

"Battle at Hearing on Internet Gambling Likely." *CongressDaily*, May 13, 2003, p. 8. An exemption for state-sanctioned gambling operations has U.S. legislators debating the passage of the House bill that would otherwise restrict credit issuers from transacting with Internet gambling web sites.

Binkley, Christina. "Atlantic City Gets a Vegas Makeover." *Wall Street Journal* (Eastern Edition), June 26, 2003, p. D1. Trying to entice younger tourists, Atlantic City is opening grand-scale casinos that offer more than just gambling.

———. "California Signs Gambling Accords." *Wall Street Journal* (Eastern Edition), June 22, 2004, p. A2. After agreeing to share a large percent of the profits, five California tribes are permitted increased casino gambling.

———. "Harrah's Makes a $917 Million Bet on Horseshoe." *Wall Street Journal* (Eastern Edition), September 11, 2003, p. A3. Harrah's Entertainment buys up the Horseshoe Gaming Holding Company to solidify its hold on the gambling markets in the South and Midwest.

———. "Missouri Mayor's Bet on Gambling Takes Unexpected Toll." *Wall Street Journal* (Eastern Edition), February 24, 2004, p. A1. Mayor Betty Burch suggests gambling as a way for Riverside, Missouri, to earn needed revenue. Probes into her background, however, reveal that some members of her own family suffer from problem gambling.

Binkley, Christina, Robert S. Greenberger, and John R. Wilke. "FTC to Review Casino Deals and How They Reshape Sector." *Wall Street Journal* (Eastern Edition), July 16, 2004, p. A5. After the merger of Harrah's and Caesar's and the MGM Mirage takeover of Mandalay Resorts, the Federal Trade Commission examines the impact on the gambling industry.

Bowen, John. "A Virtual Pandora's Box: What Cyberspace Gambling Prohibition Means to Terrestrial Casino Operators." *Gambling Research & Review Journal*, vol. 7, no. 1, 2003, p. 59. Land-based casino operators may think that legislation against Internet gambling will eliminate the competition, but the laws created may set a dangerous precedent that could then be used against casinos and other common forms of legalized gambling.

Briggs, Joe Bob. "Socialized Gambling." *Reason*, vol. 35, no. 3, July 2003, p. 16. In an effort to limit gambling and reap the lion's share of the profits, Illinois governor Rod Blagojevich proposes that either the state take over casino management or the casinos owners bow to a 70 percent tax of their profits.

Broder, John M. "More Slot Machines for Tribes, $1 Billion for California." *New York Times*, June 22, 2004, p. A15. Against his campaign promises, California governor Arnold Schwarzenegger allows the expansion of tribal gaming in exchange for a percentage of the profits.

Buchthal, Kristina. "Racing Clout Still Runs Strong; In Revenues and Taxes, Horses Finish Last—but Lawmakers Still Pony Up." *Crain's Chicago Business*, vol. 27, no. 47, November 22, 2004, p. 2. While horse racing in Illinois generates the least profits of the state's legalized gambling ventures, the industry still has enough clout to ensure that favorable bills pass the legislature.

Calvert, Guy, and Robert E. McCormick. "Gambling and the Good Society: Gambling May Be Risky but Government Regulation Would Be, Too." *World & I*, vol. 15, no. 7, July 2000, p. 40. Gambling is both popular and sanctioned by the government. To ban it or limit it would be a Herculean task that might engender more problems than it solves.

Carr, David. "Deal Them In." *New York Times*, September 23, 2004, p. E1. Poker has captured the nation's attention for several reasons, not the least of which is the televised broadcasting of high-stakes poker tournaments.

"Casino Project Near Chicago Is Endangered by Accusations." *New York Times*, April 14, 2004, p. A24. After the city of Rosemont, Illinois, unveiled plans to build a casino, accusations that the mayor is tied to organized crime have threatened to stall the project.

Cauchon, Dennis. "Slots Prove Lucky for Many States." *USA Today*, July 26, 2004, p. 3. The addition or expansion of slot machines at racetracks and casinos has been profitable for many state treasuries.

Claburn, Thomas. "Dicey Business." *Information Week*, vol. 1001, August 9, 2004, p. 14. Major Internet service providers are the target of a class-action lawsuit in California for tolerating Internet gambling advertisements.

"College Students Roll the Dice." *Perspective*, vol. 19, no. 9, September 2004, p. 5. Gambling among college students is typically not detrimental, but for those who are problem gamblers, academic success and mental health can suffer.

Cooper, Michael, and Al Baker. "Court Overturns State Law Allowing Racetrack Slots." *New York Times*, July 8, 2004, p. B5. An appeals court in New York declared that the state's plan to install video slots at racetracks is unconstitutional.

Cummins, David. "The Gambler." *British Medical Journal*, vol. 329, no. 7467, September 18, 2004, p. 674. The gambler discussed in this article was so addicted to gambling that his health suffered, and he died of a heart attack on his way from the hospital to his favorite gambling haunt.

Dao, James. "Two States Trying to Keep Gambling Money at Home." *New York Times*, March 22, 2004, p. A16. Legislators in Maryland and Pennsylvania are trying to pass measures to legalize gambling because they believe residents are crossing borders to visit casinos in neighboring states.

Desai, Rani, et al. "Health Correlates of Recreational Gambling in Older Adults." *American Journal of Psychiatry*, vol. 161, no. 9, September 2004, p. 1672. Unlike findings in younger age groups, older adults have not experienced negative health problems from recreational gambling.

Deverensky, Jeffrey L., Rina Gupta, and Maggie Magoon. "Adolescent Problem Gambling: Legislative and Policy Decisions." *Gambling Law Review*, vol. 8, no. 2, April 2004, p. 107. Evidence shows that problem gambling begins at a young age. Adolescents are likely to engage in unregulated gambling and even sneak into casinos or illegally partake of other forms of legal gambling.

Emshwiller, John R., and Christina Brinkley. "As Indian Casinos Grow, Regulation Raises Concerns." *Wall Street Journal* (Eastern Edition), August 23, 2004, p. A1. As tribal gaming expands, critics fear that the lack of government regulation could spell disaster.

Engwell, Douglas, Robert Hunter, and Marvin Steinberg. "Gambling and Other Risk Behaviors on University Campuses." *Journal of American College Health*, vol. 52, no. 6, May/June 2004, p. 245. A study at Connecticut State University revealed that 18 percent of male students and 4 percent of female students had some negative experience with gambling while on campus.

"Few Treatment Options for Problem Gamblers." *Health & Medicine Week*, July 5, 2004, p. 443. A survey claims that few treatment programs exist for problem gamblers and that not enough is being done to educate young people against the dangers of gambling.

Fine, Howard. "Win or Lose, Casinos, Racetracks Keep Up Fight for Slots." *Los Angeles Business Journal*, vol. 26, no. 40, October 4, 2004, p. 3. California card-house and racetrack owners vow to win the right to have slots at their establishments. Their stance is a reaction to the expansion of tribal casinos that already have the authority to run slot machines and video gaming machines.

Finley, Bill. "With Addition of Slots, Racing Is Horse of Another Color." *New York Times*, January 28, 2004, p. D2. The addition of slot machines at Saratoga Springs has brought patrons to the track, but has the character of horse racing changed if the majority of visitors are playing slots rather than watching the races?

Frey, Kelly L., and Carolyn W. Schott. "Sink or Swim." *Tennessee Bar Journal*, vol. 40, no. 7, July 2004, p. 14. Having just passed the legislature, Tennessee's new Charitable Gaming Implementation Law tolerates some form of gambling for nonprofit organizations.

"Gambling Hits the Jackpot in a Few States." *State Legislatures*, vol. 29, no. 9, October/November 2003, p. 4. Nevada and North Carolina are just two states reaping huge profits from legalized gambling. Many other states are also using gaming to fatten state treasuries.

"Gambling on the Reservation." *Christian Science Monitor*, April 23, 2004, p. 8. Lured by big profits, many Native American tribes are doing anything they can to get recognition to run casinos.

Gewertz, Catherine. "PA Wagers on Slot Machines to Pay for Property-Tax Relief." *Education Week*, vol. 23, no. 42, July 14, p. 26. Pennsylvania governor Edward G. Rendell signs legislation to allow slot machines in the state. The hope is that the gaming revenues will fund education and remove the burden from property taxes.

Grant, Peter. "More Gamblers Flock to the Web." *Wall Street Journal* (Eastern Edition), June 8, 2004, p. D6. Internet casinos and gaming sites are attracting many visitors and raking in huge profits.

Gray, Geoffrey. "A Sport Fighting for Survival." *New York Times*, June 12, 2004, p. D1. Professional jai alai has lost fans and money in recent years. Promoters are seeking new sources of gambling revenues to lure back spectators.

Grover, Ron, and Monica Roman. "Roll Them Bones." *Business Week*, vol. 3889, June 28, 2004, p. 57. Billionaire Kirk Kerkorian, the majority stockholder of MGM Mirage, launches his scheme to acquire Mandalay Resorts.

Harman, Danna. "Gambling on Tribal Ancestry." *Christian Science Monitor*, April 14, 2004, p. 15. The Pechanga Indians of California are facing infighting and feuds over tribal membership. Banishment has severe economic consequences because members share in their casino's profits.

Hart, Ariel. "South Carolina: Tribe Pursues Gambling." *New York Times*, May 6, 2004, p. A31. The Catawba Indians are petitioning the state to let them open an electronic bingo hall, but if that fails, the tribe plans to establish a video poker operation.

Hernandez, Raymond. "Connecticut Indians Denied Tribal Status, Dimming 3rd Casino's Chances." *New York Times*, June 15, 2004, p. B6. The federal government rejected the Golden Hill Paugussetts' bid for tribal status, leaving them unable to propose legally the building of a casino.

Hewitt, William L., and Barbara Beaucar. "State v. Tribe: How the Indian Gaming Controversy Began." *Social Education*, September 2003, Supplement 18, p. M3. The current controversies over Indian gaming have a history that stretches back nearly three decades.

"Indian Gaming: Tribal Leaders Tell of Benefits from Revenues." *Native American Report*, vol. 9, no. 15, September 2004, p. 147. According to several tribal leaders, Indian gaming revenues have helped reservations as well as state treasuries and local businesses.

Janes, Patricia L., and Jim Collison. "Community Leader Perceptions of the Social and Economic Impacts of Indian Gaming." *Gaming Research & Review Journal*, vol. 8, no. 1, 2004, p. 13. Eight community leaders were asked about their perceptions of the impact of the expansion of Indian gaming in Michigan. All thought the economic benefits were welcome, but many expressed concerns that the community may suffer long-term social problems.

Janke, James, and Jerry Gerlach. "Native American Casino Gambling in Wisconsin and Minnesota." *Focus on Geography*, vol. 47, no. 2, Winter 2002, p. 14. Both Wisconsin and Minnesota have seen rapid development of Indian casinos. Thanks to beneficial compacts between the states and the tribes, and the lack of non-tribal competition for gambling dollars, Indian gaming is likely to prosper in these states.

Johnston, David Clay. "A Texas Bid to Shift School Financing to 'Sin Taxes.'" *New York Times*, April 21, 2004, p. A14. Texas governor Rick Perry unveils a plan to reap education revenues from casinos, tobacco, and other vices.

Kahn, Jeremy. "Place Your Bets—On War." *Fortune*, vol. 147, no. 4, March 3, 2003, p. 48. Several Internet sites allow visitors to wager on the outcome of political events. The U.S. Defense Department is even planning to host a site that creates a fictional futures market based on political turns in the Middle East.

Kennedy, John W. "The New Gambling Goliath." *Christianity Today*, vol. 48, no. 8, August 2004, p. 50. Christian activists in California are organizing to fight the growth of Indian casinos in that state.

Kilborn, Peter T. "Casinos Revive a Town, but Poverty Persists." *New York Times*, October 20, 2002, p. 1. While Tunica, Mississippi, has benefited from casino revenues, not all residents are sharing in the profits, and poverty and crime are still rampant.

Kilgannon, Corey. "Win or Lose, a Place to Show." *New York Times*, May 15, 2004, p. B1. Off-track betting in New York is still popular but perhaps mainly for the social-club atmosphere of the betting parlors.

Krantz, Matt. "Gambling Drives Passion for Ponies." *USA Today*, June 6, 2003, p. 1B. Simulcasting and the advent of "racinos" have reshaped the horse-racing industry. Those tracks that don't adapt to these trends face obsolescence.

———. "Gaming Companies Rolling Up Big Wins." *USA Today*, June 8, 2004, p. 3B. Renewed media interest and a rise in the economy is increasing Las Vegas casino profits.

———. "Indian Tribe Bets on Diversification for Longevity." *USA Today*, January 30, 2004, p. 5B. The San Manuel Indian Nation has prospered from casino revenues, but leaders are concerned about the future of Indian gaming and are looking to diversify into other businesses to sustain economic growth.

Kurlantzick, Joshua. "Gambling's Royal Flush." *U.S. News & World Report*, May 20, 2002, p. 34. Nevada's resorts are facing competition from riverboats and tribal casinos that are giving patrons more Las Vegas–style entertainments and resort accommodations. Instead of fearing the competition, Las Vegas and Reno are fighting for tourist dollars with more attractive gambling campaigns.

Ladouceur, Robert. "Gambling: The Hidden Addiction." *Canadian Journal of Psychiatry*, vol. 49, no. 8, August 2004, p. 501. A psychologist offers a psychiatric model of gambling addiction in which gamblers' perceptions of reality are distorted.

Lampman, Jane. "In a Classic David-and-Goliath Matchup, Grass-roots Groups Push Back against the Gambling Industry: 'Enough!'" *Christian Science Monitor*, February 18, 2004, p. 15. While many state officials are backing gambling as a way of raising revenues, grassroots organizations have successfully defeated gambling measures in 30 states.

Larson, Megan. "Gambling Pays Off." *MediaWeek*, vol. 14, no. 34, September 27, 2004, p. 12. The success of televised poker tournaments has spurred cable networks to focus more attention on this popular pastime.

"Lemons in a Row." *New York Times*, July 13, 2004, p. A18. More states are contemplating plans to legalize slot machines to pay for education costs.

Levine, Samantha. "Betting the Budget." *U.S. News & World Report*, vol. 134, no. 10, March 31, 2003, p. 55. Because of a weak economy and a fear of raising taxes, state legislatures are reviewing three times as many gambling revenue bills in 2003 than in the previous year. Not everyone, however, is sure that gambling is the panacea to budget deficits.

Maich, Steve. "The Folly of the Field Bet." *Maclean's*, vol. 117, no. 38, September 20, 2004, p. 26. The stock market and gambling have much in common, including the types of people who risk their money.

Marcial, Gene G. "As Gambling Grows, So Does Wells-Gardner." *Business Week*, vol. 3894, August 2, 2004, p. 98. A major supplier of video gaming machines earns more than $12 million in sales but posts profits of only 4 cents.

Marshall, Patrick. "Gambling in America." *CQ Researcher*, vol. 13, no. 9, March 7, 2003, p. 203. Gambling is immensely popular and pervasive in America. While states try to benefit from gaming revenues, critics are concerned that the costs may be higher than the gains.

Martin, Edward. "Reservations: Gambling Has Changed Life for the Cherokee. Some Say They've Lost More than They've Won." *Business North Carolina*, vol. 24, no. 3, March 2004, p. 44. Clans within the Cherokee Nation are split on the issue of gambling. The more religious clans will not touch the revenues brought in by the tribe's casinos.

"Mass. Agency Launches Gambling Awareness Campaign." *Alcoholism & Drug Abuse Weekly*, vol. 16, no. 24, June 21, 2004, p. 7. The Massachusetts Council on Compulsive Gambling stages a public-service campaign.

McDonald, Marci. "Betting the House." *U.S. News & World Report*, vol. 129, no. 15, October 16, 2000, p. 44. Attempts to dissuade credit card companies from transacting with Internet gaming sites may simply prompt some new form of cybercash that will skirt this attempt to halt the growing industry.

McGowan, Richard A. "Snake Eyes or a Seven?" *America*, vol. 189, no. 9, September 29, 2003, p. 12. Gambling interests are tempting states with the promise that gambling revenues will fix budget deficits. Once states get hooked on this idea, though, they come to rely on gambling as a necessary source of income.

McLaughlin, Abraham. "Despite Gambling's Riches, States Play Cautiously." *Christian Science Monitor*, April 22, 2003, p. 1. While 34 states have expanded gambling Measures on the table, few have made any progress due to fears of the resulting social costs.

Mercer, Gordon E., et al. "Policy Point-Counterpoint: State Lotteries." *International Social Science Review*, vol. 79, no. 1–2, 2004, p. 63. Advocates of state lotteries insist that without the revenues, public works and education funding would suffer. Detractors say they are a regressive form of taxation that has no overall benefit to public funds.

Miller, Donald E. "Schools Lose out in Lotteries." *USA Today*, April 15, 2004, p. 13A. While legislatures sell constituents on gambling measures by promising that the income will be used to fund education, some of the revenues are being used to pay for other, nonacademic projects.

Miller, Matthew. "House Wins." *Forbes*, vol. 174, no. 2, July 26, 2004, p. 62. The MGM Mirage takeover of Mandalay Resort Group in 2004 has left

MGM with control of half the hotel rooms and more than a third of the games in Las Vegas.

Miller, Scott, and Christina Binkley. "Trade Body Rules against U.S. Ban on Web Gambling." *Wall Street Journal* (Eastern Edition), March 25, 2004, p. A2. The World Trade Organization upheld claims by Antigua and Barbuda that the U.S. ban on Internet gambling was unfairly damaging their economies.

Murphy, Dean E., Carolyn Marshall, and Nick Madigan. "California Deal Authorizes Huge Casino Near Oakland." *New York Times*, August 20, 2004, p. A14. Governor Arnold Schwarzenegger has signed a deal to allow the Pomono Indians to build the first urban casino in California.

Napolitano, Jo. "Plan for Indian Casino Splits Illinois Town." *New York Times*, June 19, 2004, p. A10. Despite promises of revenues and jobs, a local interest group fights the building of a casino in Illinois.

Nelson, Michael, and John Lyman Mason. "The Politics of Gambling in the South." *Political Science Quarterly*, vol. 118, no. 4, Winter 2003/2004, p. 645. The gambling industry in the South wields strong political clout—enough to floor grassroots resistance movements and topple uncooperative office holders.

Nguyen, Tomson H. "The Business of Illegal Gambling: An Examination of the Gambling Business of Vietnamese Cafés." *Deviant Behavior*, vol. 25, no. 5, September/October 2004, p. 451. Vietnamese cafes in Southern California have special video poker machines that the café owners can illegally switch to a full-range gambling mode.

Norton, Stephen J., and Jon Cranford. "WTO Rule on Gambling Ban Draws Fire." *CQ Weekly*, vol. 62, no. 14, April 3, 2004, p. 784. U.S. trade officials speak out against the World Trade Organization's decision that banning Internet gambling sites in America is an unfair trade policy.

O'Brien, Timothy L., and Eric Dash. "The Midas Touch, with Spin on It." *New York Times*, September 8, 2004, p. C1. Donald Trump's businesses are showing warning signs of financial difficulties. Among them, his casinos are filing for bankruptcy protection.

———. "Trump Must Ante Up $55 Million to Hold on to 25% of His Casino." *New York Times*, August 11, 2004, p. C1. With Trump Hotels and Casino Resorts in bankruptcy, Trump will have to invest his own money to save his stake in the business.

Palmeri, Christopher. "Little Guys with Big Plans for Vegas." *Business Week*, vol. 3894, August 2, 2004, p. 49. The profits of independent casino owners are examined in the wake of corporate sales and takeovers in Las Vegas.

Palmeri, Christopher, and Ira Sager. "How Casinos Are Hogging the Chips." *Business Week*, vol. 3853, October 13, 2003, p. 16. California governor Arnold Schwarzenegger demands that tribal casinos no longer be given the tax concessions afforded by previous administrations.

"Panel Approves Legislation Aimed at Curbing Internet Gambling." *CongressDaily*, July 31, 2003, p. 8. The U.S. Senate Banking Committee passes legislation to curb Internet gambling by prohibiting credit institutions from transacting with gambling sites.

Parke, Adrian, and Mark Griffiths. "Aggressive Behavior in Slot Machine Gamblers: A Preliminary Observational Study." *Psychological Reports*, vol. 95, no. 1, August 2004, p. 109. A study finds that slot machine players are likely to exhibit aggressive behavior as they gamble. This supports other evidence of a possible link between gambling and aggression.

Peterson, Iver. "Atlantic City Seeks New Image: Las Vegas's." *New York Times*, May 9, 2004, p. 28. New Jersey plans to remake Atlantic City into a shopping, tourist, and gambling community that will be modeled on Las Vegas.

———. "Despite Promise of Easy Money, Indian Casinos Meet Resistance." *New York Times*, February 1, 2004, p. 29 (Metro Section). Antigambling lobbies have repealed the charitable gaming laws in Connecticut in hopes of thwarting Native Americans from using them to spread casino gambling. Now these groups are fighting casino expansion head-on.

———. "Reluctantly, a Tribe Starts to See Casinos as Being Imperative." *New York Times*, May 9, 2003, p. A1. After years of declaring itself a nongaming tribe, the Cayuga Nation of New York is contracting to build a casino.

———. "Would-Be Tribes Entice Investors." *New York Times*, March 29, 2004, p. A1. Native American tribes seeking recognition from the federal government are being watched by investors who anticipate that gambling ventures will follow.

Piner, Judie M., and Thomas W. Paradis. "Beyond the Casino: Sustainable Tourism and Cultural Development on Native American Lands." *Tourism Geographies*, vol. 6, no. 1, February 2004, p. 80. Although many Native American tribes view casino gambling as a means of empowerment, gaming should be only one facet of a larger economic and cultural plan.

"Problem Gambling." *Harvard Mental Health Letter.* Vol. 20, no. 9, March 2004, p. 1. Problem gambling is on the rise and can severely impact career and home environments. Treatment options mirror other addiction therapies.

"Ralph Reed Attracts Indian Casino Cash, Hypocrisy Charges." *Church & State*, vol. 57, no. 8, September 2004, p. 17. A former director of the Christian Coalition once condemned the spread of gambling, but now he works as a political consultant for a Native American tribe in Louisiana that is trying to stifle opposing casino competition.

Ramirez, Anthony. "Salamanca: Senecas Open Second Casino." *New York Times*, May 3, 2004, p. B6. The Seneca tribe unveils its second casino in New York.

"Reid Blocks Bill Changing Indian Gaming Law Revisions." *CongressDaily*, April 7, 2004, p. 8. Senate Minority Whip Harry Reid blocked consideration of a bill that would make changes to the Indian Gaming Regulatory Act. Reid maintains the bill would deprive the states of potential revenues.

Richard, Alan. "States Bet on Gambling to Raise Money for Schools." *Education Week*, vol. 23, no. 26, March 10, 2004, p. 18. States suggest that gambling revenues could fund education, but naysayers argue that the income may be unstable and lead to other social ills.

Richtel, Matt. "An Industry That Dares Not Meet in the Country of Its Best Customers." *New York Times*, May 17, 2004, p. C4. The federal government is taking action against Internet casinos and sports wagering sites. Even some Internet servers are buckling to the pressure and ousting gambling sites.

———. "Companies Aiding Internet Gambling Feel U.S. Pressure." *New York Times*, March 15, 2004, p. A1. The Justice Department is cracking down on companies doing business with Internet gambling sites. Major corporations have bowed to threats that they could face "aiding and abetting" charges in future lawsuits.

———. "Electronic Arts to Stop Advertising for Online Casinos on Its Web Site." *New York Times*, June 12, 2004, p. C1. The video game company Electronic Arts announces that it will ban gambling ads from its web site after federal investigators target online gaming.

———. "Lawsuit Claims Free Speech for Online Casino Ads." *New York Times*, August 23, 2004, p. C3. Casino City, an Internet casino advertiser, sues the Justice Department and claims that gambling ads fall under the protection of the Second Amendment.

———. "Web Engines Plan to End Online Ads for Gambling." *New York Times*, April 5, 2004, p. C1. Internet service providers Yahoo! and Google agree to ban gambling ads on their sites in the United States.

Rivlin, Gary, and Richard Barnes. "The Chrome-Shiny, Lights-Flashing, Wheel-Spinning, Touch-Screened, Drew-Carey-Wisecracking, Video-Playing, 'Sound Events'-Packed, Pulse-Quickening Bandit." *New York Times Magazine*, May 9, 2004, p. 42. The slot machine remains one of the most popular forms of gambling in America.

Rose, I. Nelson. "Gambling and the Law: Is It Bingo, or a Slot Machine?" *Gaming Law Review*, vol. 7, no. 2, April 2003, p. 99. A new video version of bingo has evaded congressional restrictions, giving Native American bingo parlors the feel of a casino.

Rotter, Joseph C. "Curing Problem of Pathological Gambling: Don't Bet on It." *Family Journal*, vol. 12, no. 1, January 2004, p. 37. A review of the literature on pathological gambling provides the history of gambling's expansion and the efforts to curtail the problems of addictive gambling behavior.

Santora, Marc. "Gambling Foes Try to Curb Growth of Connecticut's 2 Casino Giants." *New York Times*, September 4, 2003, p. B1. Regional opposition is trying to halt the expansion of tribal casinos in Connecticut.
———. "Pataki Proposes the Creation of a State Gambling Commission." *New York Times*, May 28, 2004, p. B6. New York governor George Pataki introduces a plan to create a state gaming commission that would change the way in which gambling is monitored.
Seligman, Dan. "In Defense of Gambling." *Forbes*, vol. 171, no. 13, June 23, 2003, p. 86. Though critics exaggerate the social costs of gambling, most Americans gamble responsibly. Problem gambling crusaders lack hard evidence to show that gambling should be curbed for the good of society.
Selim, Jocelyn. "Win Some, Lose More." *Discover*, vol. 25, no. 8, August 2004, p. 14. Studies suggest that problem gamblers may be more rewarded by the depressive feeling of losing than the thrill of winning.
Shaffer, Howard J., and Rachel Kidman. "Shifting Perspectives on Gambling and Addiction." *Journal of Gambling Studies*, vol. 19, no. 1, Spring 2003, p. 1. Since it is unclear whether compulsive gambling is an addiction, psychologists approach the problem with a variety of treatment strategies.
Shigley, Paul. "Concerns Grow with Indian Casinos: Vegas-style Resorts Moving into State's Urban Areas." *California Planning & Development Report*, vol. 18, no. 7, July 2003, p. 1. Some Native American tribes in California are shopping for land to build casinos near urban areas. While some local officials welcome the revenues, others fear the problems that casinos could bring to these areas.
Silverman, Fran. "Gambling for Classes." *District Administration*, vol. 40, no. 2, February 2004, p. 10. Using lottery proceeds to fund education remains a controversial issue in America. The promise of aiding schools appears worthy, but critics ask how much of the funds are actually being channeled into the school system.
Sirhal, Maureen. "Justice Official Raises Questions about Online Gaming Bill." *CongressDaily*, March 18, 2003, p. 6. Members of the U.S. Department of Justice are concerned that the antigambling bills in Congress do not give law enforcement the latitude it needs to curb illegal gambling.
"States Resist More Gambling." *Christian Science Monitor*, June 23, 2004, p. 8. Courts, legislatures, and grassroots organizations are stymieing gambling initiatives in many states.
Stein, Joel, and Laura A. Locke. "The Strip Is Back!" *Time*, vol. 164, no. 4, July 26, 2004, p. 22. The disposable income of young people is bolstering profits of casinos and other commercial industries in Las Vegas.
Stitt, Grant B., Mark Nichols, and David Giacopassi. "Does the Presence of Casinos Increase Crime? An Examination of Casino and Control Communities." *Crime & Delinquency*, vol. 49, no. 2, April 2003, p. 253. A study

of communities with and without casinos reveals no distinct differences in crime statistics.

Stone, Peter H. "A New Twist on Casino Lobbying." *National Journal*, vol. 36, no. 34, August 21, 2004, p. 2,497. Heated competition between rival gaming tribes in the United States has turned the spotlight on the powerful lobbying organizations of the tribal casinos.

———. "Odd Bedfellows on Internet Betting." *National Journal*, vol. 35, no. 24, June 14, 2003, p. 1,862. Unlikely allies have joined together to either lobby for or against the Internet gambling bill that is up for vote in the House of Representatives.

Strasser, Jason. "Poker that Needs No Poker Face." *Business Week*, vol. 3896, August 16, 2004, p. 99. Poker has increased in popularity, especially online where, on some of the largest sites, millions of dollars are wagered each day.

"Student Gambling: Studies Answer 'Who?' but Not 'How Much?'" *National On-Campus Report*, vol. 32, no. 14, July 15, 2004, p. 3. Recent studies on college gambling identify some problem gamblers but are limited in addressing other concerns about gambling among students.

"Survey Finds Widespread Gambling among U.S. Adults." *Alcoholism & Drug Abuse Weekly*, vol. 15, no. 3, January 20, 2003, p. 5. A study indicates that American adults are gambling more than in past years. The study also examines the economic background of the most frequent players and the degree to which problem gambling afflicts the lowest income players.

"Survey Suggests Fewer Gambling Problems Among College Students." *Alcoholism & Drug Abuse Weekly*, vol. 16, no. 20, May 17, 2004, p. 3. A study concludes that student gambling is not as rampant as some have assumed.

Sweeney, James P. "A High-Stakes Gamble." *California Journal*, vol. 35, no. 7, July 2004, p. 28. Measures to increase tribal gaming in California are up for vote in California.

"Taking Chances: Mid-western Casinos." *The Economist* (U.S.), vol. 371, no. 8372, April 24, 2004, p. 33. The governors of Illinois and Indiana are attracted to the revenues that new casinos could bring to their states, but accusations of crime syndicate involvement and muddled business deals are stalling efforts to get casino plans finalized.

Timmons, Heather. "Can Slot Machines Rescue Racing?" *Business Week*, December 2, 2002, p. 76. Several U.S. racetracks have built video gaming halls to bring in more patrons. The increased proceeds of these video slots are being used to create bigger racing purses.

Toneatto, Tony, and Goldie Millar. "Assessing and Treating Problem Gambling: Empirical Status and Promising Trends." *Canadian Journal of Psychiatry*, vol. 49, no. 8, August 2004, p. 517. The diagnosis and treatment of problem gambling is improving, but many of the contributing factors are still unclear or poorly measured.

"Tribes Challenge Schwarzenegger on Gambling." *New York Times*, July 18, 2004, p. 24. A group of Native Americans is proposing a bill that will give tribes free reign in expanding gambling operations without acquiescing to Governor Arnold Schwarzenegger's new deal to take more tribal gaming profits.

Viser, Matt. "Rhode Island: Court Rules against Casino." *New York Times*, August 13, 2004, p. A14. Rhode Island's Supreme Court rules that creating legislation to approve a resort casino is unconstitutional.

Von Zielbauer, Paul. "Hartford Moves to Curb Gambling and Stop a Casino." *New York Times*, January 7, 2003, p. B1. The Connecticut State Legislature has voted to ban Las Vegas Nights and other charity games in an attempt to thwart Indian tribes' efforts to build casinos that feature Las Vegas–type games.

Walters, Lawrence G. "Advertising Online Casinos: An Analysis of the Legal Rights and Risks." *Gaming Law Review*, vol. 7, no. 2, April 2003, p. 111. The government crackdown on online casino advertisers engenders debate about the possible encroachment on the right to free speech.

Weir, Tom. "Online Sports Betting Spins out of Control." *USA Today*, August 22, 2003, p. A1. Many Americans—including students and athletes—are losing millions on online sports betting. The secrecy afforded by Internet gambling makes the problem hard to detect before financial ruin sets in.

Welte, John W., et al. "Gambling Participation in the U.S.—Results from a National Survey." *Journal of Gambling Studies*, vol. 18, no. 4, Winter 2002, p. 313. A phone survey reveals the popularity of various forms of legalized gambling. It also examines the age and racial and economic background of problem gamblers.

———. "Risk Factors for Pathological Gambling." *Addictive Behaviors*, vol. 29, no. 2, February 2004, p. 323. Several risk factors—such as substance abuse, socioeconomic status, and gambling patterns—may predicate an individual's likelihood to suffer from problem gambling.

Whalen, Bill. "The New Special Interest." *Campaigns & Elections*, vol. 25, no. 6, July 2004, p. 19. Wealthy Indian gaming tribes in the United States have become powerful lobbying groups with enough clout to be courted by presidential candidates.

Will, George. "'Electronic Morphine': Gambling Has Been a Common Feature of American Life Forever, but for a Long Time It Was Broadly Considered a Sin. Now It Is a Social Policy." *Newsweek*, November 15, 2002, p. 92. Americans should be troubled that the nation is host to many problem gamblers, yet the government actively promotes gambling and is often hog-tied when trying to legislate against gambling's expansion.

York, Anthony. "Native-American Tribes." *California Journal*, vol. 35, no. 9, September 2004, p. 43. The growth of tribal gaming has given California's tribes more political power. Governor Arnold Schwarzenegger is trying to negotiate new deals with gaming tribes.

Zampirripa, Mark, and Harvey N. Chin. "Should State Governments Be in the Lottery Business?" *CQ Researcher*, vol. 13, no. 9, March 7, 2003, p. 217. States raise large amounts of money through lotteries, but critics charge that governments have a moral and legal responsibility to refrain from entering the business realm where they must entice citizens to play.

INTERNET DOCUMENTS

American Gaming Association (AGA). "Annual Survey Shows More Americans Visiting Casinos." American Gaming Association web site. Available online. URL: http://www.americangaming.org/Press/press_releases/press_detail.cfv?ID=283. Posted May 27, 2004. According to this press release, an AGA survey from 2004 found that more than 53 million Americans visited U.S. casinos in 2003. The report also cites studies that indicate that the majority of Americans believe gambling is an acceptable behavior.

———. "Study Shows Gaming Industry Leading the Way in Creating Employment Opportunities for Minorities." American Gaming Association web site. Available online. URL: http://www.americangaming.org/Press/press_releases/press_detail.cfv?ID=256. Posted March 9, 2004. In this press release, the AGA asserts that the gaming industry employs more minorities in executive and service positions that any other business in the United States.

Bell, Tom W. "Internet Gambling: Prohibition v. Legalization." Cato Institute web site. Available online. URL: http://www.cato.org/testimony/ct-tb052198.html. Posted May 21, 1998. Internet gambling poses many obstacles to prohibition policies. It is ubiquitous and can evade domestic laws by using foreign Internet domains. Therefore, it is better to legalize Internet gambling, which would allow regulation and invite healthy competition with other forms of legitimized gambling.

California Nations Indian Gaming Association (CNIGA). "California's Gaming Tribes Share More Than $30 Million with Other Tribes." California Nations Indian Gaming Association web site. Available online. URL: http://www.cniga.com/media/pressrelease_detail.php?id=6. Posted August 28, 2001. In this press release, CNIGA reveals the results of its agreement to share the profits of successful gaming tribes with nongaming or small-scale gaming tribes throughout the state of California.

———. "Growth in Tribal Employment Nears 20 Percent." California Nations Indian Gaming Association web site. Available online. URL: http://www.cniga.com/media/pressrelease_detail.php?id=34. Posted August 12, 2003. This brief press release claims that, according to California government employment figures, tribal governments are showing a growth in job rates that exceed those posted by all other private sector businesses.

———. "*Time* Misses the Point of Tribal Government Gaming." California Nations Indian Gaming Association web site. Available online. URL: http://www.cniga.com/media/pressrelease_detail.php?id=18. Posted December 13, 2002. In response to a *Time* magazine cover story that was critical of Indian gaming, CNIGA refutes some of the errors in the article and explains how the Indian Gaming Regulatory Act of 1988 gave Native Americans back their sovereignty and has enhanced tribal self-reliance after decades of government and industry neglect.

Chambers, Wally. "2004 State of the Industry Report." American Gaming Association web site. Available online. URL: http://www.americangaming.org/Press/speeches/speeches_detail.cfv?ID=317. Posted December 7, 2004. At a governors' conference, the vice president of the AGA maintains that recent casino mergers and plans for more elaborate casino complexes in Nevada illustrate that the industry is healthy and prospering.

Fahrenkopf, Frank J., Jr. "Testimony before the Maryland House Ways & Means Committee." American Gaming Association web site. Available online. URL: http://www.americangaming.org/Press/speeches/speeches_detail.cfv?ID=225. Posted August 19, 2003. The president of the AGA enumerates the positive impact of the gambling industry on state and local treasuries and on job prospects in host communities. He also debunks what he believes are popular myths about the presumed negative social consequences of gambling.

———. "Unifying the Industry on Responsible Gaming." American Gaming Association web site. Available online. URL: http://www.americangaming.org/Press/speeches/speeches_detail.cfv?ID=312. Posted November 4, 2004. In this radio conference testimony, the president of the AGA states that the gaming industry recognizes that problem gambling is a detriment to personal lives and communities. He maintains that the AGA and other industry affiliates are promoting responsible gaming and helping to disseminate information about treatment programs for problem gamblers.

Institute of Governmental Studies at the University of California. "Indian Gaming in California." Institute of Governmental Studies Library web site. Available online. URL: http://www.igs.berkeley.edu/library/htIndianGaming.htm. Posted November 2004. This web document lays out a thorough history of tribal gaming in California.

Kelly, Timothy A. "Gambling Backlash: Time for a Moratorium on Casino and Lottery Expansion." Family Research Council web site. Available online. URL: http://www.frc.org/get.cfm?i=IS00C1. Archived March 13, 2003. Government promotion of gambling coupled with its widespread availability is making gambling an acceptable phenomenon in American society. With all the problems inherent to gambling, the country's policy makers must have the courage to stall gambling's growth and reassess its value to America.

Nash, Doug. "Indian Gaming." FindLaw web site. URL: http://profs.lp.findlaw.com/gaming. Copyright 1999. Downloaded June 17, 2004. The future of Indian gaming will continue to be based on the strength and resilience of the Indian Gaming Regulatory Act of 1988. Since that document has stood against all challenges thus far, Indian gaming is likely to keep expanding.

National Coalition Against Legalized Gambling (NCALG). "Facts about Gambling and Addiction." National Coalition Against Legalized Gambling web site. Available online. URL: http://www.ncalg.org/library/pdf/Facts%20about%20Gambling%20and%20Addiction1.pdf. Posted June 28, 2004. This fact sheet cites various research reports that claim that gambling can be an addictive behavior. NCALG maintains that problem gambling affects thousands of people and that the gaming industry has come to rely on profits generated by addicted players.

———. "Legalized Gambling: The Inside Story." National Coalition Against Legalized Gambling web site. Available online. URL: http://www.ncalg.org/library/pdf/Inside%20Story%20brochure.pdf. Posted September 2004. This brief brochure lists many of the presumed ills of legalized gambling, including rising crime rates and damage to local economies.

———. "Lottery Fact Sheet." National Coalition Against Legalized Gambling web site. Available online. URL: http://www.ncalg.org/library/pdf/NCALG%20Lottery%20Fact%20Sheet1.pdf. Posted July 19, 2004. This fact sheet cites various authorities who have commented on how state lotteries have greatly expanded gambling in America and promoted an attitude that gambling is good for society. NCALG then claims that, in reality, lotteries prey on low-income players, and the funds generated do not significantly affect the social services (such as education) to which they are allocated.

———. "The Tide of Indian Gambling Begins to Turn." National Coalition Against Legalized Gambling web site. Available online. URL: http://www.ncalg.org/library/pdf/NCALG%20June%2004%20Newsletter.pdf. Posted June 2004. This newsletter argues that the right to Native American tribal sovereignty is being abused by tribes who are using the freedom to build casinos across the country—often without consulting the nearby communities that must contend with the social and economic impact of these huge gambling complexes. However, NCALG spokesman Guy C. Clark is optimistic that current government leaders will reassess the open-door policies toward Indian gaming.

———. "The True Face of Gambling." National Coalition Against Legalized Gambling web site. Available online. URL: http://www.ncalg.org/library/pdf/August%2004%20newsletter.pdf. Posted August 2004. This newsletter recounts how in one Kansas family, a man committed suicide over gambling addiction, his sister had to declare bankruptcy to pay off her own gambling debts, and her son ended up working for a local casino and was subsequently jailed for embezzling funds. In response to such tragedies, NCALG pushes legislators to stand up against gambling lobbies and address the dangers of legalized gambling.

Palmeri, Christopher. "Now, Big Casinos Bet on the Indians." *Business Week Online*. Available online. URL: http://www.businessweek.com/bwdaily/dnflash/jun2004/nf20040614_5430_db035.htm. Posted June 15, 2004. Many Native American casinos are run by large corporations that generate millions of dollars in revenue.

Spilde, Katherine A. "Why Media Matters: Indian Gaming in the News." National Indian Gaming Association web site. Available online. URL: http://www.indiangaming.org/library/newsletters/newsletter_04-01.html. Posted April 2001. The former director of research of the National Indian Gaming Association argues that the media attention on Indian gaming is significant since it helps determine how Native Americans are perceived by the public, and it can be used to substantiate claims made by politicians who are either for or against the expansion of Indian gaming.

Strumpf, Koleman. "Why Prohibitions on Internet Gambling Won't Work." Cato Institute web site. Available online. URL: http://www.cato.org/dailys/02-19-04.html. Posted February 19, 2004. Attempts to ban Internet gambling will ultimately fail because prohibition will entice more public curiosity and will simply drive purveyors to offshore locations where they can evade regulation and accountability.

VIDEOS

Dubrowsky, Ed. *Handling Gambling* (1998). Video Knowledge Learning Library, VHS, 1998. Educator and media producer Ed Dubrowsky examines the question of whether gambling can be addictive, and if so, who should ultimately regulate the problem.

Gambling Mania (1999). A&E Entertainment, VHS, 2000. An episode of the popular History Channel cable show *The Twentieth Century with Mike Wallace*, this documentary looks into the expansion of gambling in America in the late 20th century. Interviewing proponents and detractors of the gambling industry, the program tries to show why gambling has become such a popular and accepted part of American culture.

High Rollers: A History of Gambling (2001). A&E Home Video, VHS, 2001. Part of the A&E cable channel's *Time Machine* series, this two-hour video edition provides an overview history of gambling in the United States since the early 17th century. It also traces the arguments for and against the continuance of gambling in America.

Investigative Reports: Teen Gambling (1991). A&E Home Video, VHS, 1991. Aired as part of the popular *Investigative Reports* series on the A&E cable channel, this video episode discusses the rise of teen gambling in America. The show is primarily composed of interviews with teenagers who roll dice at school, place wagers at the track, and partake of other legal and illegal forms of gambling.

CHAPTER 8

ORGANIZATIONS AND AGENCIES

This chapter provides a list of advocacy organizations, government agencies, Native American associations, and other collectives that are connected to the issue of legalized gambling in America. Each listing will provide (if available) the organization's web site (URL) and e-mail address, phone and fax numbers, and postal address. The contact information entries are followed by a brief description of the organization's mission or purpose.

Researchers should be aware that contact information for an organization might change over time as the group relocates its headquarters or changes its Internet address. Occasionally, an organization may disband entirely or become dormant for a time. The best method of keeping up with such changes is to try and locate the desired organization through an Internet search engine and check the most recent posting of its contact information.

NATIONAL ORGANIZATIONS

American Gaming Association (AGA)
URL: http://www.americangaming.org
E-mail: info@americangaming.org
Phone: (202) 637-6500
Fax: (202) 637-6507
555 13th Street, NW
Suite 1010 East
Washington, DC 20004

The AGA was founded in 1995 to represent the interests of the commercial gaming industry. As such, the AGA has organized research and compiled facts about gaming in America and presented these to the general public, government officials, and the media with the aim of maintaining a positive image for the industry. The AGA is also committed to addressing troubling issues such as problem gambling and underage gambling in hopes of alleviating their burden on society.

The association has published a few academic studies of the gaming industry and its social impact. These are available for free to AGA members and for a fee to nonmembers. In addition to these publications, the AGA offers many press releases and articles that can be read or downloaded free from its web site.

American Quarter Horse Association (AQHA)
Phone: (806) 376-4811
P.O. Box 200
Amarillo, TX 79168
The AQHA is devoted to interest in the quarter horse. The AQHA maintains a registry of quarter horses and offers other services to those involved in breeding, riding, and racing the breed. The AQHA web site has racing information, including venues, race dates, and prizes. The organization also publishes several magazines, one of which is the *American Quarter Horse Racing Journal.*

Association of Racing Commissioners International (ARCI)
URL: http://www.arci.com
E-mail: support@arci.com
Phone: (859) 224-7070
Fax: (859) 224-7071
2343 Alexandria Drive
Suite 200
Lexington, KY 40504
Begun in 1934, ARCI aims to enforce a uniform code of rules and regulations (including those related to pari-mutuel wagering) in the sports of horse racing, greyhound racing, and jai alai. Twenty-one U.S. states and five foreign territories are currently members of the organization. The Association of Racing Commissioners International publishes newsletters, fact sheets, and rulebooks. Some of these can be downloaded free from the ARCI web site; others are available only to paying members of the organization.

The Cato Institute
URL: http://www.cato.org
E-mail: webmaster@cato.org
Phone: (202) 842-0200
Fax: (202) 842-3490
1000 Massachusetts Avenue, NW
Washington, DC 20001-5403
Founded in 1977, the Cato Institute is a nonprofit public-policy research foundation. Its libertarian agenda is to promote public debate about the virtues of personal liberty and limited government. The organization has voiced its opinion on a variety of public-policy issues, including legalized gambling. The institute's web site has archived a handful of gambling policy analysis reports and other gambling-related articles written by Cato members.

Focus on the Family
URL: http://www.family.org
Phone: (800) 232-6459
Colorado Springs, CO 80995
Begun in 1977, Focus on the Family is a nonprofit Christian organization that seeks to strengthen traditional values and preserve the institution of the family. The organization publishes a magazine entitled *Focus on the Family*, broadcasts a radio program, and orchestrates a variety of ministries that contend with family issues, community outreach, and government policy. Focus on the

Family stands firmly against legalized gambling, and the "Focus on Social Issues" section of its web site has many fact sheets and opinion pieces on the ills of gambling—especially on what it views as the dangers of compulsive gambling and its destructive effects on families. The organization also publishes books, audiotapes, and videos on problem gambling, and these materials are available for a "suggested donation" fee.

Gamblers Anonymous (GA)
URL: http://www.gamblersanonymous.org
E-mail: isomain@gamblersanonymous.org
Phone: (213) 386-8789
Fax: (213) 386-0030
P.O. Box 17173
Los Angeles, CA 90017

Gamblers Anonymous is a self-supporting fellowship of men and women who come together to share their personal experiences with problem gambling. GA is not affiliated with any religious organization, but, according to the group's mission statement, its 12-step recovery program is based on "ancient spiritual principles and rooted in sound medical therapy." GA also espouses no cause beyond the desire to help its members deal with and overcome the compulsion to gamble.

Gamblers Anonymous has branches in all 50 states and in 36 countries. Its web site outlines the organization's 12-step program and provides a list of 20 questions that gamblers can use to evaluate whether their own gambling has become problematic. GA also publishes some books, pamphlets, and handouts that can be obtained by contacting the Gam-Anon International Service Office for an order form (Gam-Anon International Service Office, Inc., P.O. Box 157, Whitestone, NY 11357; Phone: (718) 352-1671; Fax: 718-746-2571; E-mail: info3@gam-anon.org).

Gambler's Book Club
URL: http://www.gamblersbook.com
E-mail: gamble@lasvegas.net
Phone: (702) 382-7555
Fax: (702) 382-7594
630 South 11th Street
Las Vegas, NV 89101

In business since 1964, the Gambler's Book Club is the largest retail store devoted to selling books, videos, and computer software on gambling. All materials can be ordered online or through toll-free phone numbers provided on the store's web site.

Harness Tracks of America (HTA)
URL: http://www.harnesstracks.com
E-mail: info@harnesstracks.com
Phone: (520) 529-2525
Fax: (520) 529-3235
4640 East Sunrise
Suite 200
Tucson, AZ 85718

HTA is an industry organization that promotes the sport of harness racing. The HTA is concerned with upholding the integrity of the sport, facilitating relations between track operators and other membership corporations, and educating the general public about harness racing and its economic impact. The HTA web site provides some general information on the sport to nonmembers; it also has an archive of press releases about racing events and achievements.

Harvard Medical School Division on Addictions
URL: http://www.hms.harvard.edu/doa
E-mail: doa@hms.harvard.edu
Phone: (617) 384-9030
Fax: (617) 384-9023
The Landmark Center
401 Park Drive
2nd Floor East
Boston, MA 02215

Established in 1990, the Harvard School on Addictions is an educational facility that conducts research on various addictive behaviors and then makes this information public. The purpose of the department is to reduce the impact of addictive behaviors on individuals and society. The school's web site has an archive of some articles, publications, and other research material related to gambling. In 2000, the school opened the Institute for Research on Pathological Gambling and Related Disorders (see next entry). This subsidiary program now contends with the bulk of Harvard's research on gambling addiction issues.

Institute for Research on Pathological Gambling and Related Disorders
URL: http://www.hms.harvard.edu/doa/institute/index.htm
Phone: (617) 384-9028
Fax: (617) 384-9023
The Landmark Center
401 Park Drive
2nd Floor East
Boston, MA 02215

Set up in 2000, the Institute for Research on Pathological Gambling and Related Disorders is a program within the Harvard Medical School Division on Addictions. The program's aim is to conduct research and publish data on the impact of pathological gambling on individuals, the economy, and society. The institute publishes the free weekly online research journal *WAGER* (http://www.basisonline.org), which keeps track of studies and new information on problem gambling.

Institute for the Study of Gambling and Commercial Gaming
URL: http://www.unr.edu/gaming/index.asp
Phone: (775) 784-1442
Fax: (775) 784-1057
College of Business Administration
University of Nevada
Reno, NV 89557-0208

Established by the University of Reno in 1989, the Institute for the Study of Gambling and Commercial Gaming was the first academic program in the United States geared toward an understanding of the gaming industry. While supporting research on various gambling issues, the institute also conducts classes on the business of gaming operation and management. The institute's web site provides access to several articles and conference papers by institute faculty.

Interactive Gaming Council (IGC)
URL: http://www.igcouncil.org
E-mail: admin@igcouncil.org
Phone: (604) 732-3833
Fax: (604) 732-3866
2906 West Broadway
Suite 175
Vancouver, British Columbia
V6K 2G8
Canada
The IGC is a nonprofit organization that provides a forum to discuss issues related to Internet gaming. The IGC was originally formed in the United States in 1996 but relocated to Canada in 2000. IGC members have testified before the U.S. Congress on matters relating to Internet gaming in hopes that such gaming could be legalized and regulated in America (where it is currently outlawed). The IGC web site has archives of news items and council member testimonies on Internet gaming. It also has a list of suggestions concerning how to ensure the legitimacy of Internet gaming sites.

International Association of Gaming Attorneys (IAGA)
URL: http://www.theiaga.org:7080/pls/lmacc/iagasys.iagahome
E-mail: iaga@cox.net
Phone: (702) 804-1492
Fax: (702) 233-8414
1930 Village Center Circle
Suite 3
Box 462
Las Vegas, NV 89134
The IAGA is a nonprofit organization of professionals interested in the study of gaming law. The IAGA web site posts some articles on topical issues concerning gaming law.

The Jockey Club
URL: http://www.jockeyclub.com/default.asp
Phone: (212) 371-5970
Fax: (212) 371-6123
40 East 52nd Street
New York, NY 10022
Formed in 1894, the Jockey Club is an industry organization dedicated to the breeding and racing of thoroughbred horses. The club manages a registry of all thoroughbred horses in North America, and its member associations (including state racing commissions and various breeding associations) seek to maintain exemplary standards in thoroughbred racing. The Jockey Club web site lists its member organizations and provides some information on thoroughbreds, including the club's rule book and a fact book on the breed.

Multi-State Lottery Association (MUSL)
URL: http://www.musl.com
Phone: (515) 453-1400
4400 NW Urbandale Drive
Urbandale, IA 50322
Formed in 1987, MUSL is a government nonprofit organization

that serves the 29 states and one U.S. territory that offer one or more MUSL games. The most prominent and popular MUSL game is Powerball, but four other lottery games are also administered by the association. While MUSL offers no research information to the general public, the MUSL web site does provide links to its five constituent lotteries. Each of these sites outlines the general play of the respective games and any newsworthy items such as winners' stories.

National Center for Responsible Gaming (NCRG)
URL: http://www.ncrg.org
E-mail: contact@ncrg.org
Phone: (202) 530-4704
P.O. Box 14323
Washington, DC 20044-4323

Founded in 1996, NCRG is a national organization that funds research on pathological and youth gambling. The mission of the organization is to increase education and inform public policy on these issues with the goal of alleviating their burden on society. NCRG publishes annual reports on the state of problem gambling research, and these reports are available on the organization's web site. NCRG also cosponsors (with the American Gaming Association) *Responsible Gaming Quarterly*, a journal available on the AGA web site, and partially funds *WAGER*, an online publication of the Institute for Research on Pathological Gambling and Related Disorders.

National Coalition Against Legalized Gambling (NCALG)
URL: http://www.ncalg.org
E-mail: ncalg@vcn.com
Phone: (800) 664-2680
Fax: (307) 587-8082
100 Maryland Avenue, NE
Room 311
Washington, DC 20002

Founded in 1978, NCALG is a charitable organization bent on educating the American public about what it believes are the dangers of legalized gambling. The coalition maintains that gambling's expansion has had a negative impact on society by increasing crime, feeding gambling addictions, encouraging youth gambling, and destroying families. The political action work of NCALG is handled by its sister organization, the National Coalition Against Gambling Expansion (NCAGE), which was set up in 1994 to combat federal and state legislation beneficial to the expansion of the gaming industry.

NCALG's web site hosts an Information Center that has links to gambling fact sheets, topical papers, and the NCALG newsletter. The Information Center also maintains archives of other documents that relate to the coalition's stand against legalized gambling.

National Congress of American Indians (NCAI)
URL: http://www.ncai.org
E-mail: ncai@ncai.org
Phone: (202) 466-7767
Fax: (202) 466-7797

1301 Connecticut Ave, NW
Suite 200
Washington, DC 20036
Founded in 1944, NCAI is the oldest and largest coalition of Native American tribes. Its intent is to inform the public about Indian affairs and to safeguard the sovereign rights of the country's tribes. Among its list of prerogatives is the right to operate gaming enterprises free of federal or state government control. NCAI has voiced its opinion on Indian gaming issues in Congress and in other public forums. Some of these testimonies, as well as other gaming-related documents, are available on the organization's web site.

National Council of Legislators from Gaming States (NCLGS)
URL: http://www.nclgs.org
E-mail: info@nclgs.org
Phone: (518) 687-0615
Fax: (518) 687-0401
385 Jordan Road
Troy, NY 12180
NCLGS is a nonpartisan collective of state lawmakers (representing 44 states and the District of Columbia) who meet regularly to discuss issues related to gaming and its regulation. The council also routinely testifies before the U.S. Congress when laws involving gaming and states' rights are debated. NCLGS has sponsored some research into the gaming industry and its impact. Most notably, the council was one backer of the Public Sector Gaming Study Commission (PSGSC), an investigative body that looked into the economic, social, and political consequences of gaming. The PSGSC's final report (issued in 2000) as well as other NCLGS press releases can be accessed through the council's web site.

National Council on Problem Gambling (NCPG)
URL: http://www.ncpgambling.org
E-mail: ncpg@ncpgambling.org
Phone: (202) 547-9204
Fax: (202) 547-9206
216 G Street, NE
Suite 200
Washington, DC 20002
The mission of NCPG is to educate the public on the hazards of problem gambling. In doing so, the organization promotes research on the causes of problem gambling and supports treatment for its sufferers. NCPG has affiliates in 34 states that increase local awareness and advocate treatment options for problem gamblers. Contact information for each of these subsidiary organizations can be found on the NCPG web site. The web site also has downloadable copies of NCPG newsletters and problem-gambling fact sheets.

National Greyhound Association (NGA)
URL: http://www.ngagreyhounds.com
E-mail: nga@ngagreyhounds.com
Phone: (785) 263-4660
P.O. Box 543
Abilene, KS 67410

Formed in 1906, the NGA is a nonprofit organization that maintains a registry of all racing greyhounds in North America. The association is recognized by all dog-racing tracks as the official record keeper of the breed. The NGA web site carries some news items that pertain to breeding and racing. It also catalogs each year's race schedules for tracks across the continent.

National Indian Gaming Association (NIGA)
URL: http://www.indiangaming.org
Phone: (202) 546-7711
Fax: (202) 546-1755
224 Second Street, SE
Washington, DC 20003

Begun in 1985, the NIGA is a nonprofit organization of Native American tribes in North America engaged in gaming enterprises. The NIGA currently represents 168 Indian nations as well as several nonvoting tribes that are also engaged in tribal gaming. The mission of the organization is to promote Indian gaming as a means of tribal self-sufficiency and to provide the public with educational information and policy-making news regarding tribal gaming. The NIGA also functions as a political advocacy group that weighs in on congressional legislation affecting Native American gaming.

The National Indian Gaming Association web site has several resources. The most useful are its fact sheets on Indian gaming in America and the association's virtual library—an Internet storehouse of testimonies, surveys, and other documents relating to tribal gaming. Several NIGA publications can also be ordered for a price through the web site.

National Indian Gaming Commission (NIGC)
URL: http://www.nigc.gov/nigc/index.jsp
E-mail: info@nigc.gov
Phone: (202) 632-7003
Fax: (202) 632-7066
1441 L Street, NW
Suite 9100
Washington, DC 20005

Set up as a provision of the Indian Gaming Regulatory Act of 1988, the NIGC is a three-person committee that oversees gaming regulation on tribal land. The commission ensures that Indian gaming is not susceptible to organized crime, that Indian tribes are the primary beneficiaries of gaming revenue, and that all gaming activities are conducted fairly and honestly. To maintain the integrity of Indian gaming, the commission has the legal power to enforce its regulations through fines and court actions. The NIGC publishes bulletins and annual reports on Indian gaming in the United States. Many of these reports are available on the NIGC web site, along with listings of the commission's powers and enforcement capabilities.

National Thoroughbred Racing Association (NTRA)
URL: http://www.ntra.com

E-mail: ntra@ntra.com
Phone: (212) 230-9500
Fax: (212) 752-3093
800 Third Avenue
Suite 901
New York, NY 10022
The NTRA promotes the sport of thoroughbred racing and keeps the public and legislators informed about the racing industry's initiatives and achievements. The NTRA web site provides news about the sport, racetrack guides and listings, and press releases concerning current events in the industry.

North American Association of State and Provincial Lotteries (NASPL)
URL: http://www.naspl.org
E-mail: NASPLHQ@aol.com
Phone: (216) 241-2310
Fax: (216) 241-4350
2775 Bishop Road
Suite B
Willoughby Hills, OH 44092
Founded in 1971, the North American Association of State and Provincial Lotteries (NASPL) is a nonprofit organization representing 47 lotteries operated throughout North America. The organization maintains public awareness of lottery issues, including disclosure of lottery profits and detailed accounts of where lottery proceeds go. All of this information is available on the NASPL web site. In addition, the organization publishes the *NASPL Lottery Handbook* (a statistical resource manual) and *Lottery Insights* (a monthly periodical).

North American Gaming Regulators Association (NAGRA)
URL: http://www.nagra.org
E-mail: info@nagra.org
Phone: (651) 203-7244
Fax: (651) 290-2266
1000 Westgate Drive
Suite 252
St. Paul, MN 55114
Organized in 1984, the NAGRA is comprised of members of federal, state, local, provincial, and tribal government agencies that are involved in regulating gaming. The NAGRA's mission is to bring some unity to the rules and regulations enacted by gaming enterprises across North America. The association holds regular meetings and publishes a newsletter that can be downloaded from its web site.

North American Pari-Mutuel Regulators Association (NAPRA)
URL: http://www.napraonline.com/PublicPages/2001web/home.asp
Phone: (701) 221-2142
Fax: (701) 255-7979
120 North Third Street
Suite 100
Bismarck, ND 58501
The NAPRA is an industry organization that promotes communication and maintains standards among pari-mutuel wagering facilities. The NAPRA strives for industry integrity by devising a book of parimutuel guidelines and by ensuring that member organizations are open and accountable in their

transactions. The association publishes press releases concerning the trade, and these are available for viewing on the NAPRA web site.

Problemgambling.com
URL: http://www.problemgambling.com
E-mail: webmaster@problemgambling.com
Fax: (702) 363-7934
10443 Noontide Avenue
Las Vegas, NV 89135

Problemgambling.com is an organization that provides resources both to individuals who suffer from problem gambling and to government and industry entities that are concerned about the issue. The organization maintains lists of counselors and treatment centers worldwide and offers this information to the public. Problemgambling.com also sells books, manuals, and videos that relate to problem gambling and its treatment.

Public Gaming Research Institute (PGRI)
URL: http://www.publicgaming.org
E-mail: info@publicgaming.org
Phone: (800) 493-0527
Fax: (425) 985-3159
218 Main Street
Suite #203
Kirkland, WA 98033

The PGRI is an organization that supports the lottery industry. The PGRI assists in marketing and career placement and hosts trade shows and conferences to promote the industry. The organization publishes *Public Gaming International* magazine, a trade journal that contends with lottery issues and innovations. The PGRI web site has an archive of this publication as well as an archive of the organization's daily reports.

United Methodist Church General Board of Church and Society (GBCS)
URL: http://www.umc-gbcs.org
Phone: (202) 488-5600
100 Maryland Avenue, NE
Washington, DC 20002

The GBCS is one of four program boards operated by the United Methodist Church. The GBCS encourages its members to work with their communities in upholding the Christian gospel. In practice, the board operates under a set of principles, one of which declares that "Gambling is a menace to society, deadly to the best interests of moral, social, economic, and spiritual life, and destructive of good government." The GBCS's antigambling doctrine is fleshed out in resolutions, press statements, and articles that are available on its web site. The board also offers a "Gambling Packet" that can be ordered for a fee from its online store.

University of Nevada at Las Vegas (UNLV) Libraries Gaming Collection
URL: http://www.library.unlv.edu/speccol/gaming/index.html
E-mail: dgs@unlv.nevada.edu
Phone: (702) 895-2242

Fax: (702) 895-2253
4505 Maryland Parkway
Box 457010
Las Vegas, NV 89154-7010
The Gaming Collection is the largest repository of materials on the history, regulation, politics, psychology, and statistical bases of gambling worldwide. As part of the UNLV Libraries' Special Collections, the entire Gaming Collection can be visited at the UNLV campus, but many of the documents, books, and periodicals in the collection can be accessed online. The Gaming Collection web site also hosts a virtual museum of art work and other visual elements relating to gambling.

STATE GAMING AGENCIES

The following is a list of state regulation agencies that oversee gaming operations within their given jurisdictions. In states where some form of casino or card-room gaming is permitted, the agencies will likely provide information on casino licensing, state taxing rates, Native American compacts, and (perhaps) state laws that pertain to legal and illegal gambling. Similarly, racing commissions may list breeding information and state-approved courses. Lottery departments typically provide game rules, odds of winning, and other information about the conduct of the lottery. Because these types of agencies do not vary much from state to state, no detailed description of each individual agency is included.

Alabama Racing Commission
URL: http://www.mindspring.com/~brc
E-mail: ledadimperio@bellsouth.net
Phone: (205) 328-7223
2101 6th Avenue North
Suite 725
Birmingham, AL 35203

Alaska Tax Division Gaming Group
URL: http://www.tax.state.ak.us/abouttax/groups.asp
Phone: (907) 269-6620
Fax: (907) 269-6644
550 West 7th Avenue
Suite 500
Anchorage, AK 99501-3555

Arizona Department of Gaming (ADG)
URL: http://www.azgaming.gov
Phone: (602) 604-1801
Fax: (602) 255-3883
202 East Earll Drive
Suite 200
Phoenix, AZ 85012

Arizona Department of Racing (ADOR)
URL: http://www.racing.state.az.us
E-mail: ador@azracing.gov
Phone: (602) 364-1700
Fax: (602) 364-1703
1110 West Washington
Suite 260
Phoenix, AZ 85007

Arizona Lottery
http://www.arizonalottery.com
Phone: (480) 921-4400
P.O. Box 2913
Phoenix, AZ 85062-2913

Arkansas Racing Commission (ARC)
URL: http://www.state.ar.us/dfa/racing
Phone: (501) 682-1467
1515 West 7th Street
Suite 505
P.O. Box 3076
Little Rock, AR 72203

California Division of Gambling Control (DGC)
URL: http://caag.state.ca.us/gambling/index.htm
E-mail: piu@doj.ca.gov
Phone: (916) 263-3408
Fax: (916) 263-3403
1425 River Park Drive
Suite 400
Sacramento, CA 95815-4509

California Gambling Control Commission (CGCC)
URL: http://www.cgcc.ca.gov
Phone: (916) 263-0700
Fax: (916) 263-0452
P.O. Box 526013
Sacramento, CA 95852

California Horse Racing Board (CHRB)
URL: http://www.chrb.ca.gov
E-mail: roym@chrb.ca.gov
Phone: (916) 263-6000
1010 Hurley Way
Suite 300
Sacramento, CA 95825

California Lottery
URL: http://www.calottery.com
Phone: (800) 568-8379

Colorado Department of State Licensing Division
URL: http://www.sos.state.co.us/pubs/bingo_raffles/main.htm
E-mail: sos.licensing@sos.state.co.us
Phone: (303) 894-2200
Fax: (303) 869-4871
1560 Broadway
Suite 200
Denver, CO

Central City/Blackhawk Offices
Phone: (303) 582-0529
Fax: (303) 582-0535
142 Lawrence Street
P.O. Box 721
Central City, CO 80427

Cripple Creek Offices
Phone: (719) 689-3362
Fax: (719) 689-3366
433 East Carr Avenue
P.O. Box 1209
Cripple Creek, CO 80813

Colorado Division of Gaming
URL: http://www.revenue.state.co.us/Gaming/home.asp
Lakewood Offices
Phone: (303) 205-1355
Fax: (303) 205-1342
1881 Pierce Street
Suite 112
Lakewood, CO 80214-1496

Colorado Division of Racing
URL: http://www.revenue.state.co.us/racing_dir/home.asp

E-mail: racing@spike.dor.state.co.us
Phone: (303) 205-2990

Colorado Lottery
URL: http://www.coloradolottery.com/home.cfm
Phone: (719) 546-2400
Fax: (719) 546-5208
Wells Fargo Building
201 West 8th Street
Suite 600
Pueblo, CO 81003

Connecticut Division of Special Revenue (DOSR)
URL: http://www.dosr.state.ct.us
E-mail: charitablegames@po.state.ct.us
Phone: (860) 594-0500
Fax: (860) 594-0696
555 Russell Road
Newington, CT 06111

Connecticut Lottery
URL: http://www.qgm.com/ctlott.html
E-mail: ct-lotto@qgm.com

Delaware Gaming Control Board
URL: http://professionallicensing.state.de.us/boards/gaming/index.shtml
Phone: (302) 744-4530
Fax: (302) 739-2711
Cannon Building
Suite 203
861 Silver Lake Boulevard
Dover, DE 19904

Delaware State Lottery
URL: http://lottery.state.de.us
Phone: (302) 739-5291
Fax: (302) 739-6706
McKee Business Park
1575 McKee Road
Suite 102
Dover, DE 19904

District of Columbia Lottery
URL: http://www.dclottery.com
Phone: (202) 645-7900
2101 Martin Luther King, Jr. Avenue, SE
Washington, DC 20020-5731

Florida Department of Agriculture and Consumer Services (DOACS)
URL: http://www.800helpfla.com/sweepstakes.html
E-mail: beachl@doacs.state.fl.us
Phone: (850) 922-2966
Division of Consumer Services
2005 Apalachee Parkway
Terry Rhodes Building
Tallahassee, FL 32399-6500

Florida Division of Pari-Mutuel Wagering
URL: http://www.myflorida.com/dbpr/pmw/index.shtml
E-mail: call.center@dbpr.state.fl.us
Phone: (850) 487-1395
Fax: (850) 921-0038
1940 North Monroe Street
Tallahassee, FL 32399-1027

Florida Lottery
URL: http://www.flalottery.com
E-mail: asklott@flalottery.com
Phone: (850) 487-7777
250 Marriott Drive
Tallahassee, FL 32301

Georgia Bureau of Investigation Bingo Unit
URL: http://www.ganet.org/gbi/idbingo.html
Phone: (404) 244-2510
3121 Panthersville Road
P.O. Box 370808
Decatur, GA 30037-0808

Georgia Lottery
URL: http://www.georgialottery.com/stc/home/index.jsp
250 Williams Street
Suite 3000
Atlanta, GA 30303

Idaho Lottery
URL: http://www.idaholottery.com
E-mail: info@idaholottery.com
Phone: (208) 334-2600
P.O. Box 6537
Boise, ID 83707-6537

Idaho State Police Racing Commission
URL: http://www.isp.state.id.us/race
Phone: (208) 884-7080
Fax: (208) 884-7098
P.O. Box 700
Meridian, ID 83680-0700

Illinois Gaming Board (IGB)
URL: http://www.igb.state.il.us/aboutus
E-mail: rigb005@revenue.state.il.us
Phone: (217) 524-0226
Fax: (217) 524-0228
101 West Jefferson
P.O. Box 19474
Springfield, IL 62794

Illinois Lottery
URL: http://www.illinoislottery.com
E-mail: lottery.info@isl.state.il.us
Phone: (800) 252-1775
101 West Jefferson Street
Springfield, IL 62702

Illinois Racing Board (IRB)
URL: http://www.state.il.us/agency/irb
E-mail: racing_board@irb.state.il.us
Phone: (312) 814-2600
100 W. Randolph
Suite 7-701
Chicago, IL 60601

Indiana Gaming Commission (IGC)
URL: http://www.state.in.us/gaming/index.html
Phone: (317) 233-0046
Fax: (317) 233-0047
115 West Washington Street
South Tower
Suite 950
Indianapolis, IN 46204-3408

Indiana Hoosier Lottery
URL: http://www.ai.org/hoosierlottery
E-mail: playersupport@hoosierlottery.com
Phone: (800) 955-6886
201 South Capitol Avenue
Pan Am Plaza
Suite 1100
Indianapolis, IN 46225

Iowa Department of Inspections and Appeals (DIA)

URL: http://www.state.ia.us/government/dia
E-mail: webmaster@dia.state.ia.us
Phone: (515) 281-7102
Fax: (515) 242-6863
Lucas State Office Building
321 East 12th Street
Des Moines, IA 50319-0083

Iowa Division of Criminal Investigation Gaming Enforcement Bureau
URL: http://www.state.ia.us/government/dps/dci/gaming.htm
E-mail: dciinfo@dps.state.ia.us
Phone: (515) 281-5138
Wallace State Office Building
Des Moines, IA 50319

Iowa Lottery
URL: dciinfo@dps.state.ia.us
Phone: (515) 281-7900
2015 Grand Avenue
Des Moines, IA 50312-4999

Iowa Racing and Gaming Commission (IRGC)
URL: http://www3.state.ia.us/irgc
E-mail: irgc@irgc.state.ia.us
Phone: (515) 281-7352
Fax: (515) 242-6560
717 East Court
Suite B
Des Moines, IA 50309

Kansas Lottery
URL: http://www.kslottery.com
E-mail: lotteryinfo@kslottery.net
Phone: (785) 296-5700
128 North Kansas Avenue
Topeka, KS 66603

Kansas Racing and Gaming Commission (KRGC)
URL: http://www.accesskansas.org/krc
E-mail: kracing@cjnetworks.com
Phone: (785) 296-5800
Fax: (785) 296-0900
700 Southwest Harrison
Suite 420
Topeka, KS 66603

Kansas State Gaming Agency
URL: http://www.accesskansas.org/ksga
Phone: (785) 368-6202
Fax: (785) 291-3798
700 Southwest Harrison
Suite 530
Topeka, KS 66603

Kentucky Office of Charitable Gaming (OGC)
URL: http://dcg.state.ky.us
E-mail: dcg.info@ky.gov
Phone: (502) 573-5528
Fax: (502) 573-6625
132 Brighton Park Boulevard
Frankfort, KY 40601

Kentucky Horse Racing Authority
URL: http://www.state.ky.us/agencies/cppr/krc
Phone: (859) 246-2040
4063 Iron Works Parkway
Building B
Lexington, KY 40511

Kentucky Lottery
URL: http://www.kylottery.com
E-mail: custsrvs@kylottery.com
Phone: (502) 560-1500

1011 West Main Street
Louisville, KY 40202

Louisiana Gaming Control Board
URL: http://www.dps.state.la.us/lgcb
Phone: (225) 295-8450
Fax: (225) 295-8479
9100 Bluebonnet Centre Boulevard
Suite 500
Baton Rouge, LA 70809

Louisiana Lottery Corporation
URL: http://www.louisianalottery.com
Phone: (225) 297-2000
555 Laurel Street
Baton Rouge, LA 70801-1813

Louisiana State Police Gaming Enforcement
URL: http://www2.dps.state.la.us/PublicLightsWeb/internetAudit.jsp
Phone: (225) 922-2534
Fax: (225) 922-2551
P.O. Box 66614, #A-17
Baton Rouge, LA 70896-6614

Maine State Lottery
URL: http://www.mainelottery.com
Phone: (800) 452-8777

Maryland Racing Commission
URL: http://www.dllr.state.md.us/racing
E-mail: racing@dllr.state.md.us
Phone: (410) 230-6330
Fax: (410) 333-8308
500 North Calvert Street
2nd Floor
Room 201
Baltimore, MD 21202-3651

Maryland State Lottery
URL: http://www.msla.state.md.us
Phone: (410) 230-8800
1800 Washington Boulevard
Suite 330
Baltimore, MD 21230

Michigan Department of Agriculture Office of Racing Commissioner (ORC)
URL: http://www.michigan.gov/mda/0,1607,7-125-1571_2527_4867-13112—,00.html
Phone: (734) 462-2400
37650 Professional Center Drive
Suite 105A
Livonia, MI 48154

Michigan Gaming Control Board (MGCB)
URL: http://www.michigan.gov/mgcb
E-mail: mgcbweb@michigan.gov
Phone: (517) 241-0040
Fax: (517) 241-0510
1500 Abbott Road
Suite 400
East Lansing, MI 48823

Michigan Lottery
URL: http://www.michigan.gov/lottery
E-mail: milottery@michigan.gov
Phone: (517) 335-5600
Fax: (517) 335-5644
101 East Hillsdale
P.O. Box 30023
Lansing, MI 48909

Minnesota Department of Public Safety Alcohol and Gambling Enforcement (AGED)
URL: http://www.dps.state.mn.us/alcgamb/alcgamb.html
Phone: (651) 296-6159
Fax: (651) 297-5259
444 Cedar Street
Suite 133
St. Paul, MN 55101-5133

Minnesota Gambling Control Board
URL: http://www.gcb.state.mn.us
Phone: (651) 639-4000
1711 West County Road B
Suite 300 South
Roseville, MN 55113

Minnesota Racing Commission
URL: http://www.state.mn.us/ebranch/racing
Phone: (952) 496-7950
Fax: (952) 496-7954
P.O. Box 630
Shakopee, MN 55379

Minnesota State Lottery
URL: http://www.lottery.state.mn.us
E-mail: lottery@winternet.com
Phone: (651) 297-7456
2645 Long Lake Road
Roseville, MN 55113

Mississippi Gaming Commission (MGC)
URL: http://www.mgc.state.ms.us
Phone: (601) 576-3800
Fax: (601) 576-3929
620 North Street
Suite 200
Jackson, MS 39202

Missouri Gaming Commission (MGC)
URL: http://www.mgc.state.mo.us
E-mail: publicrelation@mgc.dps.mo.gov
Phone: (573) 526-4080
Fax: (573) 526-1999
3417 Knipp Drive
Jefferson City, MO 65109

Missouri State Lottery
URL: http://www.molottery.state.mo.us
Phone: (573) 751-4050
Fax: (573) 751-5188
1823 Southridge Drive
Jefferson City, MO 65109

Montana Department of Justice Gambling Control Division
URL: http://www.doj.state.mt.us/department/gamblingcontroldivision.asp
E-mail: gcd@state.mt.us
Phone: (406) 444-1971
2550 Prospect Avenue
P.O. Box 201424
Helena, MT 59620-1424

Montana Department of Livestock Board of Horse Racing
E-mail: livemail@state.mt.gov
Phone: (406) 444-4287
P.O. Box 202001
Helena, MT 59620-2001

Montana Lottery
URL: http://www.montanalottery.com

E-mail: montanalottery@mail.com
Phone: (406) 444-5825
2525 North Montana Avenue
Helena, MT 59601-0598

Nebraska Charitable Gaming
URL: http://www.revenue.state.ne.us/gaming/index.htm
Phone: (877) 564-1315
Fax: (402) 471-5600
P.O. Box 94855
301 Centennial Mall South
Lincoln, NE 68509

Nebraska Lottery
URL: http://www.nelottery.com
E-mail: lottery@nelottery.com
Phone: (402) 471-6100
P.O. Box 98901
301 Centennial Mall South
Lincoln, NE 68509

Nevada Gaming Commission and State Gaming Control Board (GCB)
URL: http://gaming.nv.gov
E-mail: gcbwebmaster@gcb.nv.gov
Phone: (775) 684-7750 (Commission); (775) 684-7700 (Control Board)
Fax: (775) 687-5817
P.O. Box 8003
Carson City, NV 89702-8003

New Hampshire Lottery
URL: http://www.nhlottery.org
E-mail: webmaster@lottery.state.nh.us
Phone: (603) 271-3391
Fax: (603) 271-1160
P.O. Box 1208
Concord, NH 03302-1208

New Hampshire Pari-Mutuel Commission
URL: http://www.nh.gov/parimutuel
Phone: (603) 271-2158
Fax: (603) 271-3381
78 Regional Drive
Building 2
Concord, NH 03301

New Jersey Casino Control Commission (CCC)
URL: http://www.state.nj.us/casinos
Phone: (609) 441-3799
Arcade Building
Tennessee Avenue & Boardwalk
Atlantic City, NJ 08401

New Jersey Division of Gaming Enforcement (DGE)
URL: http://www.nj.gov/lps/ge
E-mail: info@njdge.org
Phone: (609) 292-9394
Fax: (609) 633-7355
P.O. Box 047
Trenton, NJ 08625

New Jersey Legalized Games of Chance Commission
URL: http://www.state.nj.us/lps/ca/lgccc.htm
E-mail: askconsumeraffairs@lps.state.nj.us
Phone: (973) 273-8000
P.O. Box 46000
Newark, NJ 07101

New Jersey Lottery
URL: http://www.state.nj.us/lottery

E-mail: publicinfo@lottery.state.nj.us
Phone: (609) 599-5800
Fax: (609) 599-5935
P.O. Box 041
Trenton, NJ 08625-0041

New Mexico Alcohol and Gaming Division
URL: http://www.rld.state.nm.us/AGD/
E-mail: agd@state.nm.us
Phone: (505) 476-4875
Fax: (505) 476-4595
P.O. Box 25101
Santa Fe, NM 87504

New Mexico Gaming Control Board (NMGCB)
URL: http://www.nmgcb.org
E-mail: webster@gcb.state.nm.us
Phone: (505) 841-9700
6400 Uptown Boulevard NE
Suite 100E
Albuquerque, NM 87110

New Mexico Lottery
URL: http://www.nmlottery.com
E-mail: custservice@nmlottery.com
Phone: (505) 342-7600
Public Information Officer
P.O. Box 93130
Albuquerque, NM 87199-3130

New Mexico Racing Commission
URL: http://nmrc.state.nm.us
E-mail: nmrc@state.nm.us
Phone: (505) 841-6400
Fax: (505) 841-6413
300 San Mateo NE
Suite 110
Albuquerque, NM 87108

New York Lottery
URL: http://www.nylottery.org/index.php
Phone: (518) 388-3300
P.O. Box 7500
Schenectady, NY 12301-7500

New York State Department of State Division of Corporations,
State Records, and Uniform Commercial Code
URL: http://www.dos.state.ny.us/corp/corpwww.html
E-mail: corporations@dos.state.ny.us
Phone: (518) 473-2492
Fax: (518) 474-1418
41 State Street
Albany, NY 12231-0001

New York State Racing and Wagering Board
URL: http://www.racing.state.ny.us/charitable/vegas.htm
E-mail: info@racing.state.ny.us
Phone: (518) 453-8460
1 Watervliet Avenue Extension
Suite 2
Albany, NY 12206

North Dakota Office of Attorney General Gaming Division
URL: http://www.ag.state.nd.us/Gaming/Gaming.htm
Phone: (800) 326-9240
Fax: (701) 328-3535
600 East Boulevard Avenue
Department 125
Bismarck, ND 58505-0040

Ohio Attorney General
URL: http://www.ag.state.oh.us/sections/charitable_law
E-mail: webmaster@ag.state.oh.us
Phone: (614) 466-4320
State Office Tower
30 East Broad Street
17th Floor
Columbus, OH 43215-3428

Ohio Lottery
URL: http://www.ohiolottery.com
Phone: (216) 787-3200
615 West Superior Avenue
Cleveland, OH 44113

Oklahoma Alcoholic Beverage Laws Enforcement Commission (ABLE)
URL: http://www.able.state.ok.us
Phone: (866) 894-3517
4545 North Lincoln Boulevard
Suite 270
Oklahoma City, OK 73105

Oklahoma Horse Racing Commission
URL: http://www.oklaosf.state.ok.us/~ohrc
E-mail: ohrc@socket.net
Phone: (405) 943-6472
Fax: (405) 943-6474
Shepherd Mall
2401 Northwest 23rd Street
Suite 78
Oklahoma City, OK 73107

Oregon Lottery
URL: http://www.oregonlottery.org/welcome.php
E-mail: lottery.webcenter@state.or.us
Phone: (503) 540-1000
Fax: (503) 540-1001
P.O. Box 12649
Salem, OR 97309

Oregon Racing Commission
URL: http://www.orednet.org/~orc
Phone: (503) 731-4052
Fax: (503) 731-4053
800 Northeast Oregon Street #11
Suite 310
Portland, OR 97232

State of Oregon Department of Justice Charitable Activities Section
URL: http://www.doj.state.or.us/ChariGroup/Howtoraffle.htm
E-mail: charitable.activities@state.or.us
Phone: (503) 229-5725
1515 Southwest Fifth Avenue
Suite 410
Portland, OR 97201

Pennsylvania Lottery
URL: http://www.palottery.state.pa.us
Phone: (717) 986-4699
Fax: (717) 986-4767
2850 Turnpike Industrial Drive
Middletown, PA 17057

Pennsylvania State Horse Racing Commission
URL: http://www.agriculture.state.pa.us/agriculture/cwp/view.asp?q=128999

Phone: (717) 787-1942
Fax: (717) 346-1546
Agriculture Building
Room 304
2301 North Cameron Street
Harrisburg, PA 17110

Rhode Island Department of Business Regulation (DBR)
URL: http://www.dbr.ri.gov
Phone: (401) 222-2246
Fax: (401) 222-6098
233 Richmond Street
Providence, RI 02903

Rhode Island Lottery
URL: http://www.rilot.com
Phone: (401) 463-6500
1425 Pontiac Avenue
Cranston, R.I. 02920

Rhode Island Office of the Secretary of State Corporations Division
URL: http://155.212.254.78/corporations.htm#chance
E-mail: corporations@sec.state.ri.us
Phone: (401) 222-3040
Fax: (401) 222-1309
100 North Main Street
1st Floor
Providence, RI 02903-1335

South Carolina Department of Revenue (SCDOR)
URL: http://www.sctax.org/Tax+Information/Beer+Wine+Liquor+and+Bingo/default.htm?wbc_purpose=Basic#miscmiscmiscaltersaluse
Phone: (803) 898-5393
P.O. Box 125
Columbia, SC 29214

South Carolina Lottery
URL: http://www.sceducationlottery.com
Phone: (803) 737-2002
Fax: (803) 737-2005
P.O. Box 11949
Columbia, SC 29211-1949

South Dakota Lottery
URL: http://www.sdlottery.org
E-mail: lottery@state.sd.us
Phone: (605) 773-5770
P.O. Box 7107
Pierre, SD 57501

South Dakota Revenue and Regulation Commission on Gaming
URL: http://www.state.sd.us/drr2/reg/gaming
E-mail: gaminginfo@state.sd.us
Phone: (605) 773-6050
Fax: (605) 773-6053
425 East Capitol Avenue
Pierre, SD 57501

Tennessee Lottery
URL: http://www.tnlottery.gov
Phone: (615) 324-6500
P.O. Box 23470
Nashville, TN 37202

Texas Lottery Commission (and Charitable Bingo Commission)
URL: http://www.txlottery.org
E-mail: customer.service@lottery.state.tx.us (lottery); bingo.services@lottery.state.tx.us (bingo)
Phone: (512) 344-5000
Fax: (512) 344-5080
P.O. Box 16630
Austin, TX 78761-6630

Texas Racing Commission
URL: http://www.txrc.state.tx.us
Phone: (512) 833-6699
Fax: (512) 833-6907
P.O. Box 12080
Austin, TX 78711-2080

Vermont State Lottery Commission
URL: http://www.vtlottery.com/cgi-bin/index.pl
E-mail: admin@vtlottery.com
Phone: (802) 479-5686
Fax: (802) 479-4294
1311 U.S. Route 302 - Berlin
Barre, VT 05641

Virginia Department of Charitable Gaming (DCG)
URL: http://www.dcg.state.va.us
E-mail: webmaster@dcg.virginia.gov
Phone: (804) 786-1681
Fax: (804) 786-1079
James Monroe Building
101 North 14th Street
17th Floor
Richmond, VA 23219

Virginia Lottery
URL: http://www.valottery.com
Phone: (804) 692-7000
Fax: (804) 692-7102
900 East Main Street
Richmond, VA 23219

Washington Lottery
URL: http://www.walottery.com
E-mail: director's_office@lottery.wa.gov
Phone: (360) 664-4739
Fax: (360) 753-2602
P.O. Box 43000
Olympia, WA 98504-3000

Washington State Gambling Commission
URL: http://www.wsgc.wa.gov
E-mail: cld@wsgc.wa.gov
Phone: (360) 486-3440
Fax: (360) 486-3629
P.O. Box 42400
Olympia, WA 98504-2400

West Virginia Lottery
URL: http://www.state.wv.us/lottery/default.htm
E-mail: mail@wvlottery.com
Phone: (304) 558-0500
Fax: (304) 558-3321
P.O. Box 2067
Charleston, WV 25327

Wisconsin Department of Administration Division of Gaming
URL: http://www.doa.state.wi.us/gaming/index.asp
101 East Wilson Street
Madison, WI 53702

Wisconsin Lottery
URL: http://www.wilottery.com/index.asp
Phone: (608) 261-4916
P.O. Box 8941
Madison, WI 53708-8941

Wyoming Pari-Mutuel Commission
URL: http://parimutuel.state.wy.us
E-mail: flamb@state.wy.us
Phone: (307) 777-5928
Fax: (307) 777-3681
Hansen Building
2515 Warren Avenue
Suite 301
Cheyenne, WY 82002

PART III

APPENDICES

APPENDIX A

THE WIRE WAGER ACT (USC 18 § 1084) (1961)

The Wire Wager Act is the cornerstone of the federal government's claim that Internet gaming is illegal in the United States. Though the act was passed in 1961, well before the advent of the World Wide Web, federal authorities maintain that the "uses of a wire communication facility" include Internet transmissions, and therefore any wagers received over Internet services or even abetted by Internet communication from a bookmaker or gaming facility are illegal. Challengers to the law argue that bets received over wireless Internet connections (which are becoming more popular and prevalent) are excluded from its provisions. They also insist that the phrase "placing of bets or wagers on any sporting event or contest" limits the scope of the law to sports wagering (that is, they hold that the adjective "sporting" modifies both "event" and "contest"). The law's defenders claim that "sporting event" and "contest" are two separate entities, and thus all contests (any game of chance) is covered by the wording. Regardless, one important note concerning the law's application is that it targets those "engaged in the business of betting or wagering" (those who receive bets) and not individual gamblers (those who place bets).

(a) Whoever being engaged in the business of betting or wagering knowingly uses a wire communication facility for the transmission in interstate or foreign commerce of bets or wagers or information assisting in the placing of bets or wagers on any sporting event or contest, or for the transmission of a wire communication which entitles the recipient to receive money or credit as a result of bets or wagers, or for information assisting in the placing of bets or wagers, shall be fined under this title or imprisoned not more than two years, or both.

(b) Nothing in this section shall be construed to prevent the transmission in interstate or foreign commerce of information for use in news reporting of sporting events or contests, or for the transmission of information assisting in the placing of bets or wagers on a sporting event or contest from a State or foreign country where betting on that sporting event or contest is legal into a State or foreign country in which such betting is legal.

(c) Nothing contained in this section shall create immunity from criminal prosecution under any laws of any State.

(d) When any common carrier, subject to the jurisdiction of the Federal Communications Commission, is notified in writing by a Federal, State, or local law enforcement agency, acting within its jurisdiction, that any facility furnished by it is being used or will be used for the purpose of transmitting or receiving gambling information in interstate or foreign commerce in violation of Federal, State or local law, it shall discontinue or refuse, the leasing, furnishing, or maintaining of such facility, after reasonable notice to the subscriber, but no damages, penalty or forfeiture, civil or criminal, shall be found against any common carrier for any act done in compliance with any notice received from a law enforcement agency. Nothing in this section shall be deemed to prejudice the right of any person affected thereby to secure an appropriate determination, as otherwise provided by law, in a Federal court or in a State or local tribunal or agency, that such facility should not be discontinued or removed, or should be restored.

(e) As used in this section, the term "State" means a State of the United States, the District of Columbia, the Commonwealth of Puerto Rico, or a commonwealth, territory or possession of the United States.

APPENDIX B

THE TRAVEL ACT (USC 18 § 1952) (1961)

Enacted in 1961, the Travel Act was intended to stamp out interstate gambling syndicates by prohibiting the use of "the mail or any facility" to conduct illegal business. It is currently being employed in conjunction with the Wire Wager Act (USC 18 § 1084) as part of the federal government's arsenal against Internet gambling. According to the government's interpretation of the law, an Internet gaming site's use of telephone lines in transacting with out-of-state wagerers violates the "interstate facility" restrictions of the law.

(a) Whoever travels in interstate or foreign commerce or uses the mail or any facility in interstate or foreign commerce, with intent to —
   (1) distribute the proceeds of any unlawful activity; or
   (2) commit any crime of violence to further any unlawful activity; or
   (3) otherwise promote, manage, establish, carry on, or facilitate the promotion, management, establishment, or carrying on, of any unlawful activity, and thereafter performs or attempts to perform —
      (A) an act described in paragraph (1) or (3) shall be fined under this title, imprisoned not more than 5 years, or both; or
      (B) an act described in paragraph (2) shall be fined under this title, imprisoned for not more than 20 years, or both, and if death results shall be imprisoned for any term of years or for life.

(b) As used in this section (i) "unlawful activity" means (1) any business enterprise involving gambling, liquor on which the Federal excise tax has not been paid, narcotics or controlled substances (as defined in section 102(6) of the Controlled Substances Act), or prostitution offenses in violation of the laws of the State in which they are committed or of the United States, (2) extortion, bribery, or arson in violation of the laws of the State in which committed or of the United States, or (3) any act which is indictable under subchapter II of chapter 53 of title 31, United States Code, or under section 1956 or 1957 of this title and (ii) the term

"State" includes a State of the United States, the District of Columbia, and any commonwealth, territory, or possession of the United States.

(c) Investigations of violations under this section involving liquor shall be conducted under the supervision of the Attorney General.

APPENDIX C

The Interstate Transportation of Wagering Paraphernalia Act (USC 18 § 1953) (1961)

The Interstate Transportation of Wagering Paraphernalia Act is the third, often-cited element of the U.S. Code used in the federal government's argument against the legality of Internet gambling. Like its counterparts—the Wire Wager Act (USC 18 § 1084) and the Travel Act (USC 18 § 1952)—the Paraphernalia Act was adopted in 1961. Unlike the other acts, however, the Paraphernalia Act is not broad in its language; instead the wording of the act focuses its restrictions directly on illegal gambling. According to the law, transporting a gambling "device" across state lines is illegal. The law has already been cited in a case involving the interstate transportation of computer software containing bookmaking programs, but the broadest interpretations of this law might include Internet web sites as a gambling "device." If this latter proscription is deemed valid in a court, then Internet service providers could forseeably be charged with "carrying" an illegal device.

(a) Whoever, except a common carrier in the usual course of its business, knowingly carries or sends in interstate or foreign commerce any record, paraphernalia, ticket, certificate, bills, slip, token, paper, writing, or other device used, or to be used, or adapted, devised, or designed for use in (a) bookmaking; or (b) wagering pools with respect to a sporting event; or (c) in a numbers, policy, bolita, or similar game shall be fined under this title or imprisoned for not more than five years or both.

(b) This section shall not apply to (1) parimutuel betting equipment, parimutuel tickets where legally acquired, or parimutuel materials used or designed for use at racetracks or other sporting events in connection with which betting is legal under applicable State law, or (2) the transportation of betting materials to be used in the placing of bets or wagers on a sporting event into a State in which such betting is legal under the statutes of that State, or (3) the carriage or transportation in interstate or foreign commerce of any newspaper or similar publication, or (4) equipment, tickets, or materials used or designed for use within a State in a lottery conducted by that State acting under authority of State law, or (5) the transportation in foreign commerce to a destination in a foreign country of equipment, tickets, or materials designed to be used within that foreign country in a lottery which is authorized by the laws of that foreign country.

(c) Nothing contained in this section shall create immunity from criminal prosecution under any laws of any State, Commonwealth of Puerto Rico, territory, possession, or the District of Columbia.

(d) For the purposes of this section (1) "State" means a State of the United States, the District of Columbia, the Commonwealth of Puerto Rico, or any territory or possession of the United States; and (2) "foreign country" means any empire, country, dominion, colony, or protectorate, or any subdivision thereof (other than the United States, its territories or possessions).

(e) For the purposes of this section "lottery" means the pooling of proceeds derived from the sale of tickets or chances and allotting those proceeds or parts thereof by chance to one or more chance takers or ticket purchasers. "Lottery" does not include the placing or accepting of bets or wagers on sporting events or contests.

APPENDIX D

EXCERPTS FROM THE SUPREME COURT'S OPINION AND DISSENT IN *CALIFORNIA V. CABAZON BAND OF MISSION INDIANS*, 480 U.S. 202 (1987)

When the Cabazon and Morengo Indians of California brought suit against county officials in 1985 for halting high-stakes bingo games on reservation land, a district court took the side of the Indians and ruled that the state had overstepped its regulatory powers. Not content with the judgment, the state fought the ruling and eventually had the case heard before the U.S. Supreme Court in 1986. That august body upheld the lower court's ruling and reaffirmed that the state had no power to shut down Indian gaming under the pretext of having violated a criminal statute. As six of the Court's justices argued, the Cabazon and Morengo had not committed a criminal infraction of California laws because bingo was tolerated in the state. Instead, the troublesome issue of the high stakes was a civil matter, and no state has the authority to enforce civil law on Indian land. Thus, the Cabazon and Morengo Indians were free to operate their games as they saw fit. Three of the Supreme Court justices, however, joined in issuing a dissenting opinion that insisted that the Court's decision was faulty and incompatable with the spirit of prior laws. The following are excerpts from both the Supreme Court's majority opinion and the minority dissent For clarity, notes and extraneous citations have been removed from the documents.

Justice Byron R. White delivered the opinion of the Court, in which Chief Justice William H. Rehnquist and Justices William J. Brennan, Thurgood Marshall, Harry A. Blackmun, and Lewis F. Powell joined.

The Cabazon and Morongo Bands of Mission Indians, federally recognized Indian Tribes, occupy reservations in Riverside County, California. Each Band, pursuant to an ordinance approved by the Secretary of the Interior, conducts bingo games on its reservation. The Cabazon Band has also opened a card club at which draw poker and other card games are played. The games are open to the public and are played predominantly by non-Indians coming onto the reservations. The games are a major source of employment for tribal members, and the profits are the Tribes' sole source of income. The State of California seeks to apply to the two Tribes Cal. Penal Code Ann. 326.5 (West Supp. 1987). That statute does not entirely prohibit the playing of bingo but permits it when the games are operated and staffed by members of designated charitable organizations who may not be paid for their services. Profits must be kept in special accounts and used only for charitable purposes; prizes may not exceed $250 per game. Asserting that the bingo games on the two reservations violated each of these restrictions, California insisted that the Tribes comply with state law. Riverside County also sought to apply its local Ordinance No. 558, regulating bingo, as well as its Ordinance No. 331, prohibiting the playing of draw poker and the other card games.

The Tribes sued the county in Federal District Court seeking a declaratory judgment that the county had no authority to apply its ordinances inside the reservations and an injunction against their enforcement. The State intervened, the facts were stipulated, and the District Court granted the Tribes' motion for summary judgment, holding that neither the State nor the county had any authority to enforce its gambling laws within the reservations. The Court of Appeals for the Ninth Circuit affirmed, 783 F.2d 900 (1986), the State and the county appealed, and we postponed jurisdiction to the hearing on the merits.

I

The Court has consistently recognized that Indian tribes retain "attributes of sovereignty over both their members and their territory," *United States v. Mazurie*, 419 U.S. 544, 557 (1975), and that "tribal sovereignty is dependent on, and subordinate to, only the Federal Government, not the States," *Washington v. Confederated Tribes of Colville Indian Reservation*, 447 U.S. 134, 154 (1980). It is clear, however, that state laws may be applied to tribal Indians on their reservations if Congress has expressly so provided. Here, the State insists that Congress has twice given its express consent; first in Pub. L. 280 in 1953, 67 Stat. 588, as amended, 18 U.S.C. 1162, 28 U.S.C. 1360 (1982 ed. and Supp. III), and second in the Organized Crime Control Act in 1970, 84 Stat. 937, 18 U.S.C. 1955. We disagree in both respects.

Appendix D

In Pub. L. 280, Congress expressly granted six States, including California, jurisdiction over specified areas of Indian country within the States and provided for the assumption of jurisdiction by other States. In [Section 2(a) of 18 U.S.C 1162(a)], California was granted broad criminal jurisdiction over offenses committed by or against Indians within all Indian country within the State. Section 4's grant of civil jurisdiction was more limited. In *Bryan v. Itasca County*, 426 U.S. 373 (1976), we interpreted 4 to grant States jurisdiction over private civil litigation involving reservation Indians in state court, but not to grant general civil regulatory authority. Id., at 385, 388–390. We held, therefore, that Minnesota could not apply its personal property tax within the reservation. Congress' primary concern in enacting Pub. L. 280 was combating lawlessness on reservations. Id., at 379–380. The Act plainly was not intended to effect total assimilation of Indian tribes into mainstream American society. Id., at 387. We recognized that a grant to States of general civil regulatory power over Indian reservations would result in the destruction of tribal institutions and values. Accordingly, when a State seeks to enforce a law within an Indian reservation under the authority of Pub. L. 280, it must be determined whether the law is criminal in nature, and thus fully applicable to the reservation under [Section 2(a) of 18 U.S.C. 1162(a)], or civil in nature, and applicable only as it may be relevant to private civil litigation in state court.

The Minnesota personal property tax at issue in *Bryan* was unquestionably civil in nature. The California bingo statute is not so easily categorized. California law permits bingo games to be conducted only by charitable and other specified organizations, and then only by their members who may not receive any wage or profit for doing so; prizes are limited and receipts are to be segregated and used only for charitable purposes. Violation of any of these provisions is a misdemeanor. California insists that these are criminal laws which Pub. L. 280 permits it to enforce on the reservations.

Following its earlier decision in *Barona Group of Capitan Grande Band of Mission Indians, San Diego County, Cal. v. Duffy*, 694 F.2d 1185 (1982), cert. denied, 461 U.S. 929 (1983), which also involved the applicability of 326.5 of the California Penal Code to Indian reservations, the Court of Appeals rejected this submission. 783 F.2d, at 901–903. In *Barona*, applying what it thought to be the civil/criminal dichotomy drawn in *Bryan v. Itasca County*, the Court of Appeals drew a distinction between state "criminal/prohibitory" laws and state "civil/regulatory" laws: if the intent of a state law is generally to prohibit certain conduct, it falls within Pub. L. 280's grant of criminal jurisdiction, but if the state law generally permits the conduct at issue, subject to regulation, it must be classified as civil/regulatory and Pub. L. 280 does not authorize its enforcement on an Indian reservation. The shorthand test is whether the conduct at issue violates the State's public policy. Inquiring into the nature of 326.5, the Court of Appeals held that it was regulatory rather than prohibitory. This was the analysis employed, with similar results, by the Court of Appeals for the Fifth Circuit in *Seminole Tribe of Florida v. Butterworth*, 658 F.2d 310 (1981), cert. denied, 455 U.S. 1020 (1982), which the Ninth Circuit found persuasive.

We are persuaded that the prohibitory/regulatory distinction is consistent with *Bryan's* construction of Pub. L. 280. It is not a bright-line rule, however; and as the Ninth Circuit itself observed, an argument of some weight may be made that the bingo statute is prohibitory rather than regulatory. But in the present case, the court reexamined the state law and reaffirmed its holding in *Barona*, and we are reluctant to disagree with that court's view of the nature and intent of the state law at issue here.

There is surely a fair basis for its conclusion. California does not prohibit all forms of gambling. California itself operates a state lottery, Cal. Govt. Code Ann. 8880 et seq. (West Supp. 1987), and daily encourages its citizens to participate in this state-run gambling. California also permits parimutuel horse-race betting. Cal. Bus. & Prof. Code Ann. 19400–19667 (West 1964 and Supp. 1987). Although certain enumerated gambling games are prohibited under Cal. Penal Code Ann. 330 (West Supp. 1987), games not enumerated, including the card games played in the Cabazon card club, are permissible. The Tribes assert that more than 400 card rooms similar to the Cabazon card club flourish in California, and the State does not dispute this fact. Brief for Appellees 47–48. Also, as the Court of Appeals noted, bingo is legally sponsored by many different organizations and is widely played in California. There is no effort to forbid the playing of bingo by any member of the public over the age of 18. Indeed, the permitted bingo games must be open to the general public. Nor is there any limit on the number of games which eligible organizations may operate, the receipts which they may obtain from the games, the number of games which a participant may play, or the amount of money which a participant may spend, either per game or in total. In light of the fact that California permits a substantial amount of gambling activity, including bingo, and actually promotes gambling through its state lottery, we must conclude that California regulates rather than prohibits gambling in general and bingo in particular.

California argues, however, that high stakes, unregulated bingo, the conduct which attracts organized crime, is a misdemeanor in California and may be prohibited on Indian reservations. But that an otherwise regulatory law is enforceable by criminal as well as civil means does not necessarily convert it into a criminal law within the meaning of Pub. L. 280. Otherwise, the distinction between 2 and 4 of that law could easily be avoided and total assimilation permitted. This view, adopted here and by the Fifth Circuit in the *Butterworth* case, we find persuasive. Accordingly, we conclude that Pub.

L. 280 does not authorize California to enforce Cal. Penal Code Ann. 326.5 (West Supp. 1987) within the Cabazon and Morongo Reservations.

California and Riverside County also argue that the Organized Crime Control Act (OCCA) authorizes the application of their gambling laws to the tribal bingo enterprises. The OCCA makes certain violations of state and local gambling laws violations of federal law. The Court of Appeals rejected appellants' argument, relying on its earlier decisions in *United States v. Farris*, 624 F.2d 890 (CA9 1980), cert. denied, 449 U.S. 1111 (1981), and *Barona Group of Capitan Grande Band of Mission Indians, San Diego County, Cal. v. Duffy*, 694 F.2d 1185 (1982). 783 F.2d, at 903. The court explained that whether a tribal activity is "a violation of the law of a state" within the meaning of OCCA depends on whether it violates the "public policy" of the State, the same test for application of state law under Pub. L. 280, and similarly concluded that bingo is not contrary to the public policy of California.

The Court of Appeals for the Sixth Circuit has rejected this view. *United States v. Dakota*, 796 F.2d 186 (1986). Since the OCCA standard is simply whether the gambling business is being operated in "violation of the law of a State," there is no basis for the regulatory/prohibitory distinction that it agreed is suitable in construing and applying Pub. L. 280. 796 F.2d, at 188. And because enforcement of OCCA is an exercise of federal rather than state authority, there is no danger of state encroachment on Indian tribal sovereignty. Ibid. This latter observation exposes the flaw in appellants' reliance on OCCA. That enactment is indeed a federal law that, among other things, defines certain federal crimes over which the district courts have exclusive jurisdiction. There is nothing in OCCA indicating that the States are to have any part in enforcing federal criminal laws or are authorized to make arrests on Indian reservations that in the absence of OCCA they could not effect. We are not informed of any federal efforts to employ OCCA to prosecute the playing of bingo on Indian reservations, although there are more than 100 such enterprises currently in operation, many of which have been in existence for several years, for the most part with the encouragement of the Federal Government. Whether or not, then, the Sixth Circuit is right and the Ninth Circuit wrong about the coverage of OCCA, a matter that we do not decide, there is no warrant for California to make arrests on reservations and thus, through OCCA, enforce its gambling laws against Indian tribes.

The dissent was delivered by Justice John Paul Stevens, with whom Justices Sandra Day O'Connor and Antonin Scalia join.

Unless and until Congress exempts Indian-managed gambling from state law and subjects it to federal supervision, I believe that a State may enforce its laws prohibiting high-stakes gambling on Indian reservations within its borders. Congress has not pre-empted California's prohibition against high-stakes bingo games and the Secretary of the Interior plainly has no authority to do so. While gambling provides needed employment and income for Indian tribes, these benefits do not, in my opinion, justify tribal operation of currently unlawful commercial activities. Accepting the majority's reasoning would require exemptions for cockfighting, tattoo parlors, nude dancing, houses of prostitution, and other illegal but profitable enterprises. As the law now stands, I believe tribal entrepreneurs, like others who might derive profits from catering to non-Indian customers, must obey applicable state laws.

In my opinion the plain language of Pub. L. 280, 67 Stat. 588, as amended, 18 U.S.C. 1162, 28 U.S.C. 1360 (1982 ed. and Supp. III), authorizes California to enforce its prohibition against commercial gambling on Indian reservations. The State prohibits bingo games that are not operated by members of designated charitable organizations or which offer prizes in excess of $250 per game. Cal. Penal Code Ann. 326.5 (West Supp. 1987). In 2 of Pub. L. 280, Congress expressly provided that the criminal laws of the State of California "shall have the same force and effect within such Indian country as they have elsewhere within the State." 18 U.S.C. 1162(a). Moreover, it provided in 4(a) that the civil laws of California "that are of general application to private persons or private property shall have the same force and effect within such Indian country as they have elsewhere within the State." 28 U.S.C. 1360(a) (1982 ed., Supp. III).

It is true that in *Bryan v. Itasca County*, 426 U.S. 373 (1976), we held that Pub. L. 280 did not confer civil jurisdiction on a State to impose a personal property tax on a mobile home that was owned by a reservation Indian and located within the reservation. Moreover, the reasoning of that decision recognizes the importance of preserving the traditional aspects of tribal sovereignty over the relationships among reservation Indians. Our more recent cases have made it clear, however, that commercial transactions between Indians and non-Indians—even when conducted on a reservation—do not enjoy any blanket immunity from state regulation. In *Rice v. Rehner*, 463 U.S. 713 (1983), respondent, a federally licensed Indian trader, was a tribal member operating a general store on an Indian reservation. We held that the State could require Rehner to obtain a state license to sell liquor for off-premises consumption. The Court attempts to distinguish *Rice v. Rehner* as resting on the absence of a sovereign tribal interest in the regulation of liquor traffic to the exclusion of the States. But as a necessary step on our way to deciding that the State could regulate all tribal liquor sales in Indian country, we recognized the State's authority over transactions, whether they be liquor sales or gambling, between Indians and non-Indians: "If there is any interest in tribal sovereignty implicated by imposition of California's alcoholic beverage regulation, it exists only insofar as the State attempts to regulate Rehner's sale of liquor to other members of the Pala Tribe on the Pala Reservation." Id., at 721. Similarly, in *Washington v. Confederated Tribes of Colville Indian Reservation*, 447 U.S. 134 (1980), we held that a State could impose its sales and cigarette taxes on non-Indian customers of smokeshops on Indian reservations.

Today the Court seems prepared to acknowledge that an Indian tribe's commercial transactions with non-Indians may violate "the State's public policy." Ante, at 209. The Court reasons, however, that the operation of high-stakes bingo games does not run afoul of California's public policy because the State permits some forms of gambling and, specifically, some forms of bingo. I find this approach to "public policy" curious, to say the least. The State's policy concerning gambling is to authorize certain specific gambling activities that comply with carefully defined regulation and that provide revenues either for the State itself or for certain charitable purposes, and to prohibit all unregulated commercial lotteries that are operated for private profit. To argue that the tribal bingo games comply with the public policy of California because the State permits some other gambling is tantamount to arguing that driving over 60 miles an hour is consistent with public policy because the State allows driving at speeds of up to 55 miles an hour.

APPENDIX E

EXCERPTS DEFINING CLASSES OF INDIAN GAMES AND THEIR OPERATION FROM THE INDIAN GAMING REGULATORY ACT (USC 25 § 2701 ET SEQ.)(1988)

Passing Congress in 1988, the Indian Gaming Regulatory Act (IGRA) was designed to bring the federal government, state governments, and Native American tribal authorities into agreement concerning the regulation of Indian gaming. One aspect of this law's regulatory power is its rigid classification of tribal games. As the following excerpts illustrate, the IGRA stipulates that there are three types of tribal games, each of which can be adopted by Native American tribes only if specific criteria are met.

2703—DEFINITIONS

(6) The term "class I gaming" means social games solely for prizes of minimal value or traditional forms of Indian gaming engaged in by individuals as a part of, or in connection with, tribal ceremonies or celebrations.

(7)(A) The term "class II gaming" means —

(i) the game of chance commonly known as bingo (whether or not electronic, computer, or other technologic aids are used in connection therewith) —

(I) which is played for prizes, including monetary prizes, with cards bearing numbers or other designations,

(II) in which the holder of the card covers such numbers or designations when objects, similarly numbered or designated, are drawn or electronically determined, and

(III) in which the game is won by the first person covering a previously designated arrangement of numbers or designations on such cards, including (if played in the same location) pull-tabs, lotto, punch boards, tip jars, instant bingo, and other games similar to bingo, and

(ii) card games that—

(I) are explicitly authorized by the laws of the State, or

(II) are not explicitly prohibited by the laws of the State and are played at any location in the State, but only if such card games are played in conformity with those laws and regulations (if any) of the State regarding hours or periods of operation of such card games or limitations on wagers or pot sizes in such card games.

(B) The term "class II gaming" does not include

(i) any banking card games, including baccarat, chemin de fer, or blackjack (21), or

(ii) electronic or electromechanical facsimiles of any game of chance or slot machines of any kind.

(C) Notwithstanding any other provision of this paragraph, the term "class II gaming" includes those card games played in the State of Michigan, the State of North Dakota, the State of South Dakota, or the State of Washington, that were actually operated in such State by an Indian tribe on or before May 1, 1988, but only to the extent of the nature and scope of the card games that were actually operated by an Indian tribe in such State on or before such date, as determined by the Chairman.

(D) Notwithstanding any other provision of this paragraph, the term "class II gaming" includes, during the 1-year period beginning on October 17, 1988, any gaming described in subparagraph (B)(ii) that was legally operated on Indian lands on or before May 1, 1988, if the Indian tribe having jurisdiction over the lands on which such gaming was operated requests the State, by no later than the date that is 30 days after October 17, 1988, to negotiate a Tribal-State compact under section 2710(d)(3) of this title.

(E) Notwithstanding any other provision of this paragraph, the term "class II gaming" includes, during the 1-year period beginning on December 17, 1991, any gaming described in subparagraph (B)(ii) that was legally operated on Indian lands in the State of Wisconsin on or before May 1, 1988, if the Indian tribe having jurisdiction over the lands on which such gaming was operated requested the State, by no later than November 16, 1988, to negotiate a Tribal-State compact under section 2710(d)(3) of this title.

(F) If, during the 1-year period described in subparagraph (E), there is a final judicial determination that the gaming described in subparagraph (E) is not legal as a matter of State law, then such gaming on such Indian land shall cease to operate on the date next following the date of such judicial decision.

(8) The term "class III gaming" means all forms of gaming that are not class I gaming or class II gaming.

(9) The term "net revenues" means gross revenues of an Indian gaming activity less amounts paid out as, or paid for, prizes and total operating expenses, excluding management fees . . . .

2710—TRIBAL GAMING ORDINANCES

(a) Jurisdiction over class I and class II gaming activity
(1) Class I gaming on Indian lands is within the exclusive jurisdiction of the Indian tribes and shall not be subject to the provisions of this chapter.
(2) Any class II gaming on Indian lands shall continue to be within the jurisdiction of the Indian tribes, but shall be subject to the provisions of this chapter.

(b) Regulation of class II gaming activity; net revenue allocation; audits; contracts
(1) An Indian tribe may engage in, or license and regulate, class II gaming on Indian lands within such tribe's jurisdiction, if—
(A) such Indian gaming is located within a State that permits such gaming for any purpose by any person, organization or entity (and such gaming is not otherwise specifically prohibited on Indian lands by Federal law), and
(B) the governing body of the Indian tribe adopts an ordinance or resolution which is approved by the Chairman [of the National Indian Gaming Commission]. A separate license issued by the Indian tribe shall be required for each place, facility, or location on Indian lands at which class II gaming is conducted.
(2) The Chairman shall approve any tribal ordinance or resolution concerning the conduct, or regulation of class II gaming on the Indian lands within the tribe's jurisdiction if such ordinance or resolution provides that—

(A) except as provided in paragraph (4), the Indian tribe will have the sole proprietary interest and responsibility for the conduct of any gaming activity;
(B) net revenues from any tribal gaming are not to be used for purposes other than —
(i) to fund tribal government operations or programs;
(ii) to provide for the general welfare of the Indian tribe and its members;
(iii) to promote tribal economic development;
(iv) to donate to charitable organizations; or
(v) to help fund operations of local government agencies . . . .

(3) Net revenues from any class II gaming activities conducted or licensed by any Indian tribe may be used to make per capita payments to members of the Indian tribe only if —
(A) the Indian tribe has prepared a plan to allocate revenues to uses authorized by paragraph (2)(B);
(B) the plan is approved by the Secretary [of the Interior] as adequate, particularly with respect to uses described in clause (i) or (iii) of paragraph (2)(B);
(C) the interests of minors and other legally incompetent persons who are entitled to receive any of the per capita payments are protected and preserved and the per capita payments are disbursed to the parents or legal guardian of such minors or legal incompetents in such amounts as may be necessary for the health, education, or welfare, of the minor or other legally incompetent person under a plan approved by the Secretary and the governing body of the Indian tribe; and
(D) the per capita payments are subject to Federal taxation and tribes notify members of such tax liability when payments are made . . . .

CLASS III GAMING

(d) (1) Class III gaming activities shall be lawful on Indian lands only if such activities are —
(A) authorized by an ordinance or resolution that —
(i) is adopted by the governing body of the Indian tribe having jurisdiction over such lands,
(ii) meets the requirements of subsection (b) of this section, and
(iii) is approved by the Chairman,
(B) located in a State that permits such gaming for any purpose by any person, organization, or entity, and

(C) conducted in conformance with a Tribal-State compact entered into by the Indian tribe and the State under paragraph (3) that is in effect.

ADOPTION AND SUBMISSION OF ORDINANCE

(2)(A) If any Indian tribe proposes to engage in, or to authorize any person or entity to engage in, a class III gaming activity on Indian lands of the Indian tribe, the governing body of the Indian tribe shall adopt and submit to the Chairman an ordinance or resolution that meets the requirements of subsection (b) of this section.

(B) The Chairman shall approve any ordinance or resolution described in subparagraph (A), unless the Chairman specifically determines that

(i) the ordinance or resolution was not adopted in compliance with the governing documents of the Indian tribe, or

(ii) the tribal governing body was significantly and unduly influenced in the adoption of such ordinance or resolution by any person identified in section 2711 (e)(1)(D) of this title.

Upon the approval of such an ordinance or resolution, the Chairman shall publish in the Federal Register such ordinance or resolution and the order of approval.

(C) Effective with the publication under subparagraph (B) of an ordinance or resolution adopted by the governing body of an Indian tribe that has been approved by the Chairman under subparagraph (B), class III gaming activity on the Indian lands of the Indian tribe shall be fully subject to the terms and conditions of the Tribal-State compact entered into under paragraph (3) by the Indian tribe that is in effect.

APPENDIX F

Excerpts Relevant to Negotiating Tribal Compacts in the Indian Gaming Regulatory Act (USC 25 § 2701 et seq.) (1988)

The Indian Gaming Regulatory Act of 1988 (IGRA) maintains that Native American tribes possess sovereignty, and therefore in order to negotiate gaming regulations with any tribes that desire to conduct class III (casino-type) games on reservation land, state governments are required to conclude compacts (or legal agreements) with tribal authorities. The following excerpts from the IGRA spell out how state and tribal governments can hammer out compacts cooperatively or how federal authorities can compel state governments to enter into compacts when the states are reluctant to negotiate.

TRIBAL STATE COMPACTS

(3) (A) Any Indian tribe having jurisdiction over the Indian lands upon which a class III gaming activity is being conducted, or is to be conducted, shall request the State in which such lands are located to enter into negotiations for the purpose of entering into a Tribal-State compact governing the conduct of gaming activities. Upon receiving such a request, the State shall negotiate with the Indian tribe in good faith to enter into such a compact.

(B) Any State and any Indian tribe may enter into a Tribal-State compact governing gaming activities on the Indian lands of the Indian tribe, but such compact shall take effect only when notice of approval by the Secretary of such compact has been published by the Secretary in the Federal Register.

(C) Any Tribal-State compact negotiated under subparagraph (A) may include provisions relating to —

(i) the application of the criminal and civil laws and regulations of the Indian tribe or the State that are directly related to, and necessary for, the licensing and regulation of such activity;

(ii) the allocation of criminal and civil jurisdiction between the State and the Indian tribe necessary for the enforcement of such laws and regulations;

(iii) the assessment by the State of such activities in such amounts as are necessary to defray the costs of regulating such activity;

(iv) taxation by the Indian tribe of such activity in amounts comparable to amounts assessed by the State for comparable activities;

(v) remedies for breach of contract;

(vi) standards for the operation of such activity and maintenance of the gaming facility, including licensing; and

(vii) any other subjects that are directly related to the operation of gaming activities.

(4) Except for any assessments that may be agreed to under paragraph (3)(C)(iii) of this subsection, nothing in this section shall be interpreted as conferring upon a State or any of its political subdivisions authority to impose any tax, fee, charge, or other assessment upon an Indian tribe or upon any other person or entity authorized by an Indian tribe to engage in a class III activity. No State may refuse to enter into the negotiations described in paragraph (3)(A) based upon the lack of authority in such State, or its political subdivisions, to impose such a tax, fee, charge, or other assessment.

(5) Nothing in this subsection shall impair the right of an Indian tribe to regulate class III gaming on its Indian lands concurrently with the State, except to the extent that such regulation is inconsistent with, or less stringent than, the State laws and regulations made applicable by any Tribal-State compact entered into by the Indian tribe under paragraph (3) that is in effect.

Appendix F

APPLICATION OF THE JOHNSON ACT

(6) The provisions of section 1175 of title 15 shall not apply to any gaming conducted under a Tribal-State compact that —
- (A) is entered into under paragraph (3) by a State in which gambling devices are legal, and
- (B) is in effect.

FEDERAL COURT ACTIONS

(7) (A) The United States district courts shall have jurisdiction over —
- (i) any cause of action initiated by an Indian tribe arising from the failure of a State to enter into negotiations with the Indian tribe for the purpose of entering into a Tribal-State compact under paragraph (3) or to conduct such negotiations in good faith,
- (ii) any cause of action initiated by a State or Indian tribe to enjoin a class III gaming activity located on Indian lands and conducted in violation of any Tribal-State compact entered into under paragraph (3) that is in effect, and
- (iii) any cause of action initiated by the Secretary to enforce the procedures prescribed under subparagraph (B)(vii).

(B)(i) An Indian tribe may initiate a cause of action described in subparagraph (A)(i) only after the close of the 180-day period beginning on the date on which the Indian tribe requested the State to enter into negotiations under paragraph (3)(A).

(ii) In any action described in subparagraph (A)(i), upon the introduction of evidence by an Indian tribe that —
- (I) a Tribal-State compact has not been entered into under paragraph (3), and
- (II) the State did not respond to the request of the Indian tribe to negotiate such a compact or did not respond to such request in good faith, the burden of proof shall be upon the State to prove that the State has negotiated with the Indian tribe in good faith to conclude a Tribal-State compact governing the conduct of gaming activities.

(iii) If, in any action described in subparagraph (A)(i), the court finds that the State has failed to negotiate in good faith with the Indian tribe to conclude a Tribal-State compact governing the conduct of gaming activities, the court shall order the State and the Indian Tribe to conclude such a compact within a 60-day period. In determining in such an action whether a State has negotiated in good faith, the court —

(I) may take into account the public interest, public safety, criminality, financial integrity, and adverse economic impacts on existing gaming activities, and

(II) shall consider any demand by the State for direct taxation of the Indian tribe or of any Indian lands as evidence that the State has not negotiated in good faith.

MEDIATION

(iv) If a State and an Indian tribe fail to conclude a Tribal-State compact governing the conduct of gaming activities on the Indian lands subject to the jurisdiction of such Indian tribe within the 60-day period provided in the order of a court issued under clause (iii), the Indian tribe and the State shall each submit to a mediator appointed by the court a proposed compact that represents their last best offer for a compact. The mediator shall select from the two proposed compacts the one which best comports with the terms of this chapter and any other applicable Federal law and with the findings and order of the court.

(v) The mediator appointed by the court under clause (iv) shall submit to the State and the Indian tribe the compact selected by the mediator under clause (iv).

(vi) If a State consents to a proposed compact during the 60-day period beginning on the date on which the proposed compact is submitted by the mediator to the State under clause (v), the proposed compact shall be treated as a Tribal-State compact entered into under paragraph (3).

PROCEDURES PRESCRIBED BY THE SECRETARY

(vii) If the State does not consent during the 60-day period described in clause (vi) to a proposed compact submitted by a mediator under clause (v), the mediator shall notify the Secretary and the Secretary shall prescribe, in consultation with the Indian tribe, procedures —

(I) which are consistent with the proposed compact selected by the mediator under clause (iv), the provisions of this chapter, and the relevant provisions of the laws of the State, and

(II) under which class III gaming may be conducted on the Indian lands over which the Indian tribe has jurisdiction.

Appendix F

SECRETARIAL APPROVAL OF TRIBAL-STATE COMPACTS

(8)(A) The Secretary is authorized to approve any Tribal-State compact entered into between an Indian tribe and a State governing gaming on Indian lands of such Indian tribe.

(B) The Secretary may disapprove a compact described in subparagraph (A) only if such compact violates —

(i) any provision of this chapter,

(ii) any other provision of Federal law that does not relate to jurisdiction over gaming on Indian lands, or

(iii) the trust obligations of the United States to Indians.

(C) If the Secretary does not approve or disapprove a compact described in subparagraph (A) before the date that is 45 days after the date on which the compact is submitted to the Secretary for approval, the compact shall be considered to have been approved by the Secretary, but only to the extent the compact is consistent with the provisions of this chapter.

(D) The Secretary shall publish in the Federal Register notice of any Tribal-State compact that is approved, or considered to have been approved, under this paragraph . . . .

TIME LIMIT FOR CHAIRMAN'S APPROVAL OF ORDINANCE

(e) Approval of ordinances

For purposes of this section, by not later than the date that is 90 days after the date on which any tribal gaming ordinance or resolution is submitted to the Chairman, the Chairman shall approve such ordinance or resolution if it meets the requirements of this section. Any such ordinance or resolution not acted upon at the end of that 90-day period shall be considered to have been approved by the Chairman, but only to the extent such ordinance or resolution is consistent with the provisions of this chapter.

APPENDIX G

The Professional and Amateur Sports Protection Act (USC 28 § 3701 et seq.) (1993)

The Professional and Amateur Sports Protection Act took effect in 1993 and thereafter outlawed the taking of wagers on all contests involving professional and amateur sports. The law targets bookmakers and gambling operators, not their patrons. Its language is broad enough to prohibit both the receiving of wagers at a physical place of business or via an Internet site. Three states—Delaware, Nevada, and Oregon—were exempt from the proscriptions of this law since they already tolerated sports wagering (in some form) prior to the law's enactment.

3701—DEFINITIONS

For purposes of this chapter —

(1) the term "amateur sports organization" means —
  (A) a person or governmental entity that sponsors, organizes, schedules, or conducts a competitive game in which one or more amateur athletes participate, or
  (B) a league or association of persons or governmental entities described in subparagraph (A),
(2) the term "governmental entity" means a State, a political subdivision of a State, or an entity or organization, including an entity or organization described in section 4(5) of the Indian Gaming Regulatory Act (25 U.S.C. 2703(5)), that has governmental authority within the territorial boundaries of the United States, including on lands described in section 4(4) of such Act (25 U.S.C. 2703(4)),

(3) the term "professional sports organization" means —
    (A) a person or governmental entity that sponsors, organizes, schedules, or conducts a competitive game in which one or more professional athletes participate, or
    (B) a league or association of persons or governmental entities described in subparagraph (A),
(4) the term "person" has the meaning given such term in section 1 of title 1, and
(5) the term "State" means any of the several States, the District of Columbia, the Commonwealth of Puerto Rico, the Commonwealth of the Northern Mariana Islands, Palau, or any territory or possession of the United States.

3702—UNLAWFUL SPORTS GAMBLING

It shall be unlawful for —

(1) a governmental entity to sponsor, operate, advertise, promote, license, or authorize by law or compact, or
(2) a person to sponsor, operate, advertise, or promote, pursuant to the law or compact of a governmental entity, a lottery, sweepstakes, or other betting, gambling, or wagering scheme based, directly or indirectly (through the use of geographical references or otherwise), on one or more competitive games in which amateur or professional athletes participate, or are intended to participate, or on one or more performances of such athletes in such games.

3703—INJUNCTIONS

A civil action to enjoin a violation of section 3702 may be commenced in an appropriate district court of the United States by the Attorney General of the United States, or by a professional sports organization or amateur sports organization whose competitive game is alleged to be the basis of such violation.

3704—APPLICABILITY

(a) Section 3702 shall not apply to —
    (1) a lottery, sweepstakes, or other betting, gambling, or wagering scheme in operation in a State or other governmental entity, to the extent that the scheme was conducted by that State or other governmental entity at any time during the period beginning January 1, 1976, and ending August 31, 1990;

(2) a lottery, sweepstakes, or other betting, gambling, or wagering scheme in operation in a State or other governmental entity where both —

(A) such scheme was authorized by a statute as in effect on October 2, 1991; and

(B) a scheme described in section 3702 (other than one based on parimutuel animal racing or jai-alai games) actually was conducted in that State or other governmental entity at any time during the period beginning September 1, 1989, and ending October 2, 1991, pursuant to the law of that State or other governmental entity;

(3) a betting, gambling, or wagering scheme, other than a lottery described in paragraph (1), conducted exclusively in casinos located in a municipality, but only to the extent that —

(A) such scheme or a similar scheme was authorized, not later than one year after the effective date of this chapter, to be operated in that municipality; and

(B) any commercial casino gaming scheme was in operation in such municipality throughout the 10-year period ending on such effective date pursuant to a comprehensive system of State regulation authorized by that State's constitution and applicable solely to such municipality; or

(4) parimutuel animal racing or jai-alai games.

(b) Except as provided in subsection (a), section 3702 shall apply on lands described in section 4(4) of the Indian Gaming Regulatory Act (25 U.S.C. 2703(4)).

APPENDIX H

EXCERPTS ON THE ROLE OF GOVERNMENT IN THE EXPANSION OF GAMBLING IN THE UNITED STATES FROM THE NATIONAL GAMBLING IMPACT STUDY COMMISSION REPORT (1999)

In issuing its report to Congress in 1999, the National Gambling Impact Study Commission (NGISC) made it clear that federal, state, and local governments have taken an active hand in shaping the scope of gambling in America. As the report notes, governing bodies sanction gaming enterprises, reap benefits from taxation of gambling revenues, and, in the case of lotteries, promote and manage gaming institutions of their own. The following is an excerpt from the first chapter of the NGISC report, in which the commission explains how government is abetting gambling's expansion.

THE ROLE OF GOVERNMENT

The public has voted either by a statewide referendum and/or local option election for the establishment or continued operation of commercial casino gambling in 9 of 11 states where commercial casinos are permitted. Similarly, the public has approved state lotteries via the ballot box in 27 of 38 instances where lotteries have been enacted. Whatever the case, whether gambling is introduced by popular referendum or by the decision of elected officials, we must recognize the important role played by government in the industry's growth and development. Government decisions have influenced the expansion of gambling in America, and influencing those decisions is the principal objective of most of the public debates on this issue.

Although some would argue that gambling is a business like any other and, consequently, should be treated as such, in fact it is almost universally regarded as something different, requiring special rules and treatment, and enhanced scrutiny by government and citizens alike. Even in the flagship state of Nevada, operation of a gambling enterprise is explicitly defined as a "privilege," an activity quite apart from running a restaurant, manufacturing furniture, or raising cotton.

Unlike other businesses in which the market is the principal determinant, the shape and operation of legalized gambling has been largely a product of government decisions. This is most obvious in the state lotteries, where governments have not just sanctioned gambling but have become its enthusiastic purveyors, legislating themselves an envied monopoly; and in Native American tribal gambling, where tribal nations own, and their governments often operate, casinos and other gambling enterprises.

But the role of government is hardly less pervasive in other forms of gambling: Governments determine which kinds of gambling will be permitted and which will not; the number, location, and size of establishments allowed; the conditions under which they operate; who may utilize them and under what conditions; who may work for them; even who may own them. All of this is in addition to the normal range of governmental activity in areas such as taxes, regulations, and so forth. And, because governments determine the level and type of competition to be permitted—granting, amending, and revoking monopolies, and restricting or enhancing competition almost at will—they also are a key determinant of the various industries' potential profits and losses.

No Master Plan

To say that gambling has grown and taken shape in obeisance to government decisions does not imply that there was a well thought-out, overall National Gambling Impact Study Commission Report plan. All too commonly, actual results have diverged from stated intentions, at times completely surprising the decisionmakers. There are many reasons for this awkward fact.

In the U.S. federalist system, use of the term "government" can easily mislead: Far from a single actor with a clear-eyed vision and unified direction, it is in fact a mix of authorities, with functions and decisionmaking divided into many levels—federal, state, local, and others, including tribal. Each of these plays an active role in determining the shape of legalized gambling. The states have always had the primary responsibility for gambling decisions and almost certainly will continue to do so for the foreseeable future. Many states, however, have delegated considerable authority to local jurisdictions, often including such key decisions as whether or not gambling will be permitted in their communities. And the federal government plays an ever-greater role: Indian gambling sprang into being as a result of federal court decisions and congressional legislation; and even the states concede that only Washington has the potential to control gambling on the Internet.

And almost none of the actors coordinate their decisions with one another. The federal government did not poll the states when it authorized Indian gambling within their borders, nor have Mississippi and Louisiana—nor, for that matter, any other state—seen fit to adopt a common approach to gambling. In fact, rivalry and competition for investment and revenues have been far more common factors in government decisionmaking regarding gambling than have any impulses toward joint planning.

Those decisions generally have been reactive, driven more by pressures of the day than by an abstract debate about the public welfare. One of the most powerful motivations has been the pursuit of revenues. It is easy to understand the impetus: Faced with stiff public resistance to tax increases as well as incessant demands for increased or improved public services from the same citizens, tax revenues from gambling can easily be portrayed as a relatively painless method of resolving this dilemma.

Lotteries and riverboat casinos offer the clearest examples of this reactive behavior on the part of legislatures. The modern history of lotteries demonstrates that when a state authorizes a lottery, inevitably citizens from neighboring states without lotteries will cross the border to purchase tickets. The apparent loss of potential tax revenues by these latter states often gives rise to demands that they institute lotteries of their own, in order to keep this money in-state, for use at home. Once any of these states installs a lottery, however, the same dynamic will assert itself in still other states further afield. This competitive ripple effect is a key reason why lotteries now exist in 37 states and the District of Columbia, with more poised to join the list.

The same pattern surfaced in legislative debates regarding riverboat casinos. As the great majority of these casinos have been sited on borders with other states, they quickly gave rise to charges of one state "raiding" the pocketbooks of its neighbors. This often prompted cries in the affected states to respond by licensing their own riverboats which, when generously distributed along their own borders, in turn, often stimulated similar reactions from other states far removed from the original instigator. For both lotteries and riverboat casinos, the immediate legislative attempt to capture fleeing tax dollars created a powerful yet usually unacknowledged dynamic for the expansion of gambling. Some believe another contributing factor has been the increasing volume of political contributions from interests with an economic stake in virtually every place expansion is sought.

Critics have asserted that this legislative pursuit of revenues has occurred at the expense of consideration of the public welfare, a serious charge indeed, albeit an unproveable one. But advocates have successfully deployed many other arguments for legalizing or expanding gambling: economic development for economically depressed areas, the general promotion of business for the investment and employment opportunities it can bring with it, undermining illegal gambling and the organized crime it supports, and so forth. There is even the eminently democratic motivation of responding to public demand: A number of election campaigns and referenda have been successfully waged on the issue of legalizing or expanding gambling.

APPENDIX I

The National Gambling Impact Study Commission Report: Recommending a Pause in the Expansion of Gambling in the United States (1999)

After conducting two years of research on the expansion and impact of gambling in the United States, the National Gambling Impact Study Commission (NGISC) released its report in 1999. In the first chapter of the report, the commission maintained that the accumulated data on the topic was not very thorough and that the growth of gambling (in all its forms) was outpacing any meaningful assessment of its positive and negative impacts. Therefore, to preempt any unforeseen or irreversible consequences, the commission recommended that federal, state, and local lawmakers temporarily halt gambling's expansion until research authorities could weigh its benefits and costs.

TIME FOR A PAUSE

It may be that the expansion of gambling accurately reflects the will of the people, as expressed in referenda, state legislatures, tribal reservations, and in Washington. The impressive financial resources already accounted for by businesses, workers, and public officials further strengthen the industry's ability to voice its interests. This Commission, however, believes that gambling is not merely a business like any other and that it should remain carefully regulated. Some Commissioners would wish it to be far more restricted, perhaps even prohibited. But overall, all agree that the country has gone very far very fast regarding an activity the consequences of which, frankly, no one really knows much about.

In an attempt to better understand those consequences, this Commission has examined many issues, received testimony from hundreds of individuals and organizations, and deliberated over a period of 2 years. This broad in-gathering of information and discussion of issues will be reflected in the following chapters, which outline the parameters of the many debates, discuss the available evidence, and offer recommendations. Inevitably for a Commission of such diverse makeup, some differences in viewpoint refuse to melt away and the existing evidence is insufficient to compel a consensus. But there is an encouraging breadth of agreement among Commissioners on many individual issues, such as the immediate need to address pathological gambling; and on one big issue: The Commissioners believe it is time to consider a pause in the expansion of gambling.

The purpose of the pause is not to wait for definitive answers to the subjects of dispute, because those may never come. Additional useful information is, of course, to be hoped for. But the continuing evolution of this dynamic industry has produced visible changes even in the short lifetime of this Commission and indicates that research will always trail far behind the issues of the day and moment. Instead, the purpose of this recommended pause is to encourage governments to do what to date few if any have done: To survey the results of their decisions and to determine if they have chosen wisely.

To restate: Virtually every aspect of legalized gambling is shaped by government decisions. Yet, virtually no state has conformed its decisions in this area to any overall plan, or even to its own stated objectives. Instead, in almost every state whatever policy exists toward gambling is more a collection of incremental and disconnected decisions than the result of deliberate purpose. The record of the federal government is even less laudatory. It is an open question whether the collective impact of decisions is even recognized by their makers, much less wanted by them. Does the result accord with the public good? What harmful effects could be remedied? Which benefits are being unnecessarily passed up?

Without a pause and reflection the future does indeed look worrisome. Were one to use the experience of the last quarter century to predict the evolution of gambling over the next, a likely scenario would be for gambling to continue to become more and more common, ultimately omnipresent in our lives and those of our children, with consequences no one can profess to know.

The Commission, through its research agenda, has added substantially to what is known about the impact of gambling in the United States. The Commission also has tried to survey the universe of information available from other sources. But it is clear that Americans need to know more. In this context, the Commission's call for a pause should be taken as a challenge—a challenge to intensify the effort to increase our understanding of the costs and the benefits of gambling and deal with them accordingly. Policymakers and the public should seek a comprehensive evaluation of gambling's impact so far and of the implications of future decisions to expand gambling. In fact, state and local versions of this Commission may be an appropriate mechanism to oversee such research. If such groups are formed they will find as did the Commission that the search for answers takes time. Therefore, some policymakers at every level may wish to impose an explicit moratorium on gambling expansion while awaiting further research and assessment.

Although some communities may decide to restrict or even ban existing gambling, there is not much prospect of its being outlawed altogether. It is clear that the American people want legalized gambling and it has already sunk deep economic and other roots in many communities. Its form and extent may change; it may even disappear altogether. But for the present, it is a reality. The balance between its benefits and costs, however, is not fixed. To a welcome extent, that appears to lie within our power to determine. We can seek to shape the world we live in or simply allow it to shape us. It is in service of the former that this *Final Report* and its recommendations are offered.

APPENDIX J

EXCERPTS OUTLINING THE ECONOMIC BENEFITS OF GAMING FROM THE NATIONAL PUBLIC SECTOR GAMING STUDY COMMISSION REPORT (1999)

The National Public Sector Gaming Study Commission (PSGSC) was organized partly in reaction to the findings of the National Gambling Impact Study Commission (NGISC), a government-sponsored body that released a cautionary report in 1999 bemoaning the unchecked and under-researched social costs of gambling expansion in the United States. The Gaming Study Commission believed that the NGISC's conclusions were skewed because NGISC failed to cull input from public sector representatives when compiling its research. After reading the NGISC report, PSGSC, a commission of state and tribal officials, undertook its own research into the social and economic impact of gambling. In 2000, the Gaming Study Commission released its own report, which was more optimistic about the state of gaming in America. In the following excerpt from the report, the PSGSC begins by detailing the positive impact of the gambling industry on host states and then goes on to enumerate the benefits of non-tribal casinos in particular. For clarity, notes and extraneous citations have been removed from the excerpt.

ECONOMIC AND SOCIAL IMPACTS OF GAMING

We begin with a discussion of the economic and social benefits of legalized gambling. The Commission found that these benefits are often large and well documented. However, later sections discuss some of the known or hypothesized costs from gambling. The challenge for policymakers is to assess the tradeoffs between benefits and costs at the state, regional, and local levels, and to use this information to manage legalized gambling so that economic and social benefits are maximized while any potential economic and social costs are minimized. The PSGSC recognizes that social and moral views must also be considered in making policy decisions, but these concerns are not easily quantified and, therefore, are not easily analyzed. The PSGSC feels that gambling policy decisions should be made at the state level to accommodate not only diverse locations and economies but also the variety of social and cultural influences present within individual states.

Of specific concern to the PSGSC are the economic issues of employment, regulation and taxation, saturation (the effect that additional gambling venues have on existing and potential gaming operations), and the social issues of gambling addictions, crime, and bankruptcy, both in the local host region and in the state as a whole. It should also be noted that, despite the apparent economic benefits for governments, legalized gambling is a relatively new industry in many areas, and its long-term effects remain to be seen.

BENEFITS OF LEGALIZED GAMBLING FOR STATE AND LOCAL GOVERNMENTS

A number of reports have been published within the past five years on the economic and social benefits from legalized gambling. Many states claim that by introducing gambling, particularly casino-style gambling, they have lowered their unemployment rates, decreased their welfare and other subsidy payments, and revitalized local economies. In addition to reducing welfare and related expenditures, legalized gambling has generated tax revenues that have been used to provide needed public services and facilities.

In New Jersey, for example, casinos employ almost 50,000 residents in full- or part-time positions and pay more than $1 billion annually in salaries; property values in Atlantic City have increased from $319 million in 1976 to more than $6 billion in 1996, with casino hotel properties accounting for almost 80 percent of the property tax base; and welfare assistance in Atlantic County declined from 6,900 persons prior to casinos to 3,200 persons by 1997, while the population increased 24 percent during the same period. In 1977, Atlantic City collected $24.5 million in real estate taxes; but, twenty years later the city collected $187.5 million in real estate taxes, $149.1 million of which came from casino properties. From the money collected for real estate taxes, casinos paid $87 million of the $109.8 million needed to operate the city's government and $38.3 million of the $48.3 million needed to run the county's school system.

In Missouri, riverboat casinos were introduced in 1994. In the first year of operation, five riverboats generated $299 million in adjusted gross receipts and attracted more than 12 million customers. By 1997, the state had a total of ten riverboats, generating adjusted gross receipts in excess of $651 million.

From just the seven riverboats in operation in Missouri in 1996, the state collected $93 million in taxes, $22 million in admission fees, and approximately $7 million in revenues generated by corporate income tax, fees and licenses, and enforcement fees. Those revenues were used to help support K–12 education programs, the Veterans Capital Improvement Fund, and the Missouri Gaming Commission. The local communities that hosted those seven riverboats received a combined total of $10 million in taxes and $22 million in admissions fees. In some areas, the money collected from the gaming venues comprised 50 percent or more of the host city's total revenues.

In Wisconsin, tribal governments contributed 70 percent of their gaming revenues to housing, health, elder care, economic development, and education programs; the remaining 30 percent was used to fund long-range plans to diversify tribal economies. Arizona tribes, between 1994 and 1997, spent approximately $204 million in construction costs, which generated an additional $340 million in economic activity within the state and created 4,000 jobs and more than $100 million in wages. In 1998, a total of $360,000 was voluntarily paid to Kansas municipalities by tribally-owned casinos to help defray the costs of such services as police and fire protection.

Similarly, state-run lotteries have also proven to be significant sources of revenue for many states. Florida's state-run lottery has contributed almost $9 billion, the entire amount of its net revenues, to education since its inception in 1988; California has also provided the total of its net revenues, more than $10 billion, to education since its inception in 1985. Georgia has contributed its net revenues of $3.3 billion to college scholarships and preschool programs. Of the almost $1.2 billion in total net revenues the Arizona lottery has generated, $374 million has been used to fund transportation related projects. The Kansas lottery has provided $308 million, from its total net revenues of $366 million, for economic development projects. The South Dakota lottery has used $226 million of its total net revenues of $569.2 million to reduce property taxes.

A third gambling sector that generates significant revenues to several states is the pari-mutuel industry, which is one of the oldest forms of gambling in the United States. The greyhound segment pays $235 million annually in taxes and fees to state and local governments. In Florida, the Thoroughbred industry generates more than $90 million annually in taxes, including property taxes, state sales taxes, and pari-mutuel taxes.

Appendix J

There is little doubt that the gambling industry contributes significantly to the national economy and to some state economies. Data from the past twenty years show that gambling has become an important form of entertainment for many people, especially recently, given the level of economic growth that the nation has experienced during the past few years. The total amount wagered in all forms of legalized gambling for 1998, including the same dollar bet many times over, was in excess of $677.4 billion, with the majority, $487.9 billion, coming from casinos. Tribal gaming facilities generated a handle of $99.4 billion, lotteries, $48.5 billion, and pari-mutuels—horse, greyhound, and Jai-Alai—$18.1 billion.

THE ECONOMIC AND SOCIAL IMPACTS OF CASINOS AND CASINO-STYLE GAMBLING

In assessing the local and regional economic and social impacts of casinos, as in any other industry, there are many factors that should be considered, including the effects that gambling facilities will have on property values, tax revenues, pollution, current infrastructure, the existing business climate, and the supply of labor. More specifically, state and local leaders need to know how any benefits or costs will be distributed among income classes, racial and ethnic groups, and neighborhoods and cities, what types of jobs will be created, the extent to which profits will be reinvested in the host community, what percentage of patrons will come from outside the host area, and how the resulting tax revenues can be most effectively spent to meet competing demands. The PSGSC does recognize that social and moral issues are also important factors to consider when setting public policy, but these issues can be difficult to quantify. For the purposes of this report, the Commission focuses on the data that is currently available.

Recent studies provide answers to many of these questions, but the answers tend to be context-specific, that is, they vary tremendously depending, for example, upon the size and population of the host community/region, the existence or absence of other non-gaming recreational opportunities, and the specific area from which both employees and patrons are recruited. In Atlantic City, most of the gamblers are visitors to the state, whereas the patrons of Wisconsin's tribally-owned casinos are primarily (80 to 85 percent) state residents. Las Vegas is a major metropolitan area, but many of the communities that host riverboat casinos in Illinois and Iowa are not. Thus, it is necessary to judge the impacts of casino gambling not only at the national level but at the state and regional levels, as well.

The employment studies published on behalf of individual states reach conclusions similar to those found in the national, macro studies. Total direct employment for the casino gaming industry was approximately 300,000 people in 1995. These jobs vary in nature and include casino positions—such as dealers, accounting personnel, slot technicians, maintenance personnel, beverage servers, and security guards—and hotel, food and beverage, and administrative positions. The average national wage, including benefits and tips, for casino gaming employees was approximately $26,000 in 1995.

The positive aspects of casino employment are delineated in a recent Coopers & Lybrand industry employee survey that encompassed 187,793 casino employees and 104 land-based, riverboat, and tribally-owned casinos within ten states. According to this survey, many casino operations offer extensive benefit packages to their employees, including health insurance and retirement options. Employees in some locations also responded that they are offered such additional benefits as on-site childcare, the flexibility to work split shifts or part-time hours, on-site training programs, and assistance with paying for external schooling. Some employees reported that because of their casino jobs they were able to leave public assistance, with 8.5 percent of survey respondents no longer receiving welfare payments and nine percent no longer receiving food stamps. Overall, sixteen percent of respondents stated that they were able to use their casino job to get off of public assistance.

A report of the New Jersey Casino Control Commission states that in 1996 the state's casinos directly employed 43,900 employees. Of these employees, women comprised more than forty percent of the service workers, professionals, and casino officials and managers and 64 percent of the sales workers; more than 40 percent of the office and clerical workers and professionals and 59 percent of the sales workers were minorities.

The Tunica Convention and Visitors Bureau (Tunica County, Mississippi) reports that the number of persons receiving Aid to Dependent Children payments has been reduced by 67 percent and food stamp distribution has decreased 58 percent between 1992, when the first casino opened, and 1998. The average per capita income rose from $11,975 in 1992 to $19,139 in 1996. Unemployment rates dropped from 13.6 percent in 1990 to 5.8 percent in 1998.

In addition to the documented employment opportunities available in the casino industry, there are also substantial indirect impacts, which occur as the spending directly associated with the building or operation of casinos are spent and re-spent, creating a ripple effect throughout the local and regional economies, and beyond. The effects of indirect impacts can be seen in industries ranging from construction to agriculture to computer manufacturing to air conditioning repair. It is estimated that the casino gaming industry indirectly generates 300,000 jobs and $10 billion in wages annually for industries that support casino operations and an additional 85,000 jobs and $2.5 billion in wages for construction-related industries. The Coopers

& Lybrand employee impact survey found that in the previous year 17 percent of the survey respondents had purchased a home, approximately 29 percent had spent money on home improvement projects, 43 percent had purchased an automobile, 30 percent had purchased a major appliance, and 51 percent had bought a home computer or other home electronic equipment. The survey also stated that the respondents patronized local restaurants approximately three times per month, ordered fast food, take-out meals, or had food delivered five times per month, and participated in recreational activities such as sporting events, bowling, concerts, and arcades about four times per month.

In the four years since the inception of riverboat casinos in Joliet, Illinois, (1992 to 1996) $121 million in commercial construction permits were issued, compared to $81 million for the four years prior to the introduction of casino gaming; housing construction doubled during this same time period. The number of hotel rooms available in Joliet increased by 50 percent, from slightly less than 1,000 in 1991 to almost 1,600 in 1996; occupancy rates rose from 47 percent in 1993 to 58 percent in 1996. Auto sales increased from $573 million in 1991 to $820 million in 1995. Retail sales for Joliet rose from approximately $750 million in 1991 to slightly more than $1 billion in 1995, and retail sales for Joliet's host county expanded almost 75 percent, from slightly more than $2 billion to $3.5 billion, during the same period of time.

In addition to these benefits, many casinos contribute to community charity campaigns, including providing computer equipment for local schools and building recreation centers for children. Gaming establishments encourage their employees to follow suit by volunteering time with worthy community causes. The Coopers & Lybrand employee impact study asserts that casino industry employees provided 884,000 hours of volunteer service to local community organizations each month and contributed more than $58 million to charitable organizations during a 12-month period from 1996 to 1997.

While there is evidence to indicate that casino gambling operations can contribute substantially to state and local economies, the positive benefits appear to be most pronounced in sluggish economies, specifically in struggling small or rural communities. For example, prior to the introduction of legalized gambling, Tunica, Mississippi, had double-digit unemployment and an undereducated workforce, the tourism industry in Biloxi and Gulfport, Mississippi, and in Atlantic City was rapidly declining, and Joliet, Illinois had lost needed manufacturing jobs. Gambling has revitalized these communities by providing a new source of revenue for state and locally funded programs and services, creating jobs with benefits and opportunities for skills training and advancement, and bringing customers into the host area who also patronize other local businesses. It should be noted, however, that the economic benefits stem primarily from the employment opportunities that gambling facilities offer.

Although communities that have casino gambling (especially in smaller and more depressed communities) appear to benefit economically from it, studies are lacking on the effect of casino gambling on neighboring communities, which may have problems with the social and economic impacts of gambling without any tax or job benefits to offset these problems. The existing research is confusing and often conflicting.

It is sometimes claimed that gambling operations pull customers away from existing local businesses. There seems to be a commonly held conception that gambling operations, particularly casinos, put small recreation- or hospitality-based businesses out of operation. Just as small, mom 'n pop retailers can not compete against retail giants like Wal-mart, critics say, locally-owned restaurants, bars, movie theaters, and other similar businesses cannot compete against large casino/entertainment complexes. This concept is based on the premise that the residents of a community have a limited amount of money to spend on recreation and must make choices on how to spend this money—either they go to a restaurant or to a movie theater or to a casino. Casinos that rely on the internal community market, that draw patrons primarily from the localized host region, are, therefore, thought to be harmful to existing local businesses, as those existing businesses are not able to effectively compete for the consumer's recreational dollars. In instances where consumers elect to gamble, they are foregoing an opportunity to see a movie; wagering is thus substituted for other non-gaming entertainment spending in an area. This situation is compounded by the fact that many casinos offer restaurants, bars, lodging, and other forms of entertainment on-site.

However, the effect of casinos on nearby businesses may involve more than just the competition for a fixed supply of local dollars. For example, riverboat casinos in New Orleans and Baton Rouge attract almost all of their patrons from the local market: 97.7 percent and 99 percent, respectively. In this scenario, the amount of money spent by local patrons at the casinos in these areas should equal the dollars displaced from other local businesses. A recent study indicates that spending by local customers at the casinos in these two markets displaced $285 million from other Louisiana businesses, but this was only about two-thirds of the total amount spent by local customers on riverboat gambling in Louisiana. The remaining one-third could have come from potential out-of-state spending, such as money put aside for out-of-state vacations or trips to other casinos, or from savings or loans, or from increased income. These sources of additional income are temporary answers and are subject to the cyclical nature of local economies. Money from savings or loans, however, will offset the effect of substitution only until the savings are depleted or the loans must be repaid; increasing incomes will offset it until the local economy experiences a downturn. Thus, some studies indicate, substitution may be an important factor in figuring the effects of casinos on other local businesses, but it is by no means the only factor.

Conversely, there is evidence that indicates that gambling establishments actually help new and existing businesses and recreational venues, such as restaurants, movie theaters, hotels, and lounges, by offering job opportunities to previously unemployed or underemployed individuals and providing an exciting attraction that lures patrons to the host area. Also, any amenities provided by the casinos, such as restaurants and bars, are a source of income for employees and will have indirect impacts as this income is spent outside the casinos. The data provided by Tunica, Joliet, and similar communities suggest that, at least in the short-run, this may be the more likely scenario. In fact, it may be that the only case where casinos actually reduce economic activities in other, local businesses, is when a casino is brought into a healthy, tourist-based economy.

In general, the information collected thus far on the economic impacts of casinos is inadequate to serve as a basis for long-term policy decisions, based partially on the fact that data have been gathered during a period of economic prosperity. The direct impacts, especially on employment, appear to be quite positive in certain circumstances, but the long-term effect of casinos on the businesses around them is not well known. The PSGSC recognizes that much of this positive economic activity has occurred during boom times and that additional longitudinal studies are needed to assess the long-term economic impacts of gambling on host communities and states.

APPENDIX K

THE NATIONAL PUBLIC SECTOR GAMING STUDY COMMISSION REPORT: EXECUTIVE SUMMARY (1999)

The National Public Sector Gaming Study Commission (PSGSC) was composed of state government officials and Native American representatives and charged with determining the impact of gaming upon the United States. The commission was organized in 1999, the same year in which the federal government's National Gambling Impact Study Commission (NGISC) released its recommendations that the expansion of gambling in America be checked until further research on the potentially damaging social and economic costs could be determined. In reaction to the NGISC's dire warning, the Gaming Study Commission conducted its own research in which it, unlike NGISC, drew data from state gaming authorities and other public sector representatives. The following excerpt from the Executive Summary of the PSGSC Final Report reveals that the Gaming Study Commission reached far different conclusions that the NGISC. For clarity, notes and extraneous citations have been removed from the document.

1. This is the Final Report of the National Public Sector Gaming Study Commission (PSGSC). The Commission was appointed by the National Council of Legislators from Gaming States (NCLGS), which is a non-partisan organization of state legislators who chair or are active members of the legislative committees responsible for gaming in their respective states. The PSGSC was created because of concerns that the National Gambling Impact Study Commission (NGISC), which was created by Congress and issued its final report in June 1999, did not include a single representative from the public sector. The members of the public sector are almost all public sector repre-

sentatives; members include a governor, three state legislators, a state attorney general, three gaming regulators, the sheriff of a large urban county, the mayor of a large city, and a representative from the National Indian Gaming Association.

2. Concerns about the NGISC turned out to be well-founded. The PSGSC and its staff found that the central thrust of the NGISC Final Report was inconsistent with the NGISC's own research. The NGISC focused on what it referred to as "convenience gambling," a term the NGISC applied to any games of chance available at gas stations, grocery stores, small food markets, and the like. However, the NGISC's research demonstrated that, despite the widespread legalization of gambling during the past twenty years, the prevalence of past-year gambling has increased only slightly. This and other findings suggest that the legalization of gambling has caused changes in social values and customs that make gambling less likely to create problems for individuals as well as communities.
3. Data from the past twenty years show that gambling has become an important form of entertainment for many people, especially recently, given the level of economic growth that the nation has experienced during the past few years. The total amount wagered in all forms of legalized gambling for 1998, including the same dollar bet many times over, was in excess of $677.4 billion, with the majority, $487.9 billion, coming from casinos. The total amount wagered was $99.4 billion at tribal gaming facilities, $48.5 billion on lotteries, and $18.1 billion at pari-mutuel facilities—horse, greyhound, and Jai-Alai.
4. The recommendations of the NGISC and its tone of alarm suggest that the problem of pathological gambling is growing, but the data on pathological gambling trends are actually inconclusive. Scientific studies conducted by the University of Michigan, the National Research Council, the National Opinion Research Center (NORC) at the University of Chicago, and the Harvard Medical School Division on Addictions demonstrate that the occurrence of pathological gambling is actually quite rare. The data from the NORC study also indicate that in many cases pathological gambling is not a primary disorder but instead a symptom of mania or depression.
5. Historically, regulation of gaming and gambling in the United States has been within the purview of the state governments. The states are fully competent to continue handling this responsibility. The federal government should exert authority over gaming and gambling only when interests beyond the state level are directly involved. Such potential areas of concern include (1) tribally-run gambling operations, due to the longstanding relationship between Indian tribes and the

federal government, (2) Internet and telephone gambling, because of the ability of gambling via telecommunication devices to circumvent traditional state boundaries and policies, and (3) parimutuel wagering to the extent that it involves interstate wagering.

6. The PSGSC recognizes the fact that the federal government has done a poor job as trustee for Indian tribes, and acknowledges that the federal government's policies have failed to address the basic needs of Indian communities. The PSGSC also recognizes that, for the few tribes who have used gambling as a means of economic development, gambling has helped to substantially raise their standard of living as no other industry has done. However, both states and tribes have expressed concerns over some sections of the Indian Gaming Regulatory Act (IGRA), the federal act that outlines the roles of federal, state, and tribal governments regarding Indian gambling. Specifically, while the negotiation process to establish tribal-state Class III gaming compacts outlined in IGRA has worked in most states and has served as a stepping stone toward improved government-to-government relationships, there have been some problems in the process, primarily over how to resolve conflicts when an impasse occurs during compact negotiations. The issue is currently being litigated. If this litigation does not settle the question, IGRA should be amended to clarify the remedies available to tribes and states when negotiations stall. In addition, to ensure that tribes cannot reclaim lands for gambling purposes that they may have been dispossessed of hundreds of years previously, the PSGSC recommends that gambling should be limited to lands already recognized as reservation lands or already being considered in the lengthy recognition process prior to the passage of IGRA.
7. While it has been the position of state governments that they typically should choose the forms of gambling they wish to legalize within their own borders, Internet gambling encompasses problems beyond the scope of state sovereignty; the Internet, by its very nature, transcends traditional state boundaries. Internet gambling is a rapidly growing and highly unregulated industry that has the potential to create untold social problems. The PSGSC believes that Internet gambling is illegal under existing law and should continue to be illegal, but that the law may need to be clarified and amplified.
8. Racing historically has been authorized and regulated at the state level. State racing regulatory commission and racing regulatory organization representatives have testified to the Commission in support of the effectiveness and responsiveness of the existing regulatory structure that governs racing at the state level. The PSGSC agrees that this level of regulation should be maintained and that the balance of the federal-

state relationship in parimutuel gambling regulation should not be disturbed. Racing regulation should remain the domain of the states, with the exceptions of those interstate segments of the industry such as wire transfers, wagering pools, and quarantine issues, and issues where uniformity is desired such as licensing or medication issues.

9. States are capable of fairly regulating lotteries just as they regulate other industries from which they receive tax revenues. States collect excise and sales tax revenues from many industries that they also regulate without creating any conflicts of interest.
10. Riverboats pose special challenges for regulation. Because riverboats have the ability to relocate, they can pull neighboring states into "bidding wars" over who offers the best arrangement for the gambling venue. These situations can make it difficult for states to set firm gaming policies, particularly with regard to taxation, sailing restrictions, and betting limits. The PSGSC believes that states should work together to maintain a balance between their own interests and the competing interests of their neighboring states. In addition, the PSGSC believes that while it is the right of each state to decide what forms of gambling are allowed within its borders, voters who are asked to decide on riverboat gambling should be made aware of what they are considering so that they do not think they are voting on a paddle wheel vessel when, in fact, they may be offered something that will look more like a land-based casino.
11. Much of the wagering that supports the sports betting industry comes from outside the three states that have legalized sports betting (Nevada, Delaware, and Oregon). Therefore, the PSGSC recommends several actions be taken with sports wagering via the Internet and other telecommunications devices. Federal law should prohibit collections on Internet sports gambling debts charged to credit cards; it should also prohibit wire transfers of money to pay for sports gambling debts. Federal law should clearly ban advertising of Internet-based amateur sports gambling on television, radio, or through Internet sites. The PSGSC also recognizes that the impact of illegal sports wagering on college campuses has impacts that reach throughout every state-supported university system and beyond. Add to the growing popularity of sports wagering the increased access to computers that universities provide students, and the results could prove very troubling. The PSGSC supports the National Collegiate Athletic Association's compulsive gambling programs for its athletes, and other similar programs, but feels that more efforts should be made to reach the broader student population. In addition, the PSGSC recognizes that sports gambling in both the amateur and professional arenas should be targeted for additional research.

12. The PSGSC received both written and oral testimony about the potentially serious short- and long-term effects of exposing young people to gambling activities and witnessed first-hand children interacting on gambling-style devices in an arcade. However, all of the information offered to the PSGSC by both gambling counseling professionals and university researchers indicates that there simply is not enough data upon which to base sound conclusions on whether such activities are harmful to children. The PSGSC feels strongly that further research—objective, long-term, longitudinal studies—should be conducted to determine whether or not children introduced to gambling or gambling-style devices at a young age will develop compulsive gambling or other harmful behaviors as adults.
13. The Johnson Act, which currently governs gambling on "cruises to nowhere," was enacted to allow American-flag vessels to offer gambling so that they could better compete with foreign flag vessels. However, the Johnson Act has serious weaknesses. While it gives states the option of prohibiting these cruises from operating, the Johnson Act does not permit any state regulation or taxation. The PSGSC recommends that the Johnson Act be amended, to the extent permitted by the U.S. Constitution, to allow states to regulate and tax these operations.
14. Because legitimate charitable gaming raises millions of dollars for worthy organizations nationwide, it provides a lure for many disreputable individuals who seek to take advantage of the benefits afforded to charitable groups. It is sometimes the case with charitable games that the named organization does not exist, or that the operator is running a fraudulent business. There have also been situations in which gaming operators claim such significant fees for their services that the charity actually receives very little, if any, of the funds raised. States should take an active role in regulating charitable games to ensure that the charities are legitimate and that the money raised benefits the organization or cause named.

APPENDIX L

EXCERPT OF THE LEACH-LAFALCE INTERNET GAMBLING ENFORCEMENT ACT (2002)

In 2002, two members of the House of Representatives, Jim Leach (R-Iowa) and John LaFalce (D-NY), sponsored legislation known as the Internet Gambling Enforcement Act. The bill attempts to bar Internet gaming sites from accepting bank or credit agency payments for clients' gambling debts. The bill also holds credit institutions potentially liable for processing such an unlawful transaction. The Leach-LaFalce bill (H.R. 556) passed the House and was sent on to the Senate for consideration. The Senate, however, held off voting on the act, pending changes. An excerpt from the text of the Internet Gambling Enforcement Act follows.

Sec. 2. Findings.
The Congress finds as follows:

(1) Internet gambling is primarily funded through personal use of bank instruments, including credit cards and wire transfers.
(2) The National Gambling Impact Study Commission in 999 recommended the passage of legislation to prohibit wire transfers to Internet gambling sites or the banks which represent them.
(3) Internet gambling is a major cause of debt collection problems for insured depository institutions and the consumer credit industry.
(4) Internet gambling conducted through offshore jurisdictions has been identified by United States law enforcement officials as a significant money laundering vulnerability.

Sec. 3. Prohibition on Acceptance of Any Bank Instrument for Unlawful Internet Gambling.

(a) IN GENERAL—No person engaged in the business of betting or wagering may knowingly accept, in connection with the participation of another person in unlawful Internet gambling —

(1) credit, or the proceeds of credit, extended to or on behalf of such other person (including credit extended through the use of a credit card);

(2) an electronic fund transfer or funds transmitted by or through a money transmitting business, or the proceeds of an electronic fund transfer or money transmitting service, from or on behalf of the other person;

(3) any check, draft, or similar instrument which is drawn by or on behalf of the other person and is drawn on or payable at or through any financial institution; or

(4) the proceeds of any other form of financial transaction as the Secretary may prescribe by regulation which involves a financial institution as a payor or financial intermediary on behalf of or for the benefit of the other person.

(b) DEFINITIONS—For purposes of this Act, the following definitions shall apply:

(1) BETS OR WAGERS—The term 'bets or wagers' —

(A) means the staking or risking by any person of something of value upon the outcome of a contest of others, a sporting event, or a game subject to chance, upon an agreement or understanding that the person or another person will receive something of greater value than the amount staked or risked in the event of a certain outcome;

(B) includes the purchase of a chance or opportunity to win a lottery or other prize (which opportunity to win is predominantly subject to chance);

(C) includes any scheme of a type described in section 3702 of title 28, United States Code;

(D) includes any instructions or information pertaining to the establishment or movement of funds in an account by the bettor or customer with the business of betting or wagering; and

(E) does not include —

(i) any activity governed by the securities laws (as that term is defined in section 3(a)(47) of the Securities Exchange Act of 934) for the purchase or sale of securities (as that term is defined in section 3(a)(0) of such Act);

(ii) any transaction conducted on or subject to the rules of a registered entity or exempt board of trade pursuant to the Commodity Exchange Act;
(iii) any over-the-counter derivative instrument;
(iv) any other transaction that —
(I) is excluded or exempt from regulation under the Commodity Exchange Act; or
(II) is exempt from State gaming or bucket shop laws under section 2(e) of the Commodity Exchange Act or section 28(a) of the Securities Exchange Act of 934;
(v) any contract of indemnity or guarantee;
(vi) any contract for insurance;
(vii) any deposit or other transaction with a depository institution (as defined in section 3(c) of the Federal Deposit Insurance Act);
(viii) any participation in a simulation sports game or an educational game or contest that —
(I) is not dependent solely on the outcome of any single sporting event or nonparticipant's singular individual performance in any single sporting event;
(II) has an outcome that reflects the relative knowledge and skill of the participants with such outcome determined predominantly by accumulated statistical results of sporting events; and
(III) offers a prize or award to a participant that is established in advance of the game or contest and is not determined by the number of participants or the amount of any fees paid by those participants; and
(ix) any lawful transaction with a business licensed or authorized by a State.

(2) BUSINESS OF BETTING OR WAGERING—The term 'business of betting or wagering' does not include, other than for purposes of subsection (e), any creditor, credit card issuer, insured depository institution, financial institution, operator of a terminal at which an electronic fund transfer may be initiated, money transmitting business, or international, national, regional, or local network utilized to effect a credit transaction, electronic fund transfer, stored value product transaction, or money transmitting service, or any participant in such network, or any interactive computer service or telecommunications service.

(3) DESIGNATED PAYMENT SYSTEM DEFINED—The term 'designated payment system' means any system utilized by any cred-

itor, credit card issuer, financial institution, operator of a terminal at which an electronic fund transfer may be initiated, money transmitting business, or international, national, regional, or local network utilized to effect a credit transaction, electronic fund transfer, or money transmitting service, or any participant in such network, that the Secretary, in consultation with the Board of Governors of the Federal Reserve System and the Attorney General, determines, by regulation or order, could be utilized in connection with, or to facilitate, any restricted transaction.

(4) INTERNET—The term 'Internet' means the international computer network of interoperable packet switched data networks.

(5) INTERACTIVE COMPUTER SERVICE—The term 'interactive computer service' has the same meaning as in section 230(f) of the Communications Act of 934.

(6) RESTRICTED TRANSACTION—The term 'restricted transaction' means any transaction or transmittal involving any credit, funds, instrument, or proceeds described in any paragraph of subsection (a) which the recipient is prohibited from accepting under subsection (a).

(7) UNLAWFUL INTERNET GAMBLING—The term 'unlawful Internet gambling' means to place, receive, or otherwise transmit a bet or wager by any means which involves the use, at least in part, of the Internet where such bet or wager is unlawful under any applicable Federal or State law in the State in which the bet or wager is initiated, received, or otherwise made.

(8) OTHER TERMS —

(A) CREDIT; CREDITOR; AND CREDIT CARD—The terms 'credit', 'creditor', and 'credit card' have the meanings given such terms in section 03 of the Truth in Lending Act.

(B) ELECTRONIC FUND TRANSFER—The term 'electronic fund transfer' —

(i) has the meaning given such term in section 903 of the Electronic Fund Transfer Act; and

(ii) includes any fund transfer covered by Article 4A of the Uniform Commercial Code, as in effect in any State.

(C) FINANCIAL INSTITUTION—The term 'financial institution' has the meaning given such term in section 903 of the Electronic Fund Transfer Act.

(D) MONEY TRANSMITTING BUSINESS AND MONEY TRANSMITTING SERVICE—The terms 'money transmitting business' and 'money transmitting service' have the meanings given such terms in section 5330(d) of title 3, United States Code.

(E) SECRETARY—The term 'Secretary' means the Secretary of the Treasury.

(c) CIVIL REMEDIES —

(1) JURISDICTION—The district courts of the United States shall have original and exclusive jurisdiction to prevent and restrain violations of this section by issuing appropriate orders in accordance with this section, regardless of whether a prosecution has been initiated under this section.

(2) PROCEEDINGS —

(A) INSTITUTION BY FEDERAL GOVERNMENT —

(i) IN GENERAL—The United States, acting through the Attorney General, may institute proceedings under this subsection to prevent or restrain a violation of this section.

(ii) RELIEF—Upon application of the United States under this subparagraph, the district court may enter a preliminary injunction or an injunction against any person to prevent or restrain a violation of this section, in accordance with Rule 65 of the Federal Rules of Civil Procedure.

(B) INSTITUTION BY STATE ATTORNEY GENERAL —

(i) IN GENERAL—The attorney general of a State (or other appropriate State official) in which a violation of this section allegedly has occurred or will occur may institute proceedings under this subsection to prevent or restrain the violation.

(ii) RELIEF—Upon application of the attorney general (or other appropriate State official) of an affected State under this subparagraph, the district court may enter a preliminary injunction or an injunction against any person to prevent or restrain a violation of this section, in accordance with Rule 65 of the Federal Rules of Civil Procedure.

(C) INDIAN LANDS —

(i) IN GENERAL—Notwithstanding subparagraphs (A) and (B), for a violation that is alleged to have occurred, or may occur, on Indian lands (as that term is defined in section 4 of the Indian Gaming Regulatory Act) —

(I) the United States shall have the enforcement authority provided under subparagraph (A); and

(II) the enforcement authorities specified in an applicable Tribal-State compact negotiated under section of the Indian Gaming Regulatory Act shall be carried out in accordance with that compact.

(ii) RULE OF CONSTRUCTION—No provision of this section shall be construed as altering, superseding, or otherwise affecting the application of the Indian Gaming Regulatory Act.

(3) EXPEDITED PROCEEDINGS—In addition to any proceeding under paragraph (2), a district court may, in exigent circumstances, enter a temporary restraining order against a person alleged to be in violation of this section upon application of the United States under paragraph (2)(A), or the attorney general (or other appropriate State official) of an affected State under paragraph (2)(B), in accordance with Rule 65(b) of the Federal Rules of Civil Procedure.

(4) LIMITATION RELATING TO INTERACTIVE COMPUTER SERVICES —

(A) IN GENERAL—Relief granted under this subsection against an interactive computer service shall —

(i) be limited to the removal of, or disabling of access to, an online site violating this section, or a hypertext link to an online site violating this section, that resides on a computer server that such service controls or operates; except this limitation shall not apply if the service is subject to liability under this section pursuant to subsection (e);

(ii) be available only after notice to the interactive computer service and an opportunity for the service to appear are provided;

(iii) not impose any obligation on an interactive computer service to monitor its service or to affirmatively seek facts indicating activity violating this section;

(iv) specify the interactive computer service to which it applies; and

(v) specifically identify the location of the online site or hypertext link to be removed or access to which is to be disabled.

(B) COORDINATION WITH OTHER LAW—An interactive computer service that does not violate this section shall not be liable under section 084 of title 8, except this limitation shall not apply if an interactive computer service has actual knowledge and control of bets and wagers and —

(i) operates, manages, supervises, or directs an Internet website at which unlawful bets or wagers may be placed, received, or otherwise made or at which unlawful bets or wagers are offered to be placed, received, or otherwise made; or

(ii) owns or controls, or is owned or controlled by, any person who operates, manages, supervises, or directs an Internet website at which unlawful bets or wagers may be placed, received, or otherwise made or at which unlawful bets or wagers are offered to be placed, received, or otherwise made.

(5) FACTORS TO BE CONSIDERED IN CERTAIN CASES—In considering granting relief under this subsection against any payment system, or any participant in a payment system that is a creditor, credit card issuer, financial institution, operator of a terminal at which an electronic fund transfer may be initiated, money transmitting business, or international, national, regional, or local network utilized to effect a credit transaction, electronic fund transfer, or money transmitting service, or a participant in such network, the court shall consider the following factors:

(A) The extent to which such person is extending credit or transmitting funds knowing the transaction is in connection with unlawful Internet gambling.

(B) The history of such person in extending credit or transmitting funds knowing the transaction is in connection with unlawful Internet gambling.

(C) The extent to which such person has established and is maintaining policies and procedures in compliance with regulations prescribed under subsection (f).

(D) The feasibility that any specific remedy prescribed in the order issued under this subsection can be implemented by such person without substantial deviation from normal business practice.

(E) The costs and burdens the specific remedy will have on such person.

(6) NOTICE TO REGULATORS AND FINANCIAL INSTITUTIONS —Before initiating any proceeding under paragraph (2) with respect to a violation or potential violation of this section by any creditor, credit card issuer, financial institution, operator of a terminal at which an electronic fund transfer may be initiated, money transmitting business, or international, national, regional, or local network utilized to effect a credit transaction, electronic fund transfer, or money transmitting service, or any participant in such network, the Attorney General of the United States or an attorney general of a State (or other appropriate State official) shall —

(A) notify such person, and the appropriate regulatory agency (as determined in accordance with subsection (f)(5)) for such person, of such violation or potential violation and the remedy to be sought in such proceeding; and

(B) allow such person 30 days to implement a reasonable remedy for the violation or potential violation, consistent with the factors described in paragraph (5) and in conjunction with such action as the appropriate regulatory agency may take.

(d) CRIMINAL PENALTY—

(1) IN GENERAL—Whoever violates this section shall be fined under title 8, United States Code, or imprisoned for not more than 5 years, or both.

(2) PERMANENT INJUNCTION—Upon conviction of a person under this subsection, the court may enter a permanent injunction enjoining such person from placing, receiving, or otherwise making illegal bets or wagers or sending, receiving, or inviting information assisting in the placing of bets or wagers.

(e) CIRCUMVENTIONS PROHIBITED—Notwithstanding subsection (b)(2), a creditor, credit card issuer, financial institution, operator of a terminal at which an electronic fund transfer may be initiated, money transmitting business, or international, national, regional, or local network utilized to effect a credit transaction, electronic fund transfer, or money transmitting service, or any participant in such network, or any interactive computer service or telecommunications service, may be liable under this section if such creditor, issuer, institution, operator, business, network, or participant has actual knowledge and control of bets and wagers and—

(1) operates, manages, supervises, or directs an Internet website at which unlawful bets or wagers may be placed, received, or otherwise made or at which unlawful bets or wagers are offered to be placed, received, or otherwise made; or

(2) owns or controls, or is owned or controlled by, any person who operates, manages, supervises, or directs an Internet website at which unlawful bets or wagers may be placed, received, or otherwise made or at which unlawful bets or wagers are offered to be placed, received, or otherwise made.

(f) POLICIES AND PROCEDURES TO IDENTIFY AND PREVENT RESTRICTED TRANSACTIONS IN PAYMENT FOR UNLAWFUL INTERNET GAMBLING—

(1) REGULATIONS—Before the end of the 6-month period beginning on the date of the enactment of this Act, the Secretary of the Treasury, in consultation with the Board of Governors of the Federal Reserve System and the Attorney General, shall prescribe regulations requiring any designated payment system to establish policies and procedures reasonably designed to identify and prevent restricted transactions in any of the following ways:

(A) The establishment of policies and procedures that —
(i) allow the payment system and any person involved in the payment system to identify restricted transactions by means of codes in authorization messages or by other means; and
(ii) block restricted transactions identified as a result of the policies and procedures developed pursuant to clause (i).
(B) The establishment of policies and procedures that prevent the acceptance of the products or services of the payment system in connection with a restricted transaction.
(2) REQUIREMENTS FOR POLICIES AND PROCEDURES—In prescribing regulations pursuant to paragraph (1), the Secretary shall —
(A) identify types of policies and procedures, including nonexclusive examples, which would be deemed to be 'reasonably designed to identify' and 'reasonably designed to block' or to 'prevent the acceptance of the products or services' with respect to each type of transaction, such as, should credit card transactions be so designated, identifying transactions by a code or codes in the authorization message and denying authorization of a credit card transaction in response to an authorization message;
(B) to the extent practical, permit any participant in a payment system to choose among alternative means of identifying and blocking, or otherwise preventing the acceptance of the products or services of the payment system or participant in connection with, restricted transactions; and

Sec. 4. Internet Gambling in or Through Foreign Jurisdictions.
(a) IN GENERAL—In deliberations between the United States Government and any other country on money laundering, corruption, and crime issues, the United States Government should —
(1) encourage cooperation by foreign governments and relevant international organizations in identifying whether Internet gambling operations are being used for money laundering, corruption, or other crimes;
(2) advance policies that promote the cooperation of foreign governments, through information sharing or other measures, in the enforcement of this Act; and
(3) encourage the Financial Action Task Force on Money Laundering, in its annual report on money laundering typologies, to study the extent to which Internet gambling operations are being used for money laundering.

(b) REPORT REQUIRED—The Secretary of the Treasury shall submit an annual report to the Congress on the deliberations between the United States and other countries on issues relating to Internet gambling.

Sec. 5. Amendments to Gambling Provisions.

(a) AMENDMENT TO DEFINITION—Section 08 of title 8, United States Code, is amended —
  (1) by designating the five undesignated paragraphs that begin with 'The term' as paragraphs (1) through (5), respectively; and
  (2) in paragraph (5), as so designated —
    (A) by striking 'wire communication' and inserting 'communication';
    (B) by inserting 'satellite, microwave,' after 'cable'; and
    (C) by inserting '(whether fixed or mobile)' after 'connection'.

(b) INCREASE IN PENALTY FOR UNLAWFUL WIRE TRANSFERS OF WAGERING INFORMATION—Section 084(a) of title 8, United States Code, is amended by striking 'two years' and inserting '5 years'.

APPENDIX M

TRIBAL GAMING STATISTICS FROM THE NATIONAL INDIAN GAMING COMMISSION (2004)

The following tables and graph present data from the National Indian Gaming Commission (NIGC) on the growth of Indian gaming and its attendant revenues during the early years of the 2st century. The NIGC is a three-member commission within the Department of the Interior that oversees the regulation of Native American gaming in the United States.

TRIBAL GAMING REVENUES

			Percentage of			
Gaming Revenue Range	Number of Operations	Revenues (in thousands)	Operations	Revenues	Mean (in thousands)	Median (in thousands)
Gaming Operations with Fiscal Years Ending in 2003						
$100 million and over	43	10,714,58	13%	64%	249,176	184,332
$50 million to $100 million	35	2,459,698	11%	15%	70,277	65,416
$25 million to $50 million	55	1,984,673	17%	12%	36,085	37,029
$10 million to $25 million	67	1,144,779	20%	7%	17,086	16,894
$3 million to $10 million	57	350,398	17%	2%	6,147	5,819
Under $3 million	73	76,019	22%	0%	1,041	833
Total	**330**	**16,730,48**				
Gaming Operations with Fiscal Years Ending in 2002						
$100 million and over	41	9,510,660	12%	65%	231,967	179,101
$50 million to $100 million	24	1,694,606	7%	12%	70,609	65,577
$25 million to $50 million	55	1,978,519	16%	13%	35,976	38,984
$10 million to $25 million	65	1,067,513	19%	7%	16,423	16,570
$3 million to $10 million	63	386,399	18%	3%	6,133	5,373
Under $3 million	100	78,359	29%	1%	784	46
Total	**348**	**14,716,056**				

(table continues)

TRIBAL GAMING REVENUES *(CONTINUED)*

Gaming Revenue Range	Number of Operations	Revenues (in thousands)	Percentage of Operations	Percentage of Revenues	Mean (in thousands)	Median (in thousands)
Gaming Operations with Fiscal Years Ending in 200						
$100 million and over	39	8,398,523	12%	65%	215,347	158,836
$50 million to $100 million	19	1,415,755	6%	11%	74,513	79,083
$25 million to $50 million	43	1,528,611	13%	12%	35,549	34,264
$10 million to $25 million	58	997,546	18%	8%	17,199	16,328
$3 million to $10 million	57	385,654	17%	3%	6,766	7,292
Under $3 million	114	96,257	35%	1%	844	575
Total	**330**	**12,822,346**				
Gaming Operations with Fiscal Years Ending in 2000						
$100 million and over	31	6,606,284	10%	60%	213,106	141,684
$50 million to $100 million	24	1,693,510	8%	15%	70,563	73,314
$25 million to $50 million	41	1,360,777	13%	12%	33,190	29,944
$10 million to $25 million	50	856,464	16%	8%	17,129	17,335
$3 million to $10 million	55	350,110	18%	3%	6,366	6,250
Under $3 million	110	91,545	35%	1%	832	541
Total	**311**	**10,958,690**				
Gaming Operations with Fiscal Years Ending in 999						
$100 million and over	28	5,845,787	9%	60%	208,778	136,897
$50 million to $100 million	19	1,323,995	6%	14%	69,684	70,412
$25 million to $50 million	33	1,193,049	11%	12%	36,153	35,990
$10 million to $25 million	59	1,028,834	19%	10%	17,438	17,562
$3 million to $10 million	54	322,268	17%	3%	5,968	5,764
Under $3 million	117	86,907	38%	1%	537	395
Total	**310**	**9,800,840**				

Source: Compiled from gaming operation audit reports received and entered by the NIGC through June 30, 2004.

Appendix M

TRIBAL GAMING REVENUES BY REGION (IN THOUSANDS)

	Fiscal Year 2003		Fiscal Year 2002		Increase (or decrease)	
	Number of Operations	Gaming Revenues	Number of Operations	Gaming Revenues	Number of Operations	Gaming Revenues
Region I	43	1,439,516	47	1,230,194	–4	209,322
Region II	54	4,699,889	51	3,678,095	3	1,021,794
Region III	43	1,898,522	40	1,782,874	3	115,648
Region IV	91	3,547,360	109	3,537,227	–18	10,133
Region V	75	822,727	79	651,841	–4	170,886
Region VI	24	4,322,134	22	3,835,825	2	486,309
Total	**330**	**16,730,148**	**348**	**14,716,056**	**–18**	**2,014,092**

Note: Region I = Alaska, Idaho, Oregon, and Washington; Region II = California, and Northern Nevada; Region III = Arizona, Colorado, New Mexico, and Southern Nevada; Region IV = Iowa, Michigan, Minnesota, Montana, Nebraska, North Dakota, South Dakota, and Wisconsin; Region V = Kansas, Oklahoma, and Texas; Region VI = Alabama, Connecticut, Florida, Louisiana, Mississippi, North Carolina, and New York.

Source: Compiled from gaming operation audit reports received and entered by the NIGC through June 30, 2004.

GROWTH IN INDIAN GAMING, 1995–2003

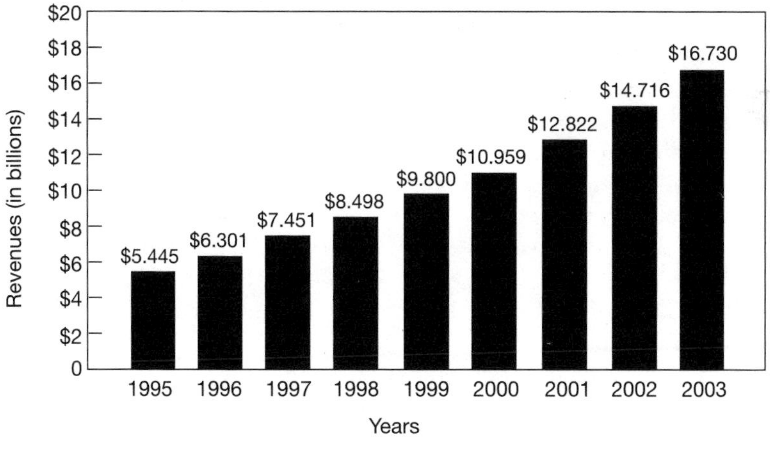

Source: National Indian Gaming Commission.

APPENDIX N

NATIONAL INDIAN GAMING COMMISSION NOTICE OF APPROVAL OF CLASS III TRIBAL GAMING ORDINANCES (2005)

The following is a list of all Native American tribes for which the chairman of the National Indian Gaming Commission has approved the issuing of Class III gaming ordinances.

Absentee-Shawnee Tribe of Oklahoma
Agua Caliente Band of Cahuilla Indians
Ak Chin Indian Community
Alturas Indian Rancheria
Apache Tribe of Oklahoma
Assiniboine & Sioux Tribes of the Fort Peck Reservation
Augustine Band of Mission Indians
Bad River Band of Lake Superior Tribe of Chippewa
Barona Band of Mission Indians
Bay Mills Indian Community
Bear River Band of the Rohnerville Rancheria
Big Lagoon Rancheria
Big Pine Paiute Tribe of the Owens Valley
Big Sandy Band of Western Mono Indians
Big Valley Rancheria of Pomo Indians
Bishop Paiute Tribe
Blue Lake Rancheria
Boise Forte Band of Chippewas
Buena Vista Rancheria of Me-Wuk Indians
Burns Paiute Tribe
Cabazon Band of Mission Indians
Caddo Indians Tribe of Oklahoma
Cahto Tribe of the Laytonville Rancheria
Cahuilla Band of Mission Indians
California Valley Mewok Indians
Campo Band of Mission Indians
Chemehuevi Indian Tribe
Cheyenne and Arapaho Tribes of Oklahoma

Appendix N

Cheyenne River Sioux Tribe
Chickasaw Nation of Oklahoma
Chicken Ranch Band of Me-Wuk Indians
Chippewa Cree Tribe of the Rocky Boy's Reservation
Chitimacha Tribe of Louisiana
Citizen Band Potawatomi Indians of Oklahoma
Cloverdale Rancheria of Pomo Indians of California
Coast Indian Community of the Resighini Rancheria
Cocopah Indian Tribe
Coeur d'Alene Tribe
Colorado River Indian Tribes
Colusa Band of Wintun Indians
Comanche Indian Tribe
Confederated Salish and Kootenai Tribes of the Flathead Reservation
Confederated Tribes and Bands of the Yakama
Confederated Tribes of the Chehalis Reservation
Confederated Tribes of the Colville Reservation
Confederated Tribes of the Grand Ronde Community
Confederated Tribes of the Siletz Indians of Oregon
Confederated Tribes of the Umatilla Indian Reservation
Confederated Tribes of the Warm Springs Reservation
Coquille Indian Tribe
Coushatta Indian Tribe of Louisiana
Cow Creek Band of Umpqua Indians
Coyote Valley Band of Pomo Indians
Crow Creek Sioux Tribe
Crow Indian Tribe
Delaware Tribe of Indians
Delaware Tribe of Western Oklahoma
Dry Creek Rancheria
Eastern Band of Cherokee Indians
Eastern Shawnee Tribe of Oklahoma
Elem Indian Colony
Elk Valley Rancheria
Enterprise Rancheria
Ewiiaapaayp Band of Mission Indians
Fallon Paiute-Shoshone Tribes
Flandreau Santee Sioux Tribe
Fond du Lac Reservation Business Committee
Forest County Potawatomi Community
Fort Belknap Indian Community
Fort McDermitt Paiute-Shoshone Indian Tribe
Fort McDowell Mohave-Apache Indian Community
Fort Mojave Tribal Council
Gila River Indian Community
Grand Portage Band of Chippewa Indians
Grand Traverse Band of Ottawa/Chippewa Indians
Greenville Rancheria
Grindstone Indian Rancheria
Gudiville Indian Rancheria
Hannahville Indian Community
Ho-Chunk Nation
Hoopa Valley Tribe
Hopland Band of Pomo Indians
Hualapai Tribe
Iowa Tribe of Kansas and Nebraska
Iowa Tribe of Oklahoma
Jackson Rancheria Band of Miwuk Indians
Jamestown S'Klallam Tribe

Jamul Band of Mission Indians
Jena Band of Choctaw Indians
Jicarilla Apache Tribe
Kaibab Band of Paiute Indians
Kalispel Tribe of Indians
Karuk Tribe of California
Keweenaw Bay Indian Community
Kickapoo Nation of Kansas
Kickapoo Traditional Tribe of Texas
Kickapoo Tribe of Oklahoma
Kiowa Tribe of Oklahoma
Klamath Tribes
Klawock Cooperative Association
Kootenai Tribe of Idaho
Lac Courte Oreilles Band of Lake Superior Chippewa
Lac du Flambeau Band of Lake Superior Chippewa
Lac Vieux Desert Band of Lake Superior Chippewa
LaJolla Band of Luiseno Indians
Lake Miwok Indian Nation of the Middletown Rancheria
La Posta Band of Mission Indians
Las Vegas Paiute Tribe
Leech Lake Band of Chippewa Indians
Little River Band of Ottawa Chippewa
Little Traverse Bay Bands of Odawa Indians
Lower Brule Sioux Tribe
Lower Sioux Indian Community
Lummi Nation
Lytton Band of Pomo Indians
Manchester Band of Pomo Indians
Manzanita Band of Mission Indians
Mashantucket Pequot Tribe
Match-E-Be-She-Wish Band of Potawatomi Indians
Mechoopda Indian Tribe of Chico Rancheria
Menominee Indian Tribe of Wisconsin
Mescalero Apache Tribe
Miami Tribe of Oklahoma
Mille Lacs Band of Chippewa Indians
Mississippi Band of Choctaw Indians
Moapa Band of Pauites
Modoc Tribe of Oklahoma
Mohegan Tribe of Indians of Connecticut
Mooretown Rancheria
Morongo Band of Mission Indians
Muckleshoot Indian Tribe
Muscogee (Creek) Nation
Narragansett Indian Tribe
Nez Perce Tribe
Nisqually Indian Tribe
Nooksack Indian Tribe
Northern Arapaho Tribe of the Wind River Indians
Northern Cheyenne Tribe
Nottawaseppi Huron Band of Potawatomi
Oglala Sioux Tribe
Omaha Tribe of Nebraska
Oneida Nation of New York
Oneida Tribe of Indians of Wisconsin
Otoe-Missouria Tribe of Oklahoma
Ottawa Tribe of Oklahoma
Pala Band of Mission Indians
Pascua Yaqui Tribe of Arizona
Paskenta Band of Nomlaki Indians
Pauma-Yuima Band of Mission Indians
Pawnee Tribe of Oklahoma
Pechanga Band of Mission Indians
Picayune Rancheria of the Chukchansi Indians
Pinoleville Indian Reservation

Appendix N

Pit River Tribe
Pokagon Band of Potawatomi Indians of Michigan
Ponca Tribe of Nebraska
Ponca Tribe of Oklahoma
Port Gamble S'Klallam
Prairie Band Potawatomi
Prairie Island Indian Community
Pueblo of Acoma
Pueblo of Isleta
Pueblo of Jemez
Pueblo of Laguna
Pueblo of Nambe
Pueblo of Pojoaque
Pueblo of Sandia
Pueblo of San Felipe
Pueblo of San Juan
Pueblo of Santa Ana
Pueblo of Santa Clara
Pueblo of Taos
Pueblo of Tesuque
Puyallup Tribe of Indians
Pyramid Lake Paiute Tribe
Quapaw Tribe of Oklahoma
Quechan Indian Tribe
Quileute Indian Tribe
Quinault Indian Nation
Red Cliff, Sokaogon Chippewa, and Lac Courte Oreilles Band
Red Cliff Band of Lake Superior Chippewa
Redding Rancheria
Red Lake Band of Chippewa Indians
Redwood Valley Rancheria
Reno-Sparks Indian Colony
Rincon San Luiseno Band of Mission Indians
Robinson Rancheria of Pomo Indians
Rosebud Sioux Tribe
Round Valley Indian Tribes
Rumsey Indian Rancheria
Sac & Fox Tribe of Mississippi in Iowa
Sac & Fox Nation of Missouri
Saginaw Chippewa Indian Tribe
St. Croix Chippewa Indians of Wisconsin
St. Regis Mohawk Tribe
Salt River Pima-Maricopa Indian Community
San Carlos Apache Tribe
San Manuel Band of Mission Indians
San Pasqual Band of Indians
Santa Rosa Band of Tachi Indians of the Santa Rosa
Santa Ynez Band of Mission Indians
Santa Ysabel Band of Mission Indians
Santo Domingo Tribe
Sauk-Suiattle Indian Tribe
Sault Ste. Marie Tribe of Chippewa Indians
Scotts Valley Band of Pomo Indians
Seminole Tribe
Seneca-Cayuga Tribe of Oklahoma
Shakopee Mdewakanton Sioux Community
Shawnee Tribe of Oklahoma
Sheep Ranch Tribe of We-Wuk Indians
Sherwood Valley Rancheria
Shingle Springs Band
Shoalwater Bay Indian Tribe
Shoshone-Bannock Tribes
Sisseton-Wahpeton Sioux Tribe
Skokomish Indian Tribe
Smith River Rancheria
Snoqualmie Tribe
Soboba Band of Mission Indians
Sokaogon Chippewa Community
Southern Ute Indian Tribe

Spirit Lake Sioux Nation
Spokane Tribe of Indians
Squaxin Island Tribe
Standing Rock Sioux Tribe
Stillaguamish Tribe of Indians
Stockbridge-Munsee Community
Suquamish Tribe
Susanville Indian Rancheria
Swinomish Indian Tribal Community
Sycuan Band of Mission Indians
Table Mountain Rancheria
Temecula Band of Luiseno Mission Indians
Three Affiliated Tribes of the Fort Berthold Reservation
Timbisha Shoshone Tribe
Tohono O'odham Nation
Tonkawa Tribe of Oklahoma
Tonto Apache Tribe
Torres Martinez Desert Cahuilla Indians Tribe
Trinidad Rancheria
Tulalip Tribes of Washington
Tule River Tribe of the Tule River Indian Reservation
Tunica-Biloxi Tribe of Louisiana
Tuolumne Band of MeWuk Indians
Turtle Mountain Band of Chippewa Indians
Twenty Nine Palms Band of Mission Indians
Tyme Maidu Tribe of the Berry Creek Rancheria
United Auburn Indian Community of Auburn Rancheria
Upper Sioux Community
Upper Skagit Indian Tribe
Ute Mountain Ute Tribe
U-tu Utu Gwaitu Paiute Tribe of Benton Paiute Reservation
Viejas Band of Mission Indians
Washoe Tribe of Nevada and California
White Earth Band of Chippewa Indians
White Mountain Apache Tribe
Wichita and Affiliated Tribes
Winnebago Tribe of Nebraska
Wyandotte Tribe of Oklahoma
Yankton Sioux Tribe
Yavapai Apache Tribe
Yavapai-Prescott Indian Tribe
Yurok Tribe

INDEX

Locators in **boldface** indicate main topics. Locators followed by *c* indicate chronology entries. Locators followed by *b* indicate biographical entries. Locators followed by *g* indicate glossary entries. Locators followed by *t* indicate graphs or tables.

Index

Index

Index

Index

Index

Index

Index

Index